THE LAST FIGHTING TOMMY

OTHER BOOKS BY RICHARD VAN EMDEN

THE LAST
FIGHTING TOMMY

The Life of Harry Patch,
the Oldest Surviving Veteran of the Trenches

Harry Patch
with
Richard van Emden

BLOOMSBURY
LONDON · BERLIN · NEW YORK

First published in Great Britain 2007
This paperback edition published 2008

Copyright © by Richard van Emden 2007, 2008

The right of Richard van Emden to be identified as the author
of this work has been asserted by him in accordance with
the Copyright, Designs and Patents Act 1988

Bloomsbury Publishing Plc
36 Soho Square
London W1D 3QY

www.bloomsbury.com

Bloomsbury Publishing, London, New York and Berlin

A CIP catalogue record for this book is available from the British Library

ISBN 978 0 7475 9336 2
10 9 8 7 6

Typeset by Hewer Text UK Ltd, Edinburgh
Printed in Great Britain by Clays Ltd, St Ives plc

FSC
Mixed Sources
Product group from well-managed
forests and other controlled sources
Cert no. SGS-COC-2061
www.fsc.org
© 1996 Forest Stewardship Council

The paper this book is printed on is certified independently in accordance with the rules of the FSC.
It is ancient-forest friendly. The printer holds chain of custody.

Dedicated to Doris Whitaker,
4 April 1914–19 March 2007,
and
Fred Patch, Lionel Morris, Harold Chivers and
Charlie Wherrett, who died during the Great War,
and George Atkins and Leslie Lush, who survived

It was the men in the trenches who won the war. What they put up with, no one will ever know. I've seen them coming out of the line, poor devils, in a terrible state, plastered with mud. They were like hermit crabs with all their equipment on and they'd plonk down in the middle of the road before somebody helped them up. How did they manage? They were at the end of their tether. They were worn out, absolutely done up. They could hardly put one foot before the other, they were gone, depleted, finished, all they wanted to do was sleep, sleep, sleep.

Air Mechanic Henry William Allingham
No. 8289, No. 12 Squadron Royal Naval Air Service
6 June 1896–

CONTENTS

Harry's father was keen on rabbiting. After he died, his sons found his gun. Nobody knew whether it had ever been licensed, so they threw it down Granny's well.

May Cooper, daughter of George Patch, and Harry's niece, born 1918

I don't think Harry wanted to fight, but he went in any case . . . I never heard him speak about the war, and I somehow doubt he ever spoke about it.

Margaret Ffoulkes, George Atkins' daughter and Harry's god-daughter

When they launched the Somerset Poppy Appeal, they had a great big cannon that shot the poppies out of the muzzle. Of course everybody jumped in shock, but Harry didn't stir a muscle. He just said, 'You haven't heard the guns like I have.'

Pauline Leyton, manager at Harry's residential home

When I first knew Harry he was the champion of local causes. He hates injustice and never hesitated to write to the council or the local newspaper, usually firing on all cylinders when he did so.

David Isaacs, son of Betty Isaacs, Harry's neighbour

I was in the living room with my back to the television. Suddenly, I heard his distinctive voice and it made me feel quite peculiar. I was very still for a moment. I remember thinking, 'Oh my goodness, it's Uncle Hal.'

June Beeching, niece to Harry's first wife Ada, born June 1933

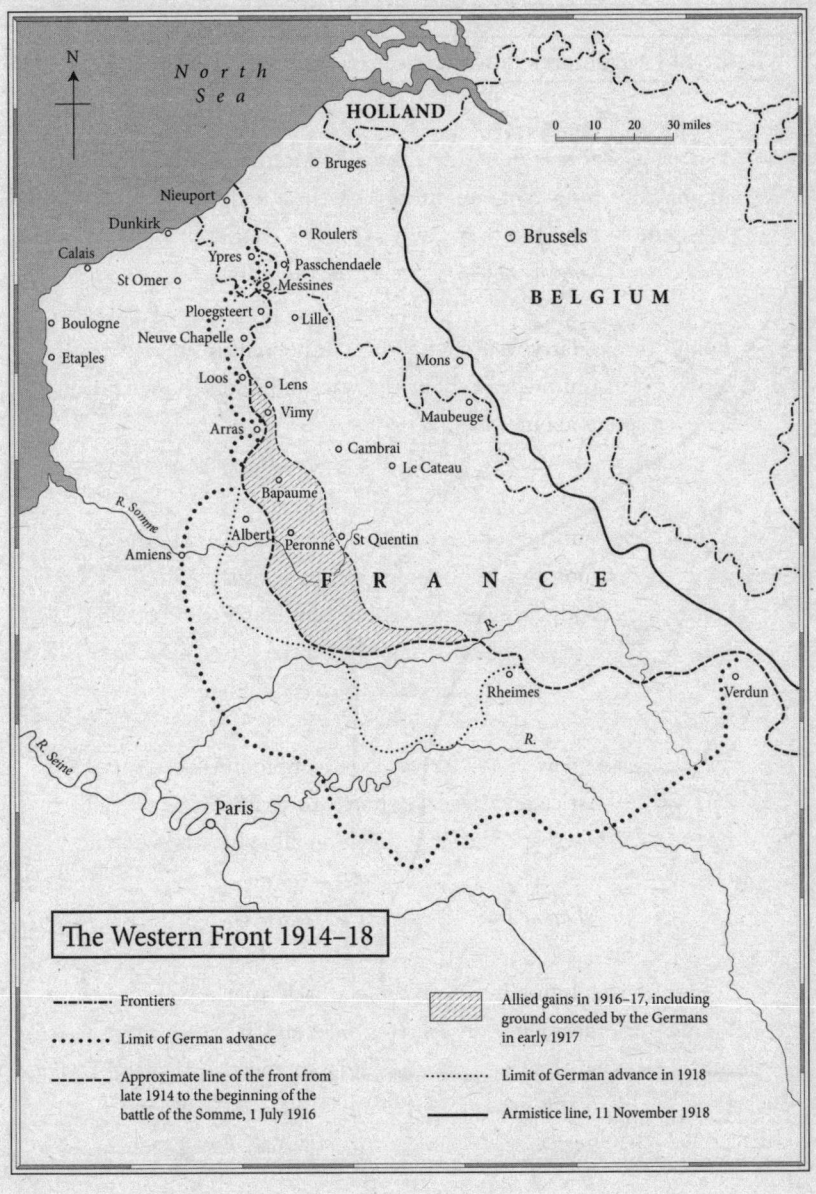

N

North Sea

HOLLAND

o Bruges

Nieuport o

Dunkirk o

Calais o

St Omer o

Boulogne o

Etaples o

Ypres o

o Roulers

o Passchendaele
Messines o

Ploegsteert o   o Lille

Neuve Chapelle o

Loos o   o Lens

Vimy o

Arras o

o Cambrai

o Le Cateau

Bapaume o

Albert o

Amiens o

Peronne o   St Quentin o

F R A N C E

R. Somme

o Brussels

B E L G I U M

o Mons

Maubeuge o

R.

Rheimes o

Verdun o

R.

R. Seine

Paris o

The Western Front 1914–18

0   10   20   30 miles

- ·–·–·– Frontiers
- •••••• Limit of German advance
- – – – – Approximate line of the front from late 1914 to the beginning of the battle of the Somme, 1 July 1916

- ▨ Allied gains in 1916–17, including ground conceded by the Germans in early 1917
- ············ Limit of German advance in 1918
- ——— Armistice line, 11 November 1918

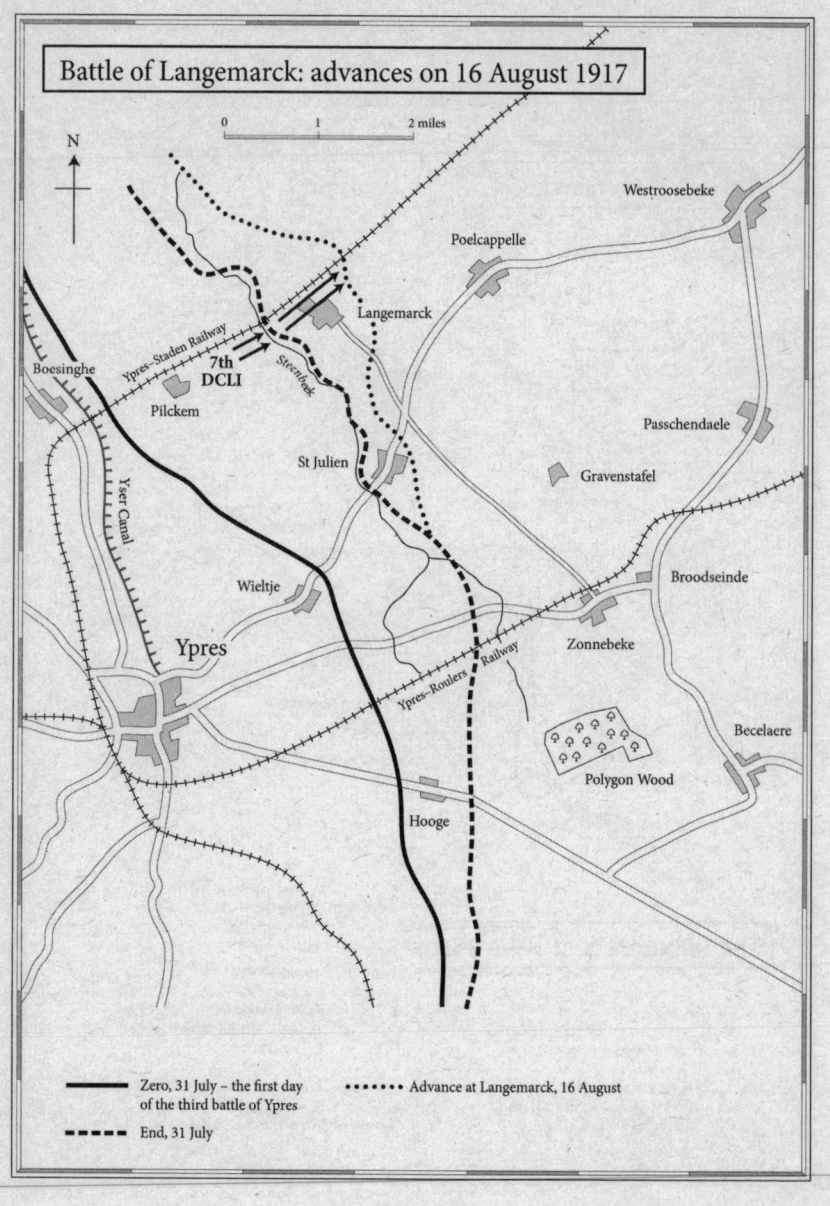

Battle of Langemarck: advances on 16 August 1917

N

0   1   2 miles

Westroosebeke

Poelcappelle

Langemarck

Ypres–Staden Railway

Boesinghe

7th DCLI

Steenbeek

Pilckem

Passchendaele

St Julien

Gravenstafel

Yser Canal

Wieltje

Broodseinde

Ypres

Zonnebeke

Ypres–Roulers Railway

Becelaere

Polygon Wood

Hooge

——— Zero, 31 July – the first day   • • • • • • Advance at Langemarck, 16 August
       of the third battle of Ypres

- - - - End, 31 July

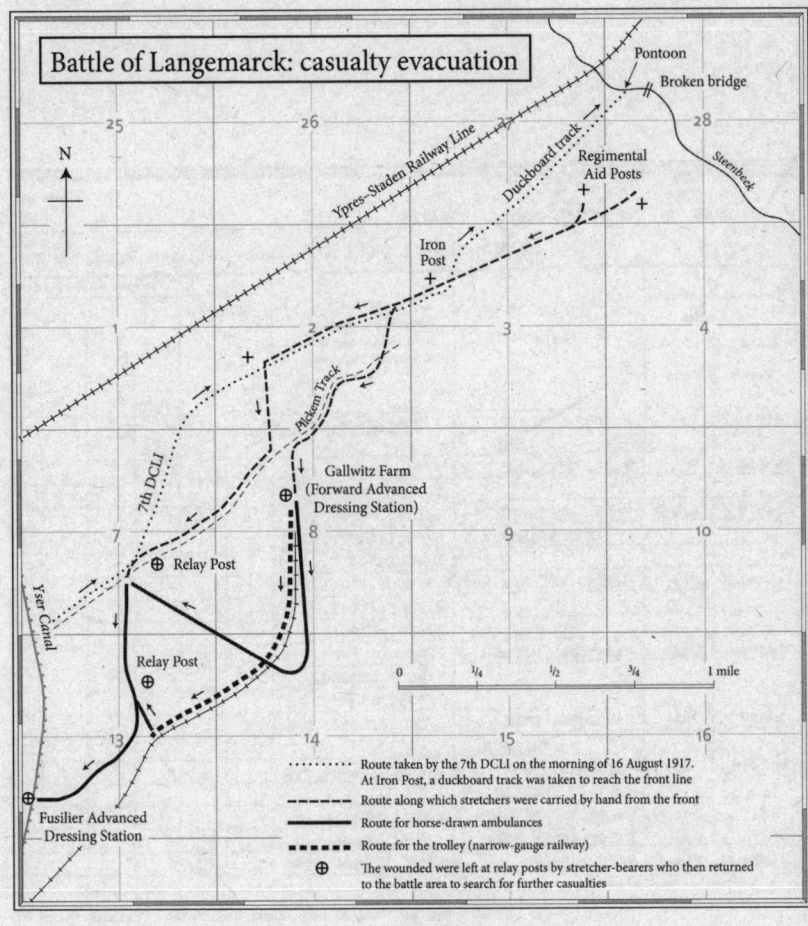

Battle of Langemarck: casualty evacuation

Pontoon
Broken bridge

Ypres–Staden Railway Line

Duckboard track

Regimental Aid Posts

Steenbeek

N

Iron Post

7th DCLI

Gallwitz Farm (Forward Advanced Dressing Station)

Relay Post

Yser Canal

Relay Post

Pilckem Track

| 0 | ¼ | ½ | ¾ | 1 mile |

Fusilier Advanced Dressing Station

.... Route taken by the 7th DCLI on the morning of 16 August 1917. At Iron Post, a duckboard track was taken to reach the front line

– – – – Route along which stretchers were carried by hand from the front

———— Route for horse-drawn ambulances

▬▬▬▬ Route for the trolley (narrow-gauge railway)

⊕ The wounded were left at relay posts by stretcher-bearers who then returned to the battle area to search for further casualties

DUKE OF CORNWALLS LIGHT INFANTRY.

ROLL OF INDIVIDUALS entitled to the Victory Medal and/or British War Medal

On 11/11/18 or on becoming non-effective		NAME	Unit previously served with. Regtl. No. and Rank in same on entry into theatre of war	Theatres of war in which served					
Regtl. No.	Rank			From	To	From	To	From	To
34934	Pte	PASCOE, WILLIAM JAMES.	1/DCLI.34934.PTE	O	RE				
23605	Pte	PASK, WILLIAM.	7/DCLI.23605.PTE 10/DCLI.23605.	O	18				
34677	L/Cpl	PASS, FREDERICK HENRY GEORGE.	6/DCLI.34677.PTE 6/DCLI.34677.HNK 1/DCLI.34677.	O	18				
17441	Pte	PASSEY, HERBERT HENRY.	2/DCLI.17441.PTE 8/DCLI.17441. 2/DCLI.17441.	X					
260089	Pte	PASSMORE, GEORGE.	2/DEVONS.1755.PTE 7/DCLI.260089. 1/DCLI.260089.		KI				
18027	Cpl	PASSMORE, HENRY WALLACE.	8/DCL I.18027.CPL	X					
201476	Pte	PASSMORE, HUGH WILLIAM	1/4.DCLI.4604.PTE	O	KS				
8461	Sgt	PASSMORE, PHILLIP.	2/DCLI.8461.SGT	X					
29295	Pte	PATCH, HENRY JOHN.	7/DCLI.29295.PTE	O	33				
21826	Pte	PATE, HEELYS.	2/DCLI.21826.PTE	X	16				

I certify that according to the Official Records the individuals named in

Place___EXETER.___

Date_____APRIL 1920.

PREFACE TO THE
PAPERBACK EDITION

Could life get any busier? I don't know, possibly, but since my book came out last July, I seem to have been out and about to the point when I have to be careful what I do. The daily batteries have only so much charge in them!

The paperback of *The Last Fighting Tommy* is now about to come out, and I'm a year older. In fact, I will celebrate my 110th birthday when it is published. I think I'll have a small party to celebrate both the book and my birthday but I'll make that family and friends only; I would prefer it that way.

In the last twelve months, I have been back to Belgium and seen the exact spot where I went over the top. I looked across the Steenbeck towards the village of Langemarck. The ground slopes up from the stream and you can just see the church on the horizon. It was ninety years to the day since I was there. In Ypres I met the mayor of the town, and I gave the oration under the Menin Gate, a very special moment for me. I also went to Langemarck Cemetery to lay a wreath on the grave of a German killed the day we attacked there, 16 August 1917.

With the proceeds from this book I have been able to buy a lifeboat for the Royal National Lifeboat Institution, and I launched it at Poole in Dorset. I would encourage everybody to support the RNLI. Anyway, it is a relief boat, meaning it travels round the United Kingdom and doesn't just stay in one place. It began its service in North Wales and my god-daughter, Margaret, was able to go along and see it. The last I heard it had launched six times and saved seven people.

I have got used to all the publicity, and I am always being photographed.

Recently, I switched on the lights in the Wills Memorial Building in Bristol, a sixty-six metre tower I helped to construct in the 1920s. Then the BBC made a programme about me earlier this year and the Poet Laureate, Andrew Motion, wrote a poem which he read to an audience at the Bishop's Palace in Wells. I very much appreciated the honour.

Lastly, I would like to say that I get requests for autographs from all over the world. I am sure people appreciate that my arthritic hands are too painful to sign now. Can I just say that at almost 110 years old, I have officially retired! Thank you.

Harry Patch, April 2008

PROLOGUE

Harry Patch is 108 years old, and Britain's second oldest man. With a good, if not a full, head of hair, and eyes that will recognize a friend at a hundred paces, his looks belie his great age. He is not a man who comes across as a potential record-breaker or statistical anomaly, but he is. He was born in 1898, one of fewer than thirty people in the United Kingdom today who can boast a nineteenth-century birth date.

Currently, there are about eight thousand centenarians, men and women, in Great Britain, compared to 102 in 1911, according to the Office of National Statistics. Nevertheless, fewer than 1 in 200 men reach the grand age of 100, and to survive to Harry's great age is, statistically, almost as rare as reaching a century in the first place. At the time of writing, April 2007, he is (without touching too much wood) just fourteen months short of passing another milestone, 110, to join the group of so-called 'supercentenarians', of whom there have been fewer than a thousand authenticated cases worldwide in the history of mankind. It is disconcerting to note that Harry has just as good a

chance of reaching such a landmark as he had of surviving
unscathed at the age of nineteen when he went over the top
with his battalion during the battle of Ypres in August
1917.

Harry has lived to become the last British trench
fighter of the Great War and, as significantly, the last
man to have gone over the top, perhaps the defining
experience of that war. Surviving the conflict was fortunate enough, but now, ninety years on, he has lived to
become the last survivor from among five million infantrymen who fought between 1914 and 1918, the last
of 1.7 million soldiers serving with the British Expeditionary Force on the Western Front in the summer of
1917, the last of the 759,615 casualties recorded by the
BEF that year and of the 77,479 men who were lost in
September, killed and wounded in the bloody salient in
front of Ypres during the battle of Passchendaele.

Harry is aware that he is heir apparent to the title of
Britain's oldest man, and while he is a little bemused
that he is alive – 'Why I'm still here, I can't fathom' –
one has a sneaking suspicion that he is quite intrigued to
see just how far he can go while he continues to enjoy
life. Until her death, he sat most days on a sofa for two,
next to his beloved Doris, his companion, some sixteen
years his junior. The two were inseparable after she came
to the home five years ago.

Doris was no ninety-two-year-old shrinking violet. A
feisty Londoner, from Angel Road, Edmonton (a street that,
sadly, no longer exists), and the daughter of a gas worker, she
learnt as a child to look after herself, and not to let others put
her down. 'My mother always told me,' Doris said firmly,
'don't let people shit on you', and so she never did, but she had

a soft side too. Her relationship with Harry was mutually supportive and caring.

It is clear that Doris was proud of Harry's achievements, but if she thought Harry might be getting too big for his boots she ran her finger up the underside of her nose, to indicate that the man beside her might have been getting just a touch too posh.

Doris died in March 2007, and this was hard for Harry. Loneliness is a recurring problem for anyone who has outlived his generation: everyone Harry knew as a child, teenager or young man has died, just one of the difficult aspects of living so long. It seems strange, more than sixty years since the end of World War II, that when Harry says 'after the war', you have to check which war he is talking about, for he served in both.

Henry John, as he was christened in 1898, is an unassuming man, now famous for four months spent on the Western Front in 1917, when as a young infantryman he served in the trenches in front of Ypres, the town that has come to symbolize the worst fighting of the Great War. His time at the front was brief in comparison with many others, but now he is the only man to have lived in the trenches who can provide a direct link to the war that forged European lives not just for a generation but for the rest of the century. He is self-effacing and self-reliant, a man born into a world where self-help and independence were expected. On the tours he has made back to Belgium since 2000, he has been the object of enormous attention but at the same time he has sought not to put anyone out; asked if there is anything anyone can do, he invariably replies, 'I'm all right, don't mind me', in his distinctive Somerset accent.

Nine years ago, few people, if any, knew about Harry. His name was just one among approximately 350 British soldiers whose identity was published in the national press when the French Government awarded surviving veterans the Légion d'Honneur for service on the Western Front. Only when the pool of soldiers dried up and the numbers in the lists were rapidly revised downwards did his name become more prominent. All of a sudden, people wanted to hear his story.

For eighty years Harry had never spoken about the war, and when he finally did there was a rawness to his voice which said as much about his former silence as it did about his service. Television took an interest. Harry could tell his story well. By this time there were perhaps seventy veterans left, but how many could tell their tale in a way that could translate easily to television screens? Not many, and most not as well as Harry. As the pool of veterans became ever smaller, so the attention grew.

All of a sudden Harry was in demand, and with fame he found the corresponding upside and downside to being public property. He was celebrated by newspapers and television locally and nationally. He spoke at the Cheltenham Literary Festival in 2001, reading to a packed and hushed audience segments from his story, and he has signed books by the hundred. He has launched poppy appeals, and opened fêtes, and other blue-ribbon events. He has had his portrait painted by the artist Jack Russell, the former Gloucestershire and England wicketkeeper, while in 2004 a special-edition sweet cider was produced in his honour by a Shepton Mallet cider company. In all, 106 bottles of 'Patch's Pride' were produced to celebrate each year of his life.

Then, in 2005, he received an honorary degree from Bristol University, conferred during a formal congregation in the Wills Memorial Building which he had helped to construct in the early 1920s.

In 2006, as his 108th birthday coincided with the World Cup, Harry was pictured in an England football shirt. 'One of Britain's Last Tommies celebrates his 108th birthday on Saturday in the midst of World Cup fever,' trumpeted the *Wells Journal*. 'To find out who Harry Patch and other mid-Somerset personalities rate as their favourite England footballer, see the centre spread.' Harry, as it turned out, was more of a rugby fan.

In the first week after Harry's appearance on BBC1's *The Last Tommy* documentary in November 2005, he received 180 letters, and since then a steady trickle has brought as many more, most speculatively addressed. 'Dear Mr Postman,' wrote one correspondent, 'Harry Patch is a Great War veteran who lives in a residential home in Wells in Somerset. Please could you see that he receives this letter, thank you.' Another letter that arrived recently was just as vague and was addressed to 'Mr Harry Patch, care of a care home, Wells, Somerset, England'. The postman has little problem finding Harry nowadays.

Fame has also offered Harry opportunities that would otherwise have remained elusive. He has been taken to visit the places of his youth; he has even returned to the battlefields of France and Flanders and laid a wreath close to the spot where he was wounded and where he lost his friends. He has spoken about his war at length, and said enough to make him feel more at ease with that time in his life. He has met a German veteran, Charles Kuentz, in an act of reconciliation that helped lay many of the private ghosts that have haunted him since the war. More recently, his television appearances have alerted long-lost relations to his continued survival. His *tour de force* on *The Last Tommy* programme was seen by a niece who had not spoken to Harry for more than thirty years. Contact has been re-established. Equally, quarrels and arguments which have fractured other family relationships in the past have also been put to one side, much to Harry's great pleasure.

Fame and great age have combined to open many doors, right up to and including those of Buckingham Palace. Harry has met the Queen on more than one occasion, as he pointed out to her on his last trip up the Mall. He met the late Queen Mother, the Prince of Wales and the Duke of Edinburgh. He has been to No. 10 and met the Prime Minister, too. He has done a balloon trip, been underground and under water. He has flown by plane and helicopter, and travelled on the footplate of a steam train to Minehead. Space remains his final frontier.

This book is based upon many interviews conducted with Harry and recorded over the summer and autumn of 2006. The idea of a biography had been proposed on a number of occasions by publishers and journalists. However, it was not until June 2006 that I approached him and asked whether he would be interested in having his memories preserved in a book. I was due to see Harry again a week later, so I asked him to think about it until the next time I saw him. When I went back I deliberately refrained from asking Harry whether he had come to any decision. As I was about to leave, he beckoned me over. 'So when are you going to bring your tape recorder, then?' He was clearly keen to tell his story.

Owing to my own deep-rooted interest in the Great War, I had frequently asked Harry about his experiences at the front in the summer of 1917, but I had rarely strayed beyond that line of questioning. I had fallen into the same groove as so many other visitors, asking Harry about four months at the front while forgetting the other $107\frac{1}{2}$ years of his life so far. However, really to understand Harry's war and his reaction to it, some context was needed, and it was only with the story of his life that I truly began to understand the effect the conflict has had on him.

There were times when Harry became subdued, depressed even. His eyes would take on the thousand-yard stare of a man who has seen much in his life, occasionally too much for his own wellbeing. I knew that he had lost his friends in the Great War but it was hard to appreciate his level of loss. Death is something everyone comes to terms with; the passing of grandparents and parents is as natural as it is painful, but the loss of children, close relations and friends, all before their time, is something few of us, mercifully, have to deal with. In a lifetime that has spanned two world wars, Harry has lived with violent death, including the premature demise of so many who were young. This was something I did not fully appreciate until I spoke to Harry about his life beyond the immediacy of the Great War. I knew he had lost friends at the front, that a cousin had been killed in the First War and a nephew in the Second, but I had not appreciated that so many of the boys from his village had been killed too, lads with whom he had rowed the rivers, explored the quarries and played rugby. He did not always state that they had been killed, and occasionally I wondered if he knew they had been, but time after time I looked up the names of those he had grown up with, and time and again their names appeared in the records of the Commonwealth War Graves Commission, and many are among the fifty-six names from the Great War on the Combe Down war memorial.

These are not all of the men and boys from Combe Down for others with connections to the village are commemorated elsewhere, so that, all in all, the community's loss stands closer to sixty-five. They were his friends, his generation, and he has outlived them all, and far too many by ninety years or more. Harry has a right to be depressed at times.

Interviews were divided so that Harry could rest and keep his energy levels up. We held one session in the morning between 10.30 and lunch time, and another in the afternoon between 2.30 and tea, in all perhaps four hours in a day. Conducting interviews was problematic. Driving from west London to Wells, I was never sure how Harry would be that day. In the very hot summer months, it was difficult for both interviewer and interviewee not to wilt in the stuffy weather (he rather took to a hand-held, battery-powered fan). On other occasions, the brightness of Harry's eyes and his general alertness indicated that a more purposeful day was ahead. Even so, Harry's voice is not as strong as it once was and I was thankful on more than one occasion that the microphone in my recording equipment proved more sensitive than my own ears.

Collating Harry's stories has demanded a multifaceted approach. There are the stories that Harry himself recalls but many had to be triggered by me, which invariably meant meeting his relations, talking to local historians and consulting local newspapers, books and historical documents so that I could go primed with stories that Harry, once prompted, recalled with his usual alacrity.

It has taken a considerable time to fathom the myriad connections between family, friends and neighbours. Teachers' names, for example, would change, but then, of course, they would, as one incumbent left and a new one arrived. For this reason, every story had to be checked for its context, related to a time and place. As far as possible, I have sought to corroborate Harry's stories and to place them in broad chronological order. Finally, when the book was complete, he was given a full copy of the text to read to ensure that he agreed with what had been written and corrected anything that I had misunderstood.

A push-button, fading-to-a-dot black-and-white television is just a memory but hardly remarkable to anyone aged thirty-five or above, and yet it may one day be worth recalling as an interesting nugget of social history. The problem always is to realize that such detail is fascinating to a new generation. For Harry, much of what we consider so quintessentially a part of the Edwardian age is so mundane to a child of that time that it is hardly worth mentioning. Human history, and not just the devil, is in the detail.

Rural poverty was rife but lack of money did not equate to a lack of fun, and for the children of that generation such as Harry, adventure, opportunity and excitement were just round the corner, and often no more than a literal stone's throw away. Children lived at a time when danger was accepted and managed, and accidents were an unavoidable fact of life and of growing up.

There is a story that Harry tells of a gooseberry bush growing at the end of his parents' walled garden, just beyond the line of potatoes. Harry was not allowed to pick the gooseberries, but, when they were ripe, they hung temptingly, too tempting to be ignored. The only way to reach them was to crawl, stomach hard to the ground, between the heaped lines of potatoes, under the nose of his mother whose kitchen window overlooked the garden. The boy's own adventure of the unobserved crawl was just as exciting, and as much the object of the exercise, as eating the fruit.

In the summer, the trees in the garden were laden with ripe, sweet fruits and they were the Mars Bars of yesteryear; they were treats. But they were also forbidden, in a quasi-biblical as well as a literal sense: they hung from the tree and tempted the onlooker or the passer-by. The fruit belonged to the Family Patch, not to any individual, Harry included, and the self-discipline needed to resist this ripe temptation was all part of growing up in Edwardian England, when spur-of-the-moment whims went un-requited because life taught you that, for the vast majority of the population, what you wanted in no way equated to what you got.

Ample meals were provided, in Harry's family three times a day, and there was no reason to pick at food in between them. Parents provided for their children as best they could, and if a child routinely supplemented his or her diet outside mealtimes, it could be seen as a lack of parental care; in a respectable middle-class family where the father was the provider, this would border on social disgrace. The fruit trees were symbols of a great divide between our society today and that of a century ago; Harry Patch is one of the very few who can cross the divide.

Harry grew up in what is now an almost forgotten world. The children who left the textile mills, or played in the narrow alleyways and back streets of northern industrial towns, were Harry's contemporaries. The clothes, the food, the traditions, the attitudes and the sights and sounds remain as familiar to him as they are remote to us. We have not quite severed all contact with a time that, for all its perils of industrial disease, child poverty and infant mortality, seems to offer a cosy sanctuary from the new and stark twenty-first-century perils such as global warming and home-grown terrorism. Back then, duty, responsibility, community and church were the pillars that upheld decent society, and paternalism, repression, secrecy, drudgery and narrow-mindedness were its straitjacket, and the ignorance and naivety that were seen as akin to bliss.

The country life into which Harry was born was parochial in the extreme. Decisions of national importance frequently failed to encroach on the rural community, and it is not surprising that events of real magnitude were forgotten or only half-remembered. Even the sinking of the *Titanic* in 1912 made little impression on children, Harry included, who were living in the heart of the countryside where trains rather than ships were the focus of excitement and debate among boys.

And what was that wider world into which little Harry Patch was born in 1898? It was just twenty-two years since Custer's Last Stand at the battle of the Little Bighorn, and nineteen years since Rorke's Drift, in time closer to Harry than the war for the Falklands is to us. The great Prime Minister William Ewart Gladstone died just a month before Harry was born; Queen Victoria still had two and a half years to reign, and Lord Salisbury, the last peer to serve as British Prime Minister, was resident at 10 Downing Street.

In 1899, when Harry was one, the Boer War broke out; he was five in 1903 when Wilbur and Orville Wright undertook the first flight controlled by power. He predates the foundation of the British Labour Party by two years, was nine when Baden-Powell formed the Scout movement, and nearly fourteen when the *Titanic* sank. He began work the year suffragette Emily Davison was filmed throwing herself under the King's horse at the Epsom Derby, the same year that stainless steel was invented in Sheffield and Canberra became the federal capital of Australia.

Harry was seventeen when the cricketer W.G. Grace died, twenty-four when Howard Carter discovered the tomb of Tutankhamun, twenty-six when John Logie Baird transmitted the first television images, and thirty-four when Adolf Hitler became Chancellor of Germany.

During Harry's lifetime so far, he has lived through the reigns of six monarchs, has voted in twenty-three general elections and, in 2007, will see off his twentieth Prime Minister.

And what of the news in 1898? Well, Henry Lindfield became the first British automobile fatality. Hawaii was annexed by the United States, while Lord Kitchener defeated the Sudanese tribesmen at the battle of Omdurman. In France, Emile Zola was brought to trial for writing *J'accuse* and Italian football played its first league games.

While 1898 as a date holds no obvious resonance for the British public, those of 1914–18 certainly do. The

Great War has held the nation spellbound for more than ninety years. As it finally passes out of direct human memory, we as a nation will say farewell to a generation of people who, for all their human failings, gave and lost so much in the prosecution of a war the effects of which we still feel today, the results still argued over, the lessons still not learnt.

Since World War II, the West has dealt in small conflicts, where casualties, while individually tragic, have nevertheless been tiny in comparison with the losses of the two world wars and especially those of the 1914–18 conflict. The horror of the fighting on the Western Front is peculiarly gripping, and continues to attract ever-increasing numbers of visitors – around a quarter of a million a year – to the battlefields of the Somme and Ypres.

The soldiers of the Great War were caught in a moment of history. A few years prior to 1914, industrial nations could not have sustained the presence of great, largely immobile armies in the field for any length of time; fifteen years after 1918, entrenched infantrymen could not have thwarted the advance of an enemy utilizing strategic bombers and the increasing mechanization of fast and armoured vehicles and tanks. The Great War, and the Western Front as we remember it, had to be fought when it was, or it would not have happened at all. No war had ever before raged for more than four years across such a narrow strip of land, and with such devastating consequences.

Harry Patch just happens to be the last witness to this remarkable moment in history, and the last of those infantrymen who held the line in front of Ypres, or 'Wipers' as it was more commonly known by the men who fought there. When he is gone, that battle and the war will enter the pantheon of other wars and battles that Britain has fought down the centuries and that are now beyond living memory. Yet Harry is hardly warlike. On the contrary, as a reluctant conscript he never wanted to fight anyone; nevertheless he did his duty and remains an unassuming gentleman, in every sense.

Richard van Emden
April 2007

VICTORIAN BORN

Harry Patch was born in Combe Down, a small rural community on the edge of the Somerset city of Bath. The name comes from two Anglo-Saxon words: Combe, from 'cume', meaning valley, and Down, from 'dun', meaning hill, which perfectly describe the local geography of steeply rising hills and green valleys where rough stone walls divide fields, and separate one house from another. The village, though its origins date back to Roman times, was hardly a village at all until industralization in the late eighteenth and early nineteenth centuries helped forge its current size and boundaries. For well over one hundred years, the exploitation of the local material, Bath stone, brought about a rapid expansion, as quarry after quarry was opened in the surrounding hills, and workers migrated from Bath to live close to their places of work.

The stone that was removed from Combe Down was a type of limestone. Underground, it was a pale yellow, but once it was exposed to the open air it turned grey and hardened, making it a perfect building block for Bath's Regency buildings.

With the expansion of the quarries came a transport infra-structure, most importantly the Somerset Coal Canal, built in the

1790s. The first great industrial landowner was Ralph Allen, who lived in Prior Park in the 1730s. He dominated quarrying, expanding Combe Down as a settlement, building cottages for his workmen that backed on to the quarries, and finding outlets for the stone not only in Bath but much further afield, in London and abroad. For over a hundred years quarrying boomed and Combe Down as an industrial village grew and grew.

The arrival of the railways heralded the end of quarrying around Combe Down. Isambard Kingdom Brunel's Great Western Railway, opened in 1841, cut a swathe of embankments and tunnels through the Wiltshire countryside revealing new sources of building stone that were easily accessible and transportable by railway. Combe Down could not compete and quarrying declined, so that by the time of Harry's birth only one mine was still in production, leaving tunnels under the village either abandoned or worked by a few independent quarrymen.

What remained was an area rich in geographical and architectural interest, where the surrounding hills were linked by viaducts, aqueducts and tunnels. Natural water resources were harnessed to supply the villages and the mills with water and power. Combe Down was a working village, but for any boy born at the end of the Victorian age it also provided an idyllic and endlessly interesting environment in which to grow up.

Why me? I'm 108 years old, and I'm amazed to be here, quite honestly. No one in my family has lived anything like this long. My eldest brother, who was judged unfit for military service in the Great War, lived to be ninety-six, and my mother lived to ninety-four, but 108! Mother was from a family of six and they all lived to be in their nineties, but no one can expect to live this long. Yet time has passed so quickly. In my mind's eye I can visualize people and places from my childhood and it's hard to realize that these memories are a century old.

I'd like to say I remember the death of Queen Victoria, the Coronation of Edward VII, or the end of the Boer War, but as I was born in June 1898 I was too young, and in any case I don't have the sort of early recall that some children have. My earliest memories are much more mundane, just small episodes around the house or garden that are now pretty much impossible to date exactly. I do recall when I was aged about five or six, there was a big pear tree in the middle of the garden, with very tempting fruit. I remember Dad saying to me, 'I know how many pears are on that tree, so don't you pick 'em.' I didn't, but when he next looked at the fruit, he found that I had taken a bite out of the back of every one I could reach. I remember that distinctly because I was given a good hiding.

My mother's name was Elizabeth and her maiden name was Morris. She was born in 1857 and raised in Monkton Combe. She had gone into service in the 1870s, becoming a cook for a well-to-do doctor in private practice, Dr Henley. He had two spinster daughters, and I used to watch them playing tennis on the lawn. My mother was a Victorian lady, tall, very upright, with a white apron, skirt, bodice and a servant's hat. She was head of the staff, which included a housemaid, kitchen maid, cook and a butler. The doctor's house stood directly opposite Fonthill, the home owned by my father and where I was born. Perhaps that is how my parents met. Otherwise I've no idea how they got together. That said, it's not hard to see how their paths might have crossed, when William, my father, was raised in the neighbouring village of Claverton, just a couple of miles from Monkton Combe.

Dad was about six years younger than Mum, and his family originally came from Wedmore, a village not far from Glastonbury. I believe my great-grandfather had a builder's business there. In fact, building was the family business on Dad's side – they were all involved in one discipline or another. There is a family legend that my great-grandfather, a carpenter by trade, made his own coffin. He hinged the lid and stood it at the top of the stairs, and until it was needed he used it as a wardrobe. I never met him; pity, really, he sounded like a real character.

The family was an extended one and by 1914 there were fourteen different families of Patches in Combe Down alone, including my father's five brothers, Herbert, Alfred, Eli, Walter and Harry.

My father, William, was a master stonemason. If you know Bath at all, there is a big hotel overlooking the weir, the Empire, the founding stone of which was laid in 1901. He was the master mason on that. Uncle Alf and Uncle Eli were also builders; Uncle Herb, who played the banjo, was employed at a nearby earthworks called Tucky Mill. Uncle Walter, and Uncle Harry, after whom I was named, were both professional gardeners, Harry working as a park superintendent in Weston-super-Mare.

On my mother's side, my grandmother (Morris) lived nearby, and had a daughter, Aunt Annie, who was disabled; for some reason she had had her leg amputated. She used to do dressmaking, and I delivered the dresses for her to earn a few pennies pocket money. She was the mother of Fred Patch, my cousin who was killed in the First War. His father was Walter, and he was a gardener.

Who else? Well, there was Minnie, an old aunt on my mother's side of the family, and Uncle John who kept a pub in Bristol. In fact, two of Mother's brothers were publicans; one was in Bristol and the other owned the Brass Knocker on Brass Knocker Hill on the edge of Combe Down.

I was born and brought up in a semi-detached house called Fonthill, with an adjoining property called Beckford Cottage. When the two houses were built, I was told that from the top of the scaffolding it was possible to see Fonthill Abbey, built by William Beckford, at one time the richest man in England, it was said, and a recluse. The Abbey was by all accounts a vast complex, but the central tower, some 300 feet high, kept falling down because of poor foundations and today there is hardly anything left of what was once an amazing but ultimately flawed house.

I had two brothers and we all more or less followed in Father's footsteps in terms of the building trade. My oldest brother, George, was a cabinet-maker, my middle brother a bricklayer, so I was a plumber. Over the years, Father had become something of a cautious entrepreneur. He owned no. 2 Gladstone Place which he rented to Mr Ford, a roadman with a wooden leg; no. 3 he sold to a butcher but in doing so he kept and divided the land and built nos. 4 and 5. No. 4 was my middle brother's house on his marriage, and no. 5 I inherited when I married in 1919. My eldest brother inherited Fonthill as well as another house, no. 2 Laurel Place, which Dad had also bought. The two houses he built cost £400 together, in about 1910.

As well as being a builder, my father was a very keen gardener, and the back garden was thoroughly turned over to provide the family with food all year round. As soon as anyone went through the gate into the garden, they passed by a blue trellis and a laburnum tree to a line of fruit trees. The first was an apricot, the second a pear, the third a peach, then there was a wall and behind that a Victoria plum: delicious. On the other side of the garden were six gooseberry bushes, a Gladstone apple, and then a Beauty of Bath apple, and another apple tree, the name of which I can't remember but a lovely eating apple nevertheless, then another apricot. In the middle of the garden there was a cooking apple, the name of which was Nonesuch As Good. Wonderful names you don't hear much any more.

Of course Father was very keen to protect his produce. Running around the garden was a high wall, at least six foot at a guess. He covered the top of the wall with broken glass, but, as a cunning scrumper could still throw a blanket over it, he built a board out from the wall, so that anyone who climbed up would have to reach right over to get at the fruit, rather than grab it from the branches closest to him. Terry, the family dog, was also around. He ran pretty much wild in the garden and would bark if anyone tried to climb over.

As well as the fruit trees there were two greenhouses. In one were grown orchids and chrysanthemums, and as children we weren't allowed in there. The other greenhouse was more of an outhouse, a lean-to attached to the kitchen. This was heated by a little boiler in the scullery with four-inch pipes passing into and around the lean-to to keep it warm. Here Father grew cyclamens and one or two cacti, but at Christmas time he carried over a mass of chrysanthemums, brought on in the other greenhouse but placed in the lean-to from one end to the other purely for my mother's pleasure. Father was an amateur gardener but, as two of his brothers were professionals, there was a strong tradition of flower growing in the family.

Most of the garden was utilized for food. Dad grew beans,

onions, potatoes, peas, broad beans, sprouts, cauliflower, cabbage, savoys, the lot, and, as if that wasn't enough, he rented the garden next door, no. 1 Oxford Terrace, where he grew more potatoes. It was Mother's job to pick all the vegetables and we would eat them over the winter, with the potatoes kept under the stairs in the dark. Father used to keep his pears until Christmas; they were still all right, but apricots you had to eat as soon as they were ripe.

We were never allowed to take anything from the garden unless we asked our parents first, but the temptation to scrump usually proved too great. I used to crawl on my stomach between the rows of potatoes up to the gooseberry bushes, and heaven help me if Mother spotted me. She had a window that looked straight out on to the back. It was great fun, until I was caught, that is. All the children used to go scrumping anywhere there was a good apple tree, plums, anything that was sweet and juicy. We knew where all the rich pickings were, and it was part of the fun to get away with it.

Alongside the fruit and vegetables were the livestock, including bantam hens, one of which was in the habit of flying at my legs and giving me a nip. We also had about half a dozen chickens, one bantam cock and two hens. Mother dealt with the poultry, that was her job, while Dad looked after the vegetables, and we kids had to weed.

My father used to keep three hives of bees. He had a machine that would separate wax from honey and then Mother would melt the wax down and sell it as floor wax. The honey would be in a bowl and I used to dip my fingers in. Dad would sell the sections of honey, about one pound weight in each section, and some of the fruit, too.

While bees were useful, wasps were simply a nuisance.

There was very little in the way of pest control except what we could buy from the chemist. He was a friendly chap and was a member of the church choir; he knew my family well. He used to sell pretty much anything over the counter: warfarin for rats or sodium chloride powder for weed killer. He couldn't sell cyanide, but he could and did give me a piece as big as a sugar cube to poison the wasps. The only condition was that I had to sign for it. I took the cyanide home and mixed it with potassium in a bucket of water or a watering can. Using a stirrup pump or a syringe, I'd spray the liquid at the nest and kill them all; those that were in the air literally dropped dead in mid-flight. The funny thing was, other than making sure I was down-wind when using the spray, I didn't take any precautions, no face mask or hood at all, but I never got stung and I never suffered any ill effects.

Close to the bees were a couple of pigsties. This worked fine until on one occasion the bees and pigs briefly became rather more than neighbours. Father was taken ill and was in hospital on the day when Spear Brothers, the bacon people in Bath, were due to come and take the pigs away for slaughter. That meant it fell to my eldest brother and me to get the pigs out and into the Spears van; one was OK, but the other took the wrong path and bumped into one of the beehives. He didn't overturn it, but he twisted it round and the damn things came out in swarms. I cleared out. My mother could handle them, but me, I daren't go near them. The pig was running around and was stung all over.

With Dad having a successful interest in so many different activities, it was almost inevitable that we were comfortable as a family, at least by the standards of the day. We had a butler, part of whose job was to wait at table, bringing in the food that was prepared by the cook. Her name was Alma, and she was named after the battle of Alma in the Crimea [1854], although she wasn't old enough to have been born then. My guess is she was about thirty when I knew her at the turn of the century. There was another housemaid, Ella, who helped out, sweeping and preparing the fire grates, and dusting and cleaning the house.

She had to dust a huge glass cabinet in the living room, containing fifty-five different species of local birds caught and stuffed by my father, from the smallest, a wren, to the largest, a peewit. They were all mounted on imitation tree trunks and branches. For many years George and I spent much of our time attempting to match eggs to each of the birds; we never succeeded. Sparrows, woodpeckers, thrushes and blackbirds were easy, but we watched a pair of king-fishers for two years with no luck. We had a pair of field glasses and, when we eventually found the nest, the off-spring had already hatched. They had built their nest right way back in an old water rat's burrow. Otherwise most eggs were up trees; you can guess who did the climbing.

At Fonthill, the staff came daily but as the family income grew we moved to a larger and grander house that has now gone, called Rosemount. This had a nursery, four bedrooms, a drawing room, dining room, kitchen, scullery and con-servatory. This meant that there was a bedroom for the housemaid and one for the cook, who moved in on a permanent basis. Dad was financially secure enough to rent rather than sell Fonthill but in doing so he proved how shrewd he was: in the lease he made sure that he kept the rights to all the fruit in the garden.

Upstairs, my brothers and I shared a bedroom but we had

our own beds. There was an open fire in the room, which you would put out just as you were turning in, then you would have a bed warmer, a pan filled with hot water on a long pole which you used to gently heat the blankets. In the morning the maid would light the fire downstairs in the dining room before we came down. Combe Down is 800 feet up, and in winter there was frost on the inside of the window every morning – you could scrape it off.

In winter, chesty coughs and colds were treated with honey and vinegar, which tasted horrible, as well as goose grease which was smeared on your chest. My mother was also a great believer in a teaspoon of quinine for colds. For anything worse, Dr Morris was the man to see, a wonderful practitioner who would come out at all hours and in all weathers to visit a patient, water dripping off his hat as he knocked on the door on a wet and windy night. He was a man who spoke his mind. Dad was given pills for rheumatism and Dr Morris used to come round and order him to take them. Dad wouldn't, being the difficult man he sometimes was, and the doctor would have no hesitation in letting fly. 'What's the bloody good of me prescribing medicine when you don't take it?' Not many people would speak to Dad like that! The doctor's surgery was his own home. On the occasions I saw him, I used to go into his front room, the waiting room, and he would call you through to the back room that was his surgery. He would always mix you up some sort of jollop or other; heaven knows what it was and whether it did you any good, but you never left empty-handed.

Life at Fonthill and Rosemount was primitive by modern standards. Light and heating in the house were basic and it wasn't until I was an apprentice plumber that I put gas lamps in for my parents. Before that, we had just oil lamps, paraffin lamps and candlesticks. We always went to bed with a tiny paraffin lamp. In the living room, there was a pendant with two weights: you pulled the lamp down, filled it with paraffin, trimmed the wick and pulled it back up. The fire helped light the room. Otherwise you walked around with a little candle in a square brass candleholder that collected the molten wax.

There was no internal plumbing. At Fonthill the toilet was next to the coal shed in the garden, and was reached by a narrow path. It was a small brick building with just a seat with a circular hole in it. Toilet paper was newspaper ripped into square sheets, fastened by a nail into the wall. Behind the toilet was a big pit that would be emptied every so often, when a cart came and took the effluent away. I expect a farmer used it. We would try not to go at night unless we were desperate, because you'd have to get dressed or put a dressing gown on and feel and fumble the way in the darkness. An outside toilet was quite normal in the countryside and that remained the case for a long time. I remember, well after World War I, when I was in Wales, living next door to a builder's merchant who did a round that ended in Shrewsbury. He was going up a place called Horseshoe Pass one night when it was very foggy. He knew there were some farmhouses along the top of the pass, so he decided to stop at one of the houses until the morning. In the night he went down to spend a penny, but as there were no matches on the candlestick he went down in the pitch-black. He told me that he'd crept down very carefully in case the stairs creaked, and felt his way along until he found the latch to what he assumed was the outside toilet, did what he wanted to do, and went back to bed. In the summer, he was doing the same round and came to the farm, and he went to see how they were getting on. Chatting to the farmer, he told him what had happened, and how he had fumbled his way around in the dark. The farmer looked at him for a moment and then went to the bottom of the stairs and shouted to his wife, 'Blodwen, you were right. That's what spoilt the Christmas puddings.' He thought he was in the toilet but had actually gone into an outside pantry.

It wasn't until after the war that my parents had an inside toilet, because they had to wait until Bath Council put the pipework in, connecting Combe Down to the sewers. Just as there were no sewers, so there was no running water. When I was very young, local people shared wells, so there had to be rights of way and access, allowing neighbours to pass along the back of each others' houses. The wells' shafts often passed through quarry workings underground.

At Fonthill our water came from a well in the garden of no. 5 Gladstone Place, at that time rented by the postman. Both neighbouring cottages had a right of way to the well, which was at least sixty feet deep and surrounded by nothing more than a rough stone wall. At the top there was a little structure with a drum and a rope tied to the bucket. You would throw the old oak bucket down until it reached the stream which ran through the bottom of the well. It was quite strenuous to wind it up when the bucket was full, so until we were much older it was Father's job to collect the water. I wasn't allowed to bring a bucket up – it was too heavy – but I was an inquisitive boy and I couldn't help trying. That was all right until one day, when I was winding, I let go of the handle, and it flew round and knocked me out cold.

A couple of full buckets would usually last a day except for when we had baths. The water was used for drinking, cooking, shaving and one face wash. Any used for drinking had to be boiled first, otherwise it tasted pretty foul. I believe there were as many as eight minerals in the water including iron, lead, silver, gold and lime, and drinking it without boiling it was asking for a stomach upset. Taking water from the well ensured that, as a family, we used it sensibly, otherwise Dad would have been making trips back and forth without end. For this reason, most people in the village made an effort to save their rainwater, drawing the water from the lead guttering. It was collected in a tank and used domestically, though not for drinking. I know that the rainwater from the vicarage was collected and discharged to a big tank and was used for washing, while the overflow from that tank went back into a well.

Because water was so limited, we bathed once a week in an old tin bath in front of the fire. There was an Eagle kitchen range: one side was the oven, in the middle the fire, and on the other side was a boiler with a brass tap on the front. The boiler was filled by hand from the well every morning so that we always had hot water. Mother would draw the steaming water from the boiler and pour it into a small tin bath. Then one brother after another got in, using the same water.

Apart from the wells, there were two iron water butts in Combe Down fed from the mains. When a handle was turned on the side of the butt, a chain ran down over a pulley and opened a stopcock at the base, bringing water out of an ornamental lion's mouth. One butt was just outside the church, the other opposite the pub, the Wheelwright Arms. If you didn't have access to a well in the garden, you could draw water from there. Behind both butts was a wooden trough into which water was poured for horses to drink from.

When I was still quite young, the Combe Down Water Company, a private firm, was established and mains water was brought to Combe Down. The wells were then condemned. Dad was upset. He was a cantankerous old sod and would have his own way, but in the end the authorities sealed the wells with two stones across the top, both two foot six in diameter. In the garden, not far from the well, was a cesspit for the sewage. The overflow from that pit was subsequently discharged into the well so it could no longer be used. I later cut a hole in the top of the well and dumped all our rubbish down there too until eventually the sides collapsed and all the rubbish and the sewage ran into one of the old quarries. As for the two butts in the village, they too were disused, but were left as a curiosity. At least one example of these survives in the neighbouring village of Monkton Combe.

From the age of five, I attended Combe Down Church of England School. My eldest brother had his education paid for; my mother used to pay 2d a week. He went to Monkton School, where there was a private schoolmaster. I wasn't worth the expense! I'm glad I didn't go elsewhere for it was at Combe Down School that I met my closest friend, George Atkins. I was about six and he was eight, and we remained great friends for seventy years. He was born in Diss, in Norfolk, but moved when his father took a job as a coachman quite close to Combe Down. For the rest of our time in school we were inseparable.

Our headmaster seemed to us, as young boys of six or seven, to be about 150 years old, although he was probably in his seventies. He sported a long white beard and, given a scythe to hang over his shoulder, you would have Father Time. His name was Henry Henwood, and he had been at the school for thirty years at least, a kindly man and by the standards of the time hardly a disciplinarian. About two hundred children were taught in four large classes of mixed boys and girls, in the same classroom, the girls in one block of desks, the boys in another. As well as learning the three Rs, there was woodwork and clay modelling for the boys while the girls did housewifery, which meant cleaning lessons, cookery and laundry. A local man by the name of Ross was the school inspector and he was responsible for checking on educational standards.

By no means were all lessons class-based. When it suited Henwood, and time allowed, he would march us to his walled garden which he rented from a Major Rawlings, and in the name of science we would turn over and weed his garden for him; we knew all about dandelions. There we learnt about snails, slugs and caterpillars, too, as well as the many vegetables we planted for him, and the soil we heaped over the potatoes that we had also planted. Our reward was minimal: a few gooseberries and then only when he wasn't looking. Henwood got by far the better deal.

There were other teachers. Lawson was the geometry master, but I was never his best student. I remember that he put two marks on the blackboard, A and B, and he asked what was the shortest distance between them. Of course the answer is a straight line. Then he drew a curve. 'What's the definition of a curve?' I had forgotten that, so I said, 'A straight line caught bending.' I had a rap on the knuckles for that, or rather my hand held out, palm up.

Another teacher, at least informally, was the vicar, the

Reverend Alfred Richardson, who was a noted antiquarian. We used to call him Duck Richards, for reasons lost in the mists of time. On Wednesdays, he would come to the school and ask us bible questions, and, if you got them right, you got a sugared almond.

History and archaeology were by far my favourite lessons. Trafalgar, and Nelson and Hardy. Waterloo and Wellington, the Indian Mutiny and the Black Hole of Calcutta — we knew about them all. Later, just before I left school, we were also taught about the recent valiant death of Scott and Oates, how they fought to reach the South Pole and how Oates left the tent and sacrificed himself for the expedition. We were taught about other great British heroes, too, which meant, more often than not, military commanders. For some boys, this derring-do may have been enthralling but none of it inspired me to be a soldier. I was content with my life.

There were only two places I wanted to go as a boy, Greece or Rome, Rome for preference. I was thrown into Roman history directly I could understand the spoken word. There was the history of their conquests and battles but, because of the influence they had on local life, there were other tales about their everyday lives. There were stories about how they had mined for metals in the area; how they had been unable to remove the silver from the lead taken from the Mendips, and how some of this lead with its high proportion of silver had been found in the Colosseum in Rome. At Charterdown, not far from Wells, it was, and still is, possible to see the old Roman flues where they used to smelt the lead to remove the dross.

This hands-on history fascinated me. Around Bath there

were innumerable Roman excavations, including a Roman villa with coins and pottery and also stone coffins, one with a horse's head inside. Near the vicarage, more stone coffins were discovered, including a skeleton with a coin lodged in its jaw. This was history found while I was at school. Later, as an apprentice plumber, I worked among the Roman remains of Bath, including the famous baths with their lead-lined bottom. When working there, we always took our swimming costumes. So as not to disrupt tourists during the day, all work was undertaken at night by the light of hurricane lamps. Then, when no one was around, we would strip off and swim in the baths, although we weren't supposed to. The pool was eighty feet long and forty feet wide, and it was a great thrill for me to swim where the ancient Romans had been. The water, I have to tell you, tasted disgusting.

In 1910, Mr Henwood retired and a new headmaster was installed and a totally new regime was brought in with him. The new master's name was Henry Collins, and he was a strict disciplinarian, so much so that in two months he lost both Lawson, the geometry master, and a Miss Shepherd, who taught mathematics. They wouldn't stick it, he was that stiff. Bertie, as we all called him – behind his back, of course – would come in each morning and the first thing he did was to tear a sheet out of a magazine, fold it and put it around his cuffs so that they wouldn't get dirty, then he opened the desk and got his cane out and placed it where everyone could see it, then started to teach. We used to get the cane pretty often; you couldn't really avoid it. It was always on the hand, half a dozen strokes, which made the hand a bit numb.

There was one boy, Vernon Bishop, a lad my own age,

who regularly caused trouble. He was always being sent to the Head for punishment, but when Henwood was around all he did was send him home from school for a week, which, of course, was what he wanted. Collins' attitude was different. The first time Bishop played up, he said, 'Now I know Henwood used to send you home, but you won't have anything of that now. If you misbehave, you will be punished.' Vernon didn't like being told and to our complete surprise he kicked Collins square on the ankle. Collins caught hold of him and put him across his knee and gave him the biggest hiding he ever had, then he said, 'Now back to your seat. You come here to learn, not to misbehave. You will never be sent home again.' The next day the boy came to school and his father was with him. 'What did you give him a tanning for?' Collins replied that Vernon had kicked him. 'Would you like me to kick you and see if you like it? That was what he was punished for. And another thing: if you can't tame him at home, leave it to us, he has only got to misbehave a couple more times and there is a remand school at Langport and we'll send him there. The teachers are ex-prison warders, they'll teach him.' This was said in front of the whole class. We were astonished. Many years later, I was to have my own confrontation with Vernon Bishop when his job as a water engineer collided with my own plumbing work, a disagreement that might have led to court action.

Collins had been at the school about six months when he started evening classes. I think he was surprised at the very average level of education, and the idea was to help those who had recently left school to improve their knowledge, but the classes were open to all. He gave lessons, two hours on a Tuesday and two hours on a Wednesday, and I signed up for them with my friend George Atkins. Collins' only condition was that if we started, we had to stick it. The first hour on a Tuesday was English, British English not Somerset! The second hour was Latin. On Wednesday, we had an hour of geometry and an hour of algebra; at thirteen years old, I was sensible enough to see that I needed more education as the time was fast approaching when I would leave school. Indeed, I found a lot of his teaching very useful when, two years later, I sat my exam to become a registered plumber.

Perhaps the most interesting aspect of growing up on Combe Down was the extent of the quarries that honeycombed the ground underneath our feet. I first became aware of them when one of the terraced houses owned by my father shifted slightly. It was built close to an old quarry which had long been abandoned. This was fine until the scullery wall my father was building moved about an inch; it put the wind up him. He found out that the only known entrance to the quarry was in the postman's garden, just the other side of the well we all used for water. He got permission to open it up and he took me down. I was ten years old and it was my first experience of being underground. First we climbed down a short ladder and then, through the second bed of stone, we found a stairway down to the third bed, about fifty feet underground, where the spring ran. I was fascinated. I could see the tool markings in the wall, but much more than that, for there were the workmen's tools, a great saw, teeth an inch long, two stones with a cut between, used to sharpen the saw, and the files stuck in a crevice. It appeared that the workmen had left a shift, never to return.

My father discovered that the walls of the kitchen were

actually resting on two pillars of stone left as supports. The men would cut into the rock about ten feet, and draw a block out, perhaps five or ten tons, and then they would leave a gap, go on and then leave another, resulting in these natural pillars that would hold the ceiling up. There had been a fall in the roof close to one of these supports, and that had caused a crack in the wall of the house above. That was nearly a hundred years ago now and that kitchen wall hasn't moved since.

As the quarries were extended, tunnels led off at all angles and unless you knew where you were going, it was perfectly possible to choose the wrong direction and get disorientated. Once, some boys from Prior Park, a Roman Catholic school, got into one of the caves. They took the outside wall on their way down and they went in thinking that if they kept the wall permanently on their left they could turn round at any time and find their way out, but before long they got lost in these passages. They were three days in there before they were found, and then it was only by a bit of luck. They came across a wall and they tapped on it, and it happened to be the wall of the cellar of the King William pub and the barman heard them tapping. Search parties hadn't found them.

Some people went down to explore the caves unravelling string as they went, but if the string got cut on a rock, you were in serious trouble. To know the way in and out of the quarries, you had to look for markings made by the quarrymen on the pillars. I would find a mark, an arrow pointing in, and after the arrow a number. That was the face the quarryman was working at. Follow it in to get to the face. Under that arrow there is an arrow pointing the other way and that was how he found his way out. Even so, these quarries often broke into each other so you would get confused as to which one you were in.

As kids, if ever a policeman was after us for anything, we used to make a beeline for a cave. Once we were in we'd run just a few feet to one of the stone pillars and hide behind it, knowing the policeman would never risk following us. We might be scrumping apples, or anything else that we'd got up to, and he would chase us. The quarries were our adventure playground and no one really thought much about the danger.

Although the workmen might be gone, the quarries were still full of life and colour. When the weather was bad, wasps would return to where they nested, and very often this was the quarries. Where the stone was a bit rough, the wasps would form a nest, sometimes as big as a football and almost as round. It was like a bees' comb, but a greyish paper-like consistency, full of grubs. Two or three might be suspended from the ceiling by a stalk. This was a tempting target and we used to go along and pelt them with stones, try to stir them up, or even bring the nest down. Of course, if that happened you had to shift and we would tear outside, but even then we frequently got stung on our arms.

All sorts of creatures lived in these caves, including bats, hanging upside down. We'd try to knock them off with a catapult, or if they were low enough we would pull them down with our hands and hold them, like holding a mouse with wings. Later, a rare species of bat was discovered there, and it cost a small fortune to make good the cave entrance so the bats could come in and out.

Outside each quarry there was rubble, stone that was no good for building. These heaps could be quite beautiful, with gooseberry bushes, wild strawberries and even a crab apple tree growing there. Ford, the one-legged roadman who lived at no. 2 Gladstone Place, used to look after the hedges and grass verges of the village. Dad had a habit of giving Ford a couple of pence to buy some seeds, aubrietia and suchlike, and he used to scatter them among the rocks in the quarry. In the autumn, they would flower and look beautiful.

Of course, if we were caught going into the quarries we were shooed off, because some of them were still being worked by independent quarrymen; if they caught us going in, they told us to leave, but in no time we would be back. We used to go in and see if we could find seashells or fossilized fern leaves in the pillars, and we'd try to carve them out. It was very difficult to get one, but that was part of the fun, being careful not to chip it. We never kept them; the entertainment was in getting them out and usually we just threw them away. We were only copying the quarrymen who for generations had cut and saved the fossils, making their own private collections as a hobby.

Bath stone, as it was quarried, had to be laid out to dry, and if it was laid in the wrong direction, it crumbled away. As it was pulled out, each stone was marked on the leading face with a black mark, and that was the way it had to be placed to dry, which might take six months. The men who worked there could tell by the grain what stone it was. My father could look at a block and tell you from which quarry it came, by all the tiny seashells that were in it and the colour. Although we were 800 feet above sea level, the area had at one time been under the sea.

Just as the coal mines used pit ponies, the quarrymen

managed horses underground. They were used to pull the rock from the shaft along a light railway until they came outside, where there was a windlass on a mound. There they coupled a horse on to a long arm and it'd go round and round, winding the rock up the hillside until it got to the flat where there was a shed. These horses spent much of their lives underground for there were stables down there where they slept, and mangers from which they were fed.

Lighting underground was by hurricane lamps or candles. These might be placed in a ledge cut into the wall, or set on anything horizontal; even three nails banged into the stone provided a ledge of sorts. Every now and again a ventilation shaft was dug to the surface; they were called 'light holes'. There were three in Richardson Avenue with just a warning notice board and a small wall to stop unsuspecting walkers from falling in. These holes gave some light in shallower quarries, but after they were closed the shafts were used by people merely to chuck any old household rubbish down. One chap, who owned a garage, used to drop old tyres down the shafts and when he had quite a pile down there, he would chuck in red ash to burn them and black smoke could be seen to rise out of the top.

One of the last men to work in the quarries did so independently although he ought not to have done this alone. One day he went home for dinner and when he came back he found that the roof had collapsed right where he was working. Among his tools was a stone coffin that had fallen through the ceiling and inside was a skeleton and various artefacts. They had an inquest and found he was a Roman soldier. When archaeologists excavated the area, they found yet another Roman villa and attached to it was a private cemetery dating from the same era.

Despite such close shaves, the quarrymen were expert at telling whether a ceiling was secure. An old miner would go in and tap the roof and from the sound alone he could tell whether it was safe or not. Injuries were not infrequent but serious accidents were much rarer. I can recall only one death from a collapse, when, just before the Great War, Fred Davidge was crushed in Vinegar Quarry, a relatively shallow quarry, really, but the ceiling gave way. It closed soon afterwards.

Above ground, the most tangible throwbacks to a once healthy mining industry were the many pubs. Within a quarter of a mile of each other there were the Red Lion, the Mason's Arms, the Hadley Arms and the Horseshoe. Each catered for the workmen from a particular quarry and if a worker from one pub ventured into another, there was a fight. Even when I was a kid, there would be regular free-for-alls.

The man who had been instrumental in the development of the quarries was Ralph Allen, and one of the most interesting places in Combe Down was his estate, Prior Park. In the late eighteenth century this magnate built not just a beautiful home but various follies in the grounds which were wonderful, almost magical, places for children. Sham Castle was one. It was a single wall with turrets, battlements and arrow slits, which he created simply to enhance the view from his house across the valley. The Castle looked enchanting from a distance although there was actually nothing behind it except a farm and ploughed fields. Another construction of his was a folly known as the

Monument. This building was triangular at the base with a circular tower on top. It was derelict even when I was a boy, and was boarded up, but there was no problem gaining access. There used to be a stairway you could climb – in poor condition and probably dangerous – that led up on to an outside platform from which you could look out across the park. On each corner of the triangular base were large decorative pinnacles around which we used to tie a rope, dropping the other end over a stone balustrade to the ground below. We would then climb over and shin down, or run back down the stairs and climb up. Either way it was potentially lethal but incredible fun. Sadly, the Monument fell into such a state of disrepair that it was pulled down in the 1950s.

It was in Prior Park, in 1912, that a string-back plane came to Combe Down to demonstrate the art of flying. It was the first plane anyone had seen, and it drew a big crowd. Its pilot charged a fairly hefty sum to take anyone up for a half-hour's flight. He took off from the grass next door to the Monument, and circled round, and the village turned out to be amazed by the spectacle, little realizing just how dangerous flying was in those days.

About the same time, perhaps a little earlier, I saw my first car. It seemed to me like a block of iron with wheels on. Just down from where we lived was the fellow who owned it. He was a songwriter and poet, Frederick Weatherly [1848–1929]. He must have been in his sixties then, I suppose. I saw him quite a bit around the village, a short, grey-haired old chap, one of the parishioners. He's largely forgotten now but he wrote the lyrics to the song 'Danny Boy', which he set to the tune of the 'Londonderry Air'. He also wrote 'Roses Are Blooming in Picardy', one of the best-known songs of the war. Fred had a friend who wrote the music, while Fred wrote the words. His friend had written the music to 'Friend of Mine', but he died while Fred was writing the words, so instead it became Fred's tribute to his old friend.

2

EDWARDIAN RAISED

Owing to the decline of the quarries, many of the men looked to earning secondary incomes, for instance by helping on farms, particularly during harvesting. Housewives could also help to bring in extra money, by dressmaking, repairing or altering clothes. Other people took in lodgers. That was the legal avenue, and then there was poaching. For many country people it was a valuable and free source of nutrition, hares, rabbits and pheasants being trapped or shot for the pot, and when I was a boy rabbits in particular were almost seen as fair game.

You didn't have to be poor to poach. In fact my old man was a poacher, and a good one too. I don't know if he was ever chased, but I doubt it. Dad had a friend on Combe Down, a police sergeant called Melewish, who liked a bit of rabbiting when off duty. As Dad was partial to rabbit stew, the two of them used to meet and go off together, quite where I don't know.

Sergeant Melewish was with the County Police, the limit of his jurisdiction running through a road called Summer Lane. There was a football club just on the other side of this county boundary, and some of the players used to make fun of him, knowing they were safe. That was until he caught one of them in his county. He took off his tunic and his hat and gave him a damn good hiding. You could get away with those things back then. Much later, when he retired, he took on the Pipers Inn on the way to Bath. Sadly, his son was lost at sea and the news of his death drove his wife blind and in the end Melewish had to give up the pub, a tragic end because he was a real character.

Poaching wasn't risk-free. In the woods, man traps with big iron teeth were still in use. They were hidden in the undergrowth so it was a question of treading carefully. One man who had several was the Reverend Percy Warrington. He owned part of a wooded hill area; well, it was church property really. There were some houses also owned by the church, proper slums, and when Jerry bombed Bath, he settled an argument between the county, who wouldn't buy them, and the vicar, who wouldn't restore them. People were living there, and after the damage he had no choice but to repair their homes.

The Reverend Warrington was not shy of causing controversy. Father helped build the chapel at Monkton Combe Senior School, a school for well-to-do boys, after one row. The chapel was built because the headmaster, the Reverend Hayward, and the Reverend Warrington just could not get on. The story went that before the chapel was built, the schoolboys were given two pews at church. After one service the vicar complained to Hayward that the boys were putting buttons in the collection and Hayward was naturally upset at the accusation. His boys would never do something like that. So the two men fell out and the resolution was the building of the chapel in the school grounds.

As children from an ordinary school, we didn't mix with the boys from Monkton Combe. We occasionally played rugby against them (and gave them a little punch behind the referee's back instead of the flat of the hand). I played at wing three-quarter, so I had to run fast, whereas I have a problem even to walk now! We used to have a fellow come Saturday afternoons to watch us. He'd stand on the touch-line with a double-barrel gun broken under his arm, and we got the reputation among away teams that if we couldn't beat them, we'd shoot them.

The pupils from Monkton Combe weren't local children; they were much posher. Theirs was a preparatory school for Oxford or Cambridge; they were the officers in the army. We didn't mix socially but you would see them walking about, sporting a cap with a white band on it and a blazer. They were smartly dressed and there was a real distinction between them and us. I don't think we were jealous of them, but the class difference was very apparent.

Church in Combe Down was central to community life. Throughout my childhood I sang in the choir, as did many local boys. In the stalls we quietly mucked about. One game was to place a marble on the bench and give it a knock, and the boy at the lowest end had to stop it with his book before knocking it back. I know we missed it once and the marble went off the end of the choirstalls and dropped to the floor, making more noise than seemed possible as it ran on down the aisle. The choirmaster came down at the end of the service to find out what had happened, as did the parson, and marbles became officially off limits.

In church, people rented pews for an undisclosed sum, a label revealing the name of the occupier. These seats were the ones nearer the chancel steps; perhaps the owners felt they were getting a bit closer to God, I don't know. Captain Daubeny rented just such a pew and used to read the lessons in church. He was a wealthy man who had worked abroad in the Government service. I presume he was a soldier of some earlier war, and he would serve again during the Great War, although never abroad. His family owned a large house built above Jackdaw Quarry, The Brow, and in Combe Down church there is a plaque to him. He was to lose his son on the Western Front.

When we were away from church and school, the countryside was our playground. We often walked along the canal side looking for eggs, or around the Midford Brook where the nests were in the long grass or in the bushes. I used to take moorhens' eggs and make a fire and cook them. They were very tasty.

Boys being boys, we made our own weapons: bows and arrows were common, as were catapults, though the trouble was getting the elastic. And woe betide any roaming cats and dogs that passed our way, or pigeons for that matter, indeed pretty much anything that ventured into our path or sat still for long enough. There was no concept of animal rights then and we were a bit cruel at times.

The meandering Midford Brook was a favourite of ours. The steep banks were ten feet across but there was one place where the sides flattened out and we could paddle. The bed then dipped sharply to a depth of fourteen feet, and was known as the 'fourteens'. It was here that we learnt to swim, wading in until it was deep enough, then, well, you sank or swam. We taught ourselves and used anything we could to keep ourselves afloat: two large empty tins, sealed and tied with string around our midriffs, would do. As long as they floated, then, we reasoned, so would we. They were prototypes of the water wings children use today.

One treat was to go to the spa in Bath. For 2d per hour we could bathe in the circular bath or, if we were brave, we could try another pool where the spring came up right in the middle. It was the hottest water of all and was called the two-penny scalder, and was just about bearable. It held about fifteen to twenty people, and you could swim in it. At the end of the hour, they would ring a bell and order you out. There was one other bath we used to call the tepid, that was 3d an hour, and it was all right but less fun. The building that housed these baths is still there but the scalder and the tepid are closed, and are just a curiosity.

There was one place on Hampton Downs, part of Combe Down – it's gone now because Bath University is built there – but there was a field where years and years ago the last duel in Bath was fought with swords. One of the duellists was killed, and someone cut a cross in the turf at the edge of a field in commemoration. As a boy, I used to go and look at it. It was never overgrown, there were no weeds at all, while round it the grass was always well cut. It stayed like that for many years. The land changed hands, and the new owner wanted to discover who attended to it, because no one was ever seen there. He used to watch but never saw anybody day or night, and in the end he set up four cameras, all on tripwires, one in a hedge, one on the footpath, one in a tree and one on the gate to the field, north, south, east and west, all looking towards the cross, while another camera was set up in a tree to cover the whole field. Nothing happened for months, then one night they were all tripped. He developed the film, but there was nothing but a shadow. It was one of the mysteries of Bath and it was never solved.

Not far from Hampton Downs was the old Somerset Coal Canal which ran through Monkton and joined the Kennet and Avon Canal. Before I was born, my grandfather on my mother's side had three barges on the Somerset Canal. They would pull in at Midford to weigh how much coal they had, then come on down through Monkton and when they got to an iron bridge, they'd throw two or three lumps of coal on to the side. My mother and her brother used to run down to collect them and use them on the open fire at home.

The Somerset Canal was closed the year I was born. The water gradually grew wild with weeds and was a wonderful habitat for animals and insects. As children, we spent hours scouring the banks catching newts in fishing nets. We would take them home and put them in an aquarium, but they were forever climbing up the glass and escaping. It was a pity when the canal was finally drained in 1907. They put a railway line next to the towpath and Monkton Combe railway station was built right in the basin of the canal.

That left us with the Kennet and Avon Canal. When we were about fourteen, my friends and I used to go down there to where an aqueduct crossed the canal, and if the lock keeper was asleep we'd pinch his punt. He left a shovel in the punt and we used that to paddle with, and away we would go as far as a swing bridge. It was all a bit of boyish fun, for we used to open the bridge so that the keeper couldn't come across, then we'd tie his punt up on the wrong side of the canal and go up from Claverton and have tea. He had to come down and walk into Claverton before he could get over the canal to walk back to get his punt. Even the Kennet and Avon Canal was very silted up by this time, with lots of weeds, and in time the train superseded the canal as a means of transport. I have a dim memory of seeing a barge come down the canal with timber on it, but that must have been one of the last and as a rule there was very little traffic. In fact there were so few boats that in winter the canal would freeze over and we often took the opportunity to ice skate down there.

As well as the canal, there was a meadow at Midford which was allowed to flood from the neighbouring brook to a depth of about eighteen inches. The water froze, making an ice rink for the children without any danger of anyone falling through the ice to a watery grave below, always a risk with a pond or river. A small charge of a couple of pence was made to skate on the meadow, quite an organized affair as it was possible to rent ice skates out for a small extra fee.

When the snow came, it could easily drift to several feet, and it was perilous even to walk down Ralph Allen's Drive to Bath, never mind drive, when the risk of skidding was extreme. In homes and shops, ice would form on the inside of the windows. Icicles would form anywhere there was a drip of water, such as a tank overflow. Just above the Somerset and Dorset Railway line was a very steep field. In deep snow we'd use it for tobogganing, and if you judged your descent correctly, at the bottom you'd end up on the rails, so we always used to watch the signal to see if anything was coming through the valley. If the signal was down, it meant a train was on its way and, if we had time, we would run up on to the bridge so that the warm, moist steam could billow up all around us. Like every boy, I was fascinated by steam trains and wanted to be an engine driver, but there was no opportunity ever to become one.

There's a train tunnel 500 feet under Combe Down. It's not used now, not since the Beeching axe of the 1960s, but it's the longest unventilated tunnel in England. The trains used to get steam up in Bath, enough to go through the tunnel as quickly as possible without opening the furnace door, in order to cut the smoke from the chimney. As a passenger, you'd go with a handkerchief over your mouth, as the air would get very stuffy, almost stifling. It was so filthy, the windows would cloud up, and you couldn't see, while your handkerchief would get smutty. The tunnel was a mile long and took at least a minute or two to pass through. As kids, we tried to walk through it, but it was very difficult to breathe because of the smoke that got trapped in there and more often than not we were forced back out into the fresh air.

The track from Midford to Bath was a single line and before the driver could take it, he had to be in possession of a pouch. The pouch itself wasn't important, it was the ownership that mattered as it gave the driver the right of way, and negated any risk that another train might be on the line. As long as the driver had it, the signals or points could be operated in his favour, otherwise no. Once the train was through the single line, the pouch was handed to the signalman. For the next train passing through, the pouch would be held out on a rod and the driver would grab it without stopping. However, if the train came too fast he could easily miss it or knock it out of the signalman's hand, in which case he would have to stop and retrieve it. At Midford the station was above a bridge, below which was the Hope and Anchor pub. If the pouch fell, the usual place to find it was on the roof of the pub. Retrieval of the pouch was absolutely essential and often took a few more minutes than expected. This was thirsty work, of course!

Despite the precautions, there was one serious crash on this line in 1929. I was very friendly with the signalman at Midford, in fact as a boy I had been quite interested in his daughter, Queenie. Anyway, what happened was that somewhere up Radstock way the driver and the fireman of a goods train believed they were about to be involved in a head-on crash with an oncoming train. It didn't happen, but they jumped from the engine, leaving the throttle full open. The train went on down through Midford, through the Combe Down tunnel at full speed, shedding two or three trucks on the way before crashing just before Bath station and killing two people. It was claimed afterwards that the driver and the stoker had fainted in the tunnel, but they weren't even on the train then. The signalman at Midford narrowly escaped with his life, as his signal box was smashed by one of the trucks that separated from the train. I had been working in the station hut the day before; I was often in there mending overflow problems in toilets, and when I returned he told me the full story. Fainted! No, they jumped.

One of the hobbies that I enjoyed in my youth was boating. Along with half a dozen of my friends, I joined the local Forrester Road Boating Club, and learnt to row. When we went there, we changed from our Sunday clothes into a vest and shirt, and a pair of rubber-soled pumps. I was number six in a crew of eight, the one behind stroke, while my friend Lionel Morris rowed at number three. We were quite good and used to compete against other teams such as Monkton Combe College.

At the Club, the boats were lined up on a jetty and were

linked to one another by a chain that ran through a screw eye at the bow. This chain was padlocked at the end in an attempt to stop boats being taken without permission. The rules on borrowing the boats were that we could paddle upriver to the next weir, but we mustn't go down in the direction of Bath. The only person with a key to the padlock was the boatman, called Bowman, who looked after the canoes, and it was to him that I, with Leslie Lush and Charlie Wherrett, used to go to borrow a canoe each, agreeing all the while to obey the Club's rules. So we would go paddling about until the boatman was busy, then, as soon as he was distracted, off we would go downstream. Three of us went in a line in the direction of Bath and the four-foot weir we were intent on shooting.

To reach the weir, we first passed beneath the three-arched Pulteney Bridge. Taking the central arch, where the water was fastest, we got ourselves ready. Then, as we approached the weir, there came urgent calls from tourists above us. They stood on the pier by the Empire Hotel and, believing we were ignorant of the drop, shouted, 'Get into the side, you'll go over the weir!' It was what we wanted to do!

As we reached the weir, paddles were raised in case we turned upside down, and over we went, before paddling down to the North Parade Bridge, where we could pull in on a sandbank. Here we would get out and empty any water from the canoes, carrying them back above the weir before paddling back to the boating station. Whenever we went back, Bowman would say, 'What bloody mischief have you been up to?' I think he knew.

Competitive rowing came on the back of many years of fun on the water when none of us took the sport particularly seriously. We were taught a few basics, such as how to right a canoe, but we would only be given an old tub because they knew we would sink it. If this didn't happen, then there was at least a good chance that one of us might end up in the drink. On one occasion when three of us were in a boat, Lionel informed us he wanted to spend a penny. He should have gone before we left, but seeing that there were families having picnics by the side of the river, we rowed until we reached a spot where there wasn't anybody around, and I pulled in under a large willow tree. Lionel was standing at the front of the boat, one hand holding on to the branch of the willow, while he was spending a penny. The boat must have been rocking slightly, because he said, 'Hold tight!' but I thought he said 'All right' and I put the oars into the water and pulled, leaving Lionel up to his waist in river water.

Looking back at my youth, I can see that it was spent in a community that was in many ways cut off from the outside world. Rural villages and small towns lived their own lives and had little interest in what happened in the wider world; at least that was my experience.

To give you an example, I was fourteen when the *Titanic* sank. We were out at play when the news arrived, and the headmaster called us in and we sang the 23rd Psalm, 'The Lord is my Shepherd': 'Yea, though I walk through the valley of the shadow of death, I will fear no evil . . .', and he gave us an address on the sinking of the *Titanic*, and we sang 'Eternal Father, strong to save . . .' with the prayer 'For those in peril on the sea'. I hardly knew about the ship, but the headmaster told us that on her maiden voyage she had been in collision with an iceberg. We were also told that she was trying to make the fastest trip across the Atlantic. Yet it didn't mean much to us; it was a ship that had sunk but when you grow up in the countryside and perhaps a few of your friends haven't even seen a ship, the significance is rather lost on you. I'm sure there were boys who lived by the coast for whom the *Titanic* meant much more.

I remember, too, the suffragette movement, what was her name? . . . Emmeline Pankhurst, but they were interested in politics and I wasn't. Day-to-day news came from the *Bath and Wells Chronicle*, that was the only paper Dad took. In other words this was Somerset, not London, and as far as I recall my mother never discussed it as an issue. A quarter of a century later, I remember the controversy over Edward and Mrs Simpson and the abdication; we had a radio at that time and we heard the news. But political events made little impression down here. I read about it, and that was it.

Eight months after the *Titanic* sank, my friends and I left school and followed our chosen careers, which usually meant leaving on the Friday and beginning whatever job it was on the Monday. Lionel Morris followed his father into painting and decorating, and Charlie Wherrett left to become a commercial artist, designing posters. I was down for an apprenticeship with Jacob Long and Sons, the firm for whom my father worked as a master mason. The 'Sons' were Charlie and George, the latter also happening to be the Mayor of Bath. With their father, Jacob, they ran one of three big building companies in the city. My father organized the apprenticeship. It would be a five-year legal contract that would be formally signed by the company, myself, my father and his solicitor.

I was allowed the Christmas of 1912 at home, then it was straight to work in the new year. The first job I was assigned to involved what is now the Spa Hotel outside Bath. It was being turned into a school, and my first job was standing at the foot of the ladder while the plumber was at the top working, and it was a damn cold January morning. This was the nature of the job. I was expected to watch, to try and follow what the plumber was doing, and then, in time, I would be given just a small job, changing a washer on a tap, perhaps, or adjusting a ballcock in a flush tank. Simple tasks.

The apprenticeship road had been followed by all us three brothers: George as a carpenter, William as a bricklayer and now me as a plumber. For William, bricklaying was not enough, and early in 1913 he suddenly announced that he was going to join the army. He had been persuaded to enlist by his great friend Alfred Logie, a Scot, a carpenter and joiner who lived in the village, the son of a well-known shoemaker. Fred was perhaps six or eight months older than my brother, and had enlisted the year before into the Royal Engineers. Having completed his initial training, he went overseas to Gibraltar. Army life suited him and he had obviously encouraged my brother to enlist and see a bit of the world, rather than simply pursue a career in the building trade.

William was keen to join up, and soon after his nineteenth birthday he too enlisted in the Royal Engineers with the idea of serving together with Fred, although they never got the chance.

My parents were certainly not at all happy about William enlisting; Mother in particular had an idea that only scruffs and villains joined up. I think that was the general reputation the peace-time army had in those days. However, they didn't try to stop him and so off he went. I don't recall seeing him again for a long time, in fact I only recall him coming home once. He was in his dress uniform, red tunic, white belt, looking every bit a soldier. In my interest, I put my fingers on his belt and marked it. William whacked me round the head for that as he had to clean it again with Blanco. Then, like Alf, he went abroad, sailing for South Africa and Pretoria, where he remained until August 1914.

3

JOINING UP

History will tell you that when the war broke out everyone
went mad, singing and marching about, welcoming the war
with Germany. It will also tell you that all the men ran to
join up as soon as they could, and that many boys aged
sixteen and seventeen enlisted. Well, I was sixteen in
August 1914 and I didn't. I didn't welcome the war at
all, and never felt the need to get myself into khaki and go
out there fighting before it was 'all over by Christmas'.
That's what people were saying, that the war wouldn't last
long. I am not saying I knew any different, but at my age I
was keen to continue my apprenticeship, rather than pick
up a gun.

Everyone knew that the war with Germany was only a
matter of when, and not if; it was in the papers and in
people's talk, but while a lot of local lads went and joined
up in the local regiment, the Somerset Light Infantry, I
never gave it a second thought as to whether to enlist or not.
It is hard with the passage of time really to remember what
I thought: I don't recall following news from the front in
the newspapers, although I was aware that my middle

brother, William, was out there, and I'm sure my parents were concerned, but I don't remember any great fear within the family. I don't suppose people knew what to expect and the long casualty lists were a while away.

On the outbreak of war in August 1914, six divisions of Britain's regular army set sail for France. These troops, numbering just eighty thousand, were all that the nation had readily available to take on the might of the German army which had invaded Belgium and was sweeping south towards Paris.

It was clear to men such as the new Secretary of State for War, Lord Kitchener, that a 'new' army would have to be created, a civilian army, trained and sent overseas, if Britain had any hope of successfully prosecuting, let alone winning, a war in which the German army could call up millions of reservists to fight.

Just days after the war started, Kitchener appealed for the immediate enlistment of 100,000 men, part of what would appropriately be called Kitchener's Army. They would form six new British divisions.

Kitchener's call to arms was answered with a mass rush to enlist from among Britain's young and middle aged. Within weeks, there were enough volunteers to fill every battalion in all six divisions, and on 11 September Kitchener sanctioned the formation of an additional six divisions, to be followed shortly afterwards by a further six.

In Somerset, the men of Combe Down were instinctively drawn to the local regiment. It had two regular battalions, one reserve battalion and two territorial battalions, five in all. In addition to these, a new 6th (Service) Battalion was formed. In the event, this was filled quickly, and in September and again in October two new battalions were formed and were numbered the 7th and 8th (Service) Battalions.

After the initial rush to enlist, the numbers dropped rapidly. It was found that an essentially rural community could not supply the numbers of men required to fill all three Kitchener battalions. Consequently the 'local' composition of each battalion gradually declined, so that while the 6th Battalion was formed with well over 80 per cent Somerset men, this fell to around 70 per cent for the 7th Battalion and to just 25 per cent for the 8th Battalion, which took as many men 'redirected' from the north-east of England as from Somerset. Many of Combe Down's men, Harry's friends, thus found themselves serving alongside men with whom they had very little in common. However, death and injury did not discriminate between backgrounds. At least twenty-four men from Combe Down were killed serving with the Somerset Light Infantry, of whom eighteen were killed serving with the three service battalions, perhaps a dozen of them more or less Harry's contemporaries.

I have only a patchy memory of the outbreak of war. The newspapers were full of it, of course, and as that first week in August was a bank holiday weekend, a few people were being patriotic, walking about Combe Down singing popular songs, among them, as I recall, another Fred Weatherly composition, 'We'll all come up from Somerset, where the cider apples grow . . .'. I think it was a song that was written for the Somerset Light Infantry, more or less as a recruitment song. A number of local lads, some of whom would never come back, were keen to go and see a bit of adventure. Reginald Whittaker was one, although I knew his brother Gus better. They lived a stone's throw from us on Landsdown View and were known to be a bit of a rough family, always fighting, always arguing. Frederick Gerrish was another who joined up, as was Albert Kellaway, a married man and neighbour of the Whittakers. Eric Barrow, from Church Cottages, was one of those who lied about his age to enlist. He was the same age as me and so could not have been older than eighteen when he was killed on the Somme in 1916, serving with the Somerset Light Infantry.

Somerset people are not warlike – it is not something in our make-up – and we are certainly different from people who live in the big cities. We heard rumours, for example, that people in the towns were being given white feathers to embarrass them into joining up, casting aspersions on their manhood if they didn't. I didn't see anyone receive one and no one tried to hand me one either; in fact I never felt any pressure to go, not then and not for the next two years until I was called up.

Soon after war was declared, soldiers began to appear in the village, including a number of men of the Royal Army Medical Corps who were billeted close by in Combe Grove. Perhaps their presence inspired a few to enlist in the RAMC, perhaps it was because we were not anxious to fight that a number of lads enlisted as medical orderlies or stretcher-bearers; I'm not sure, but my close friend George Atkins chose the RAMC as did my mate Leslie Lush and his brother Lewis, both of whom preferred the RAMC to a regiment of the line. In time, almost all the local lads served in one way or another. A few, like my eldest brother, were deemed unfit for the army and worked on the home front in munitions, but most of us were healthy enough and as a consequence the village paid a terrible price for its willingness to serve the country. Lionel Morris, the lad who had spent a penny in the river, he joined up, as did my friend Charlie Wherrett, and both were killed serving with the Somerset Light Infantry, and Lewis Lush, too, was killed sometime towards the end of the war.

I didn't want to join up. I came from a very sheltered family. I didn't want to go and fight anyone, but it was a case of having to. When it came, army life didn't appeal to me at all and when I found out how rough-and-tumble it could be, I liked it even less. I had no inclination to fight anybody. I mean, why should I go out and kill somebody I never knew, and for what reason? I wasn't at all patriotic. I went and did what was asked of me and no more.

I was about eighteen months into my apprenticeship when war broke out. Over the next few months, all the able-bodied plumbers on the firm either joined up or after a couple of years were called up to fight when conscription became law. The firm lost key staff and in the end there were just four men who were over military age and four apprentices. This meant that there was more than enough work to go around for those of us who were left, and inevitably the lads, like me, were sent out to do jobs which normally we wouldn't have been allowed to touch until we had finished our apprentice-ship. We undertook these jobs, working fourteen hours a day, and made a lot of mistakes, being cursed for all eternity by the older men who then had to be sent out to put them right. Nevertheless I gained a lot of experience and with evening classes twice a week to learn the technical details of the job, I was, by the age of seventeen and a half, competent enough to sit for the London Guild of Registered Plumbers exam at the

Merchant Venturer's Hall in Bristol. I passed it, my first examination to become a registered plumber.

Throughout 1914 and 1915, William, my middle brother, was away fighting in France. He had left Pretoria within days of war being declared and had entrained for Cape Town, from where his unit, the 55th Field Company, Royal Engineers, sailed for England, arriving in mid-September. The news from the front was not good: we heard all about the battle of Mons and the famous retreat, and how our small regular army had held the enemy near Paris. Since then the war had bogged down and my brother and his unit were needed at the front. As soon as they were properly kitted out, his unit was turned around and sent straight over to France sometime in early October 1914. I didn't see him before he left and I don't believe my parents did either, and although they heard from him often, it would be the best part of two years before they saw him again.

William's letters home told us something about his time at the front. He had taken part in the first fighting around Ypres, a town that meant nothing to me then. He had been doing all sorts of work: making wire entanglements, repairing the front line, digging communication trenches, mending roads, filling in shell holes, and various other jobs, including making primitive hand grenades for the infantry. He really went through it, by all accounts, although we only heard the full story when he came home wounded, by which time he had taken part in most of the big battles of 1915, including Neuve Chapelle and Loos.

George, my eldest brother, remained at home. He was in his mid-twenties in 1914, had been rejected because of asthma, and began work just outside Bath station. J. Long and Sons had a big builders' yard there and he was charged with making wooden storage cases for 18-pounder shells. Each case had a copper lining which had to be made waterproof. Every screw was soldered at the top, as was every join, so as to stop water seeping in and damaging the shells.

There were just a few casualties from Combe Down in the first year of the war. I don't suppose there were many local men in the regular army other than my brother William and his friend Fred Logie, and in 1914 and 1915 the village wasn't hit hard. I don't think it was until Christmas time 1914 that the village lost its first son, a married man called Bright, a regular: his family still live locally today.

Only in 1916 did the losses become much more serious. The local men who had enlisted in the new battalions of the Somerset Light Infantry were overseas by then, and that summer, when the battle of the Somme began, a lot of casualties began to be reported in the local press, lads that everybody knew. My brother was one of them. He may have come home on leave from the front before he was injured, but if he did I don't remember. Then, in early July, my parents received a letter informing them that William had been wounded, not on the Somme but up at Ypres. He had been hit by shrapnel while revetting trenches and was on his way back to England. He was already in Netley Hospital when my parents went down to see him. He had been wounded in the legs, not too badly because in the long term his wounds did not affect his walking. However, he never went back to France. He had reached the rank of sergeant while abroad and, because of his technical knowledge serving with the Royal Engineers, he was kept back as an instructor.

It would have been August or possibly September when he left hospital and came home on leave. People were beginning to understand what the war was about, and not just because of the long lists of casualties in the papers. At Combe Park, a large war hospital looked after hundreds of injured men, many of whom could be seen, dressed in their hospital blues, walking around Bath city or being pushed in wheelchairs.

William gave me all the details I needed to know about the front line. He used to tell me how lousy and dirty the trenches were, and about the mud and the shrapnel. I knew what I was going into, but being the sort of person I am, I would always have preferred to be told rather than be left in the dark.

There was no getting out of it. In 1915 the Government introduced National Registration when everyone above a certain age, fifteen years, had a legal duty to give the authorities details of their age, occupation and address. Everyone was then issued with a registration card which was to be carried at all times. There was pressure to get more men into the army and this information would be used when conscription came in, to call up the country's manpower, starting with single men. In June 1916, I turned eighteen years of age and from that time onwards I knew that a telegram requiring my service was only months or perhaps weeks away.

Notification came by post and with it a railway warrant from Bath to Taunton, to report by such and such a time the following day. This would have

been around October 1916, and five of us from the
village went down from Bath to Tolland Barracks. Here
we were roughly kitted out and our civilian clothes sent
home. Then, after a few days, it was off to Exmouth
where we did our basic training, squad drill out on the
square, with route marches to build up our strength and
stamina. Quite early on, I was picked out, for reasons
unbeknown to me, and made a lance corporal and given
a stripe. This was the winter of 1916/17, one of the
coldest that I can recall, and we used to go down to the
sand dunes to do physical training and it was perishing.
We did square bashing, left and right turns, about turn,
and were glad of the physical exercise just to keep
warm.

At Exmouth I was put in a billet in Sandwell Road, I
think that was the name. It was a residential house
commandeered by the Government for lodging. This was
not unusual. The size of the army had left the authorities
with a terrible shortage of accommodation and, well before
I joined up, I can remember dozens of soldiers living in
several big houses in Pulteney Street in Bath, all of which
had been taken over by the army.

Our billet was practically empty, no carpets or anything except beds which consisted of three boards on a
trestle and a couple of blankets each. Every room was
full of men of all backgrounds and characters. It was here
that I learnt the first lesson of the army: lock everything
up if you can, or keep a close eye on it if you can't, for it
wasn't very long before someone pinched my boots. I
knew enough to realize that I would not only be in
trouble but indented for a new pair. I made a search and
found out who'd taken them. The thief wouldn't own

up, which meant either I backed off or I fought for them, so I did what I was called up to do – fight. We went outside the house and got stuck in with fists, and after a scrap I got my boots back, plus one rather obvious black eye. It was a silly argument really, but you had to stick up for yourself in the army, or else. Unfortunately for me, the fight was witnessed and I was taken before the officer in charge. The upshot of this was that I lost my lance corporal's stripe over the incident and never regained it.

In early 1917 we went to Sutton Veny near Warminster where I joined the 33rd Training Reserve Battalion. At this point we weren't attached to any regiment, although before we joined the 33rd I wore several different regimental cap badges, the Warwickshire Regiment being one, so I must have been shifted around.

Our training was the usual left, right, turn by numbers. We did quite a bit of route marching around Salisbury Plain with full pack, including an overcoat, water bottle, bayonet, and entrenching tool at the back. We had gas masks issued too, known as box respirators. Nobody liked wearing them. They were a damned nuisance; they misted up and you could neither see nor even breathe properly with them on. I never wore one abroad, but in England we trained in them, going through a chlorine gas-filled hut, putting them on before we went in and then taking the horrible things off once we'd reached the other side.

Bayonet fighting was taught with special vigour by our training sergeants. Go for the shoulders, the two lungs, the heart or groin, though if you had one up the spout, as we called it, which was a live round in the rifle breech, you gave him that instead of the bayonet. If he parried you off with his rifle and bayonet, you went for him with the butt in the crotch or the leg or, if you had a chance to get it up, smash it into his face and knock him out that way. We were always taught that if you got to hand-to-hand fighting it was him or you, and with that in mind you fought with real spirit because anything less was probably fatal. It was him or you: which would it be?

That winter was not just cold but stayed cold for months. The huts we slept in had a Tortoise stove, a round stove in the middle of the room, but unless your bed was close to it, the heat dissipated long before it reached you. Each hut had a coal ration but when our company was on guard over the coal dump, supplies improved significantly! We used to go down; if it was our people, they'd turn their back and we would pinch the coal. The coal dump was behind a gated enclosure on the edge of the camp and this led to an unfortunate incident. An officer came down to check on the guard. He must have been challenged but for some reason he didn't answer and in the dark he was shot in the leg. Of course the sentry faced a court martial, but what happened to him I don't know.

It was at Sutton Veny that we really started training with rifles, firing on the ranges, learning about not only the rifle itself but the slight vagaries that each one had: perhaps yours fired slightly high, or right. At one point, I had a rifle that grouped shots to the left-hand side of the bull at about eleven o'clock, so the only way to get a bull's-eye was to fire down at five o'clock and keep your sights slightly lower.

We were on the ranges on Salisbury Plain, and I wanted

one or two more bulls to get the sought-after Crossed Guns, the badge of a marksman. I needed eight more points but the rifle I was using was firing high, and we were on the 600-yard range. I said to the sergeant in charge, 'Can I lower these sights?' He had a word with the officer. 'Tell him to put it down to five hundred and fifty,' replied the officer. I had five rounds left; my next two shots were bulls, twelve points, four more than I needed, my next shot was an inner, that was another four, and the other two I didn't trouble a damn where they went. It was something to be given the badge to wear on your forearm, but if the truth be told it was the 6d a day extra pay that I was after. Being a marksman meant one of two things: I could be a sniper or I could be sent to a Lewis gun team. I could never have been a sniper – it was far too cold and clinical – so I was sent for training on the machine gun. Here they gave us a badge to go on our sleeve, a wreath of laurels with LG for Lewis gun in the middle. As I was to discover, the badge was known to the machine-gun crews as the 'suicide badge', because if you were taken prisoner by the enemy then more than likely you would be shot.

Throughout my training at Sutton Veny we were given occasional weekend passes out of camp. For those of us who came from Wiltshire or Somerset, it was possible to go home. From the camp, a friend and I walked to Warminster from where, for half-a-crown, we could hire bicycles and ride home for the weekend, just as long as we were back in camp at midnight on Sunday. It was lovely to head back to Combe Down and see our families.

Just as I was about to finish my training, at the start of May 1917, I received the news of the death of one of my cousins. My aunt Lizzie Patch, a widow, who lived a stone's throw from my parents, had heard that her son Fred was missing, believed killed during the fighting at Arras. Fred was just a few months older than me so I knew him well, although we weren't close. He wasn't a sportsman like me, he didn't go boating or play down in the quarries. Instead, he was something of a quiet boy, and a gardener by profession. His body was never found. I was very sad, and his death only brought home the feeling that the war was getting very close.

4

IN THE TRENCHES

A couple of weeks later we were informed that our training was over and we would soon be leaving for the Western Front. After six months' training, yes, I think we did feel prepared to go to France; we were fit and strong but, equally, we were young and some were still keen. Unlike most, I had, of course, been told much by my brother but even so nothing could prepare me for the reality.

As was the custom when soldiers were warned for overseas service, we were given a week's embarkation leave. I went home with Charlie Wherrett and Stanley Pearce to visit our respective families in Combe Down. It was difficult to say goodbye; even today I find it hard to talk about. My mother had seen Bill go overseas and return wounded and now she had to watch me leave. I only understood how difficult that was when, twenty-five years later, I watched my own son leave for war. I can't recall what I did that week. I was no doubt preoccupied with thoughts of going to France; either way, one morning, my leave over, I got up and took the electric tram through Combe Down to Bath station and from there to Taunton. My parents didn't walk me to the tram; instead they saw me leave from the house and after the usual embrace, goodbye and good luck, I went. I know that I met up with Stanley to catch the tram. He had attended the same school as me, but was a few years older and was no more than an acquaintance. In civilian life, he had become a baker's boy, in the family business. Although we had trained together in the 33rd Training Reserve Battalion, we would soon be split up when we arrived in France. He went off to the 8th Somerset Light Infantry and I never saw him again, for he was killed just a few weeks later on the opening day of the third battle of Ypres. Charlie Wherrett accompanied me to France, but we too were parted and never met again.

Yet none of us could have predicted our fates when, in the second week of June, our small group walked up a narrow gangway and was packed together on an old paddle steamer. As the men crowded on board, the group that I was with moved to stand by the port-side paddle. As we pulled out of Folkestone harbour, we watched England and the white cliffs gradually recede into the darkness. I wasn't the only one who wondered whether we would ever set foot on her soil again. Would I come home and, if I did, would I be in one piece? We all knew what we were going to; there were no illusions any more, no excited chatter or joviality. All the lights on board were extinguished and we were forbidden even to smoke, for there was a genuine threat from submarines and an escort of two destroyers would shepherd us across. This was what we were told, but it may have been to make us feel better because in the pitch-dark we saw nothing but the waves breaking around the boat.

I got talking to Jack Fisher, a stoker by trade and a

member of the crew who had previously been in the Mediterranean. He told me that while on the island of Malta he had been ordered to change from one convoy to another. The transport he left then sailed and the next day it was sunk with all hands. He was lucky, and I idly wondered if some of his luck might wipe off on me. That night we slept on deck, if there was room. Lookouts were posted, while the ship zigzagged all the way across the Channel so as not to give any enemy submarines a broadside view.

It was daylight when we arrived in Boulogne, and we disembarked and marched up a steep hill into St Martin's Camp. The sound of guns was just about audible. The sight of soldiers had ceased to arouse any interest among local civilians and we disembarked without fanfare. As we marched away from the dock, I was judged not to be carrying enough, so I was given a fifteen-pound pack of bully beef to carry into camp. We lived in tents, but soon after arrival we were separated and drafted to various regiments. It was at this moment that Charlie and I were parted; there was no choice in the matter. I went into the Duke of Cornwall's Light Infantry, and he was sent to the Somerset Light Infantry and was drafted to a regiment in Egypt, and he died out in India in 1919. My new battalion would be the 7th, a service battalion in the 61st Brigade, 20th (Light) Division, a brigade that, as it turned out, also contained the 7th Somerset Light Infantry and, of course, some of the lads from Combe Down.

When the new draft arrived in France, we were selected for whatever regiment happened to be short of men. That was the fate of conscripts: you couldn't pick your regiment as the volunteers had, otherwise I would have chosen the Somerset Light Infantry. We were lined up and they asked if anyone there knew anything about the Lewis gun. Having had some training, I said 'yes'. The 7th DCLI had a team, and the no. 2 had gone home to England on compassionate leave and so I was sent to join them. On the way over, I had carried a Lee-Enfield rifle but from the moment I was chosen to join the Lewis gun team I was ordered to hand it over and was issued instead with a Webley revolver. As a no. 2 on the team, I would be responsible for carrying the spare parts for the machine gun, enough to build another one if needs be, and so I was not expected to cart around a rifle, too.

A sergeant introduced me to my new friends. At the time, the battalion was out of the line and we were sent to work on the ranges, training, to see how quickly we could do the job. I'd been thoroughly rehearsed on how to take a Lewis gun apart and, if it jammed, what I could do. What I didn't know, Bob Haynes, the no. 1 on the gun, soon taught me. He insisted absolutely, 'You've got to be quick and accurate, our lives and your life depend upon it', and he kept on practising me, when out on rest, changing the magazine and stripping down the gun. I had to know what to do automatically when anything went wrong.

The team was very close-knit and it had a pact. It was this: Bob said we wouldn't kill, not if we could help it. He said, 'We fire short, have them in the legs, or fire over their heads, but not to kill, not unless it's them or us.'

The 7th Duke of Cornwall's Light Infantry had been fighting on the Western Front since late July 1915. Despite the battalion's Cornish connections, many of those who served with the unit were not Cornishmen at all. Just as the Somerset Light Infantry had taken in men from the north-east, so the DCLI incorporated men from almost as far away. Looking at the backgrounds of the first one hundred men killed with the battalion, it is interesting to note that only sixteen were from the Royal Duchy, while as many were from Birmingham, and eleven were from towns such as Leeds, Blackburn and Sunderland. However, by far the largest number were Londoners, some fifty-seven in total. By the time Harry joined the 7th Battalion in June 1917, it was even more diluted, so that his not coming from Cornwall was the norm rather than the exception.

When Harry arrived in France at the end of the first week of June 1917, he joined a battalion resting after an exhausting time in the line. The 7th DCLI was already some three hundred men under strength following its involvement in the battle of Arras in April. Then, in late May, on its last tour in the line, the battalion had suffered a number of casualties from German shelling. C Company in particular had lost a disproportionate number, twenty-six men being killed or wounded, with the other three companies collectively losing just seven. The following month, the Battalion War Diary noted the arrival of three officers and seventeen other ranks, one of whom was almost certainly Harry. Not surprisingly, he, along with a number of other men, was sent to C Company. In July, a further 195 other ranks and one officer were sent out to join the battalion as it prepared for its involvement in the forthcoming third battle of Ypres.

Although the 7th DCLI was out at rest, the word 'rest' itself was something of a misnomer, for the men were not allowed time to recuperate. Rather, they were expected to supply working parties for the trenches. In June, a number of men were required to help the tunnelling companies which were digging deep dugouts in the vicinity of a village called Lagnicourt. On 13 June, the battalion was relieved once again and retired further back to a place referred to in the War Diary as 'Camp A', close to the village of Vaulx. Here the men underwent further refitting and training, with drill, musketry and lectures followed by instruction in map reading, patrolling and bayonet fighting.

The weather had been very blustery and showery when we were ordered up to the front line before Ypres. I know I passed through the shell-shattered town, and I can clearly remember the Cloth Hall in ruins, smashed to pieces.

It was my first time in the trenches and it just about coincided with my nineteenth birthday. Understandably I was nervous, but I didn't want to reveal any feelings to the others in my team; it wouldn't have helped me, and it would certainly not have helped them, and it was important to show them that I was reliable. They had all seen front line action and they needed to know that I was no danger to them; a windy or nervous soldier was as much danger to the rest as he was to himself. They had lost a member of the team and I was the new boy. It can't have been easy for a Lewis gun team to lose anyone under any circumstances, and I was aware that I had to prove myself before I was accepted.

No. 1 carried the gun and I carried the spare parts. The gun weighed thirty-eight pounds and the spare parts weren't much under, including one spare barrel, so it was quite a weight. Going into the line, nos 3, 4 and 5 carried panniers on straps over their shoulders, two on their chests and two on their backs, fully loaded, which meant they were carrying two hundred rounds.

We moved up with the company, along a muddy communication trench, halting at intervals until we got into the line and the men spread out. We were a little group on our own, five of us, although we were part of C Company, and under the same discipline as everyone else, but we were excused the ordinary duties, such as fatigue parties; that was the job of the infantrymen. As they were being organized by their NCOs, the Lewis gun teams were allowed to find their own spot, more or less, and we set up the gun where Bob directed and patrols were sent out into no-man's-land. The Germans may have been aware that a relief was under way, as it wasn't long before a number of shells landed close to our trenches, followed by some mortars, and enemy aircraft were active overhead. How did I feel? Well, how would anyone feel? It doesn't matter how much training you've had, you can't prepare for the reality, the noise, the filth, the uncertainty and the calls for stretcher-bearers. We took a number of casualties in the company before we were relieved.

At Ypres the land was low lying and the water table very high. It was only possible to dig down a foot or two before hitting water, and as such it reminded me very much of the Somerset Levels. The trenches were hardly below ground at all, and most of the protection was a breastwork built above ground level. The conditions were frequently awful. I quickly got used to sitting on the firing step with my feet up against the trench wall opposite, watching the water flowing underneath the duckboards. Where the floor was particularly bad, we used to get an empty box of ammunition and stand on it until it gradually sank in the mud, when you'd put another on top and stand on that. The ground was absolutely full of boxes lost in the mud.

Because we were Lewis gunners and relieved of the jobs

that the infantry were expected to do, almost our entire occupation was making sure that the machine gun functioned properly. The main problem with the machine gun was an unexpected jam at a vital moment. As a bullet travelled up the barrel, gas was sucked back on to the piston, forcing it back ready for the next round. However, should the gun get too hot, the piston wouldn't come back and compress the recoil spring and it was that recoil spring that was used to fire the next round. As it was my job to sort out any problems, I might have to replace the barrel, no easy job when the metal was hot enough to blister your fingers.

If it was raining, we wore a groundsheet which we could use as a cape, but it was more important to keep the gun dry and we'd cover that first before we covered ourselves. The Lewis gun was our job – lose the gun and we lost the point of our being there – so our main concern was to make sure the gun was clean, oiled, and ready for immediate use: loaded, magazine on.

Ensuring that we remained efficient was the job of the officer who would come down every morning. 'Stand to, right inspection.' The officer would take my Webley revolver out, snap it open and if there was a round missing you had to say who ordered you to fire it, where it had gone and why you fired it. Similarly, if the revolver was in the holster with the safety catch off, I could be on a charge for that because of the danger of shooting myself in the foot, and a self-inflicted wound was always looked on very dimly. Ammunition was hard to bring into the front line so you had to account for almost every round. The rifles belonging to the ammunition carriers were also checked before the Lewis gun was inspected. The officers were very particular that the gun and the spare parts were kept scrupulously clean, otherwise you were put on a charge. If any of the brass cartridges were damaged, then they wouldn't be ejected from the gun, jamming it; likewise a little bit of mud could render the gun unusable, and there was plenty of that around, so they were ensuring that we were ready if the Germans mounted an attack.

I served at Ypres during the summer, June to September; what it was like in the winter I hate to think. But even in the summer it was chilly, too, with occasional storms and frequent squally showers. About three to five in the morning it would get very cold, and you'd do what you could to keep yourself warm, clapping your hands together, moving your feet about, or, if you weren't on watch, moving up and down the trench. The night seemed endless, but then if the sun came out you were all right and as the sun rose, so your spirits rose a little, too.

Each morning at dawn, we stood to, the sergeants and corporals would give the order and the men would climb up on the firestep and look, just to make sure the Germans weren't up to anything, planning a sudden attack or raid. We'd be up there for half an hour, after which you stood down. In the morning, the rum ration would come round. Rum was brought up in a big pottery jar. I don't know what the measure was meant to be exactly because they poured a bit into the lid of your mess tin and you drank out of that. It burnt all the way down, especially if you weren't a drinker, but it warmed you up beautifully. Breakfast followed, then there might be a chance to go to sleep or doze off in the sunshine. If we got peckish we carried something like a square dog biscuit. It was so hard that you had to soak it in water to get your teeth into it.

If we were lucky, the mail might come up. One of the first parcels I ever had contained some of my brother William's wedding cake. It had been packed with an ounce of tobacco, but in transit both had got mixed up together, so it was a case of sitting down and meticulously picking at the cake to separate one from the other if I was to enjoy the cake and smoke the tobacco. I used to write home about once a week, but you got writing paper when you could. To send a private letter required what was known as a green envelope, which you signed saying that you had written nothing untoward, otherwise everything was censored by one of the company officers.

Despite all the rain, there was little fresh water in the front line as everything we needed had to be carried up. Ration parties would bring the water up in petrol cans which were rarely washed out. There was a standing joke that if you were out there long enough you could tell the difference in taste as to whether the water came in a British Petroleum or a Shell can. Washing was almost impossible. Behind the support lines, if you were lucky, you might find an old shell hole where the mud had gradually settled, and, the top of the water being reasonably clear, you would get a wash in that. In the trenches you might get a little lukewarm tea from which you might save a drop to have a shave, but washing in the conventional sense was out of the question. The army did provide baths well behind the lines, but I never got the chance to bathe. Indeed, from the time I landed in France in June until I came away in September, I never had a bath, and I never had any clean clothes.

There was no sanitation at all, and the place used to stink like hell. The latrine was a little recess somewhere in the trench with a piece of wood across it to sit on. Toilet roll was a bit of torn-up *Punch* magazine or newspaper.

Boredom was the real problem. We used to sit there and make up poems about the army, based on the old nursery rhymes, such as 'Jack and Jill' and 'Mary had a Little Lamb'. It was one way of whiling the time away. You would be on lookout for two hours, then off, and someone else took your place. It was so boring; you have no idea how boring it was. You'd think about what you were before you joined the army, and you'd think about the men around you. Up to a point, you slept. I mean, when they wanted sleep everyone slept, perhaps on the firestep or in a funkhole scooped out of the trench wall so you could get out of the way. You might keep awake for hours on end, but eventually you dropped off, into a fitful sleep of sorts, perhaps for an hour, two hours maybe, head in your hands, but the least noise and you would be awake and wonder for a moment where the hell you were and what you were doing there.

We took it in turns to keep lookout. You stood on the firestep and, if you saw anything you thought was a German working party, you would nudge a friend. 'What do you think?' Any doubt and we would report what we'd seen, or thought we'd seen, to the officer and he would have a look with his field glasses, to see if anyone was showing a white face or a hand. If he was even a bit doubtful, he would order a star shell to be sent up. This shell used to break into half a dozen lights which floated down, shimmering in the night sky, and they lit up the whole area. When it was sent up, we were told always to lean forward and keep our faces well down, with our arms and particularly our hands tucked in under our bodies so that nothing white could be seen. Peering out from underneath our helmets, we would try and count how many lumps we could see in no-man's-land. About five minutes after that light had died, we sent up a Very light, which lit up a much smaller area. Once again we would count; perhaps there would be the same number, well, all right, but perhaps there would be one lump less, or one more. If we knew that none of our men were out there on patrol, then the officer would say, 'Right-ho, give them a burst!' If it was just a bush, then the bush stayed where it was. Bob, as the no. 1, would fire half a magazine at them, then, straightaway, we would move from our position down the trench. It was important not to fire a magazine from the same position because the Germans could see the flash from the Lewis gun and take a bearing on the position. Firing again from that spot was asking for half a dozen whizz-bangs. So we'd always move, perhaps twenty, perhaps thirty, yards either way in the trenches and have another go, and then perhaps, later on, you'd go back to the same part of the line again. While the infantry worked at night, our duty was to carry on watching, watching, watching. Oh yes, the darkness played hell with you, with your eyesight.

After three days, a new battalion came into the line and we would be relieved, making our way out down the communication trench, which was often far from easy. You daren't let anything tinkle, like a cup, or any of your equipment rattle. Not that one person making a slight noise made any difference, but if you have a company moving into position the accumulated rattle would alert the enemy to the fact that a changeover was under way and that was an invitation for a few whizz-bangs. We were being relieved by a Scottish regiment one night, and there was only just about room for two of us to get by one another in the narrow communication trench; what with the machine gun and all the equipment, we damn near had a battle of our own to pass, pushing and shoving and swearing under our collective breath.

Once out of the trenches we took a duckboard track. This was a hazardous journey in itself. We were always told, going up or coming back, that, if a fellow slipped into a shell hole filled with water, to leave him there because it was liquid mud; if you tried to get him out you'd go in yourself and that was it. I thank God it didn't happen, because the thought of leaving anyone stuck in the mud, possibly to drown, would test anyone's resolve. Such orders were not as heartless as they seem; there was a logic to it. A company coming in or out of the line stretches back a long way, and in the dark hold-ups could cause confusion, men could get split up and hopelessly lost. Equally, no one wanted to linger on those tracks longer than they had to, just in case the Germans decided to have a little fun with their guns.

After four days in the line we went back to billets and got ourselves cleaned up. The billets varied, but one I vividly recall was on a farm, close to Poperinge, and still occupied by the owner. You never knew with the Belgian farmers: some were good and some were bad to the Tommies.

The owner of this farm had a pump in the farmyard that was used to draw fresh water from a deep well. Everybody was going to the well to draw water, and this began to grate on the farmer. He complained, and in the finish they put a guard on the well. To resolve the problem, the company was split up into groups of seven, and each one was given a permit to draw one bucket of water a day. From that bucket we could fill our water bottles; the rest was to be used for shaving and washing. Of course it depended on who was on guard – if you knew them, OK, help yourself.

At the start, the farmer left us alone when a guard was put on. However, in the end he was afraid we would pump the well dry, worried enough that he took the handle off so that we couldn't use it. I was a plumber in civilian life, so I got to work. I got a strip of wood, coupled it up to the piston that goes up and down inside the pump barrel, bored a hole and put a pin through. As long as that piston was working, it drew water; when we left, one of our men put a round through the suction pipe. That, of course, destroys the vacuum, and once air got in there was no water. I was sure the farmer would find someone to solder over the holes to make the suction pipe tight again, but for the time being he couldn't use that damn pump. I'm certain he was more than a little annoyed about that. I also made sure I took my handle with me as well, in case we wanted it somewhere else.

Out of the line, the only rest you were getting was a rest from the shells. For most of the men, those few days were spent on fatigues of one form or another, carrying duck-boards up the line, or rations, mending roads; the army never liked you to relax if it could help it. Bored soldiers are restless soldiers and restless soldiers get up to no good, and so a regime was organized to keep us occupied.

You couldn't really relax unless you had the chance to go down to Poperinge into Talbot House, or Toc H as it was known to us. A lot of us used to call it 'the haven' because that's exactly what this place was to the men – a place of peace where you could relax, and that's the only time you could forget the strains of war for a couple of hours.

Poperinge was a busy, medium-sized town, I should say

ten miles west of Ypres, and, although it was shelled occasionally by the big German guns, I don't remember that it was badly knocked about, not in comparison with Ypres. Men would come back to 'Pop' if they were going on leave, or they would go there when they were out on rest, and so you always felt comparatively safe there.

Toc H (gunners' signalling code) was named after Lieutenant Gilbert Talbot, the son of the Bishop of Winchester, who was killed during the fighting in front of Ypres at the end of July 1915. His brother, the Reverend Neville Talbot, a senior Church of England chaplain, had been given the task of selecting chaplains to join various battalions, and met the affable Philip 'Tubby' Clayton, whom he attached to the East Kent Regiment and the Bedfordshire Regiment. Clayton arrived in Poperinge in late 1915. With Neville's help and approval, he sought out a house which could be used by all soldiers, irrespective of rank, as a hostel and home from home, 'where friendships could be consecrated, and sad hearts renewed and cheered, a place of light and joy and brotherhood and peace', as Clayton later wrote. The building he chose was an empty mansion rented from a wealthy brewer for 150 francs a month on condition that the house was kept in good order. It had in fact been hit by shellfire in 1915, which had caused serious but not irreparable damage to the building, smashing windows and also badly damaging one corner of a hop loft at the top of the building, which was soon earmarked as a chapel. This room was repaired by the Royal Engineers, and in December 1915 the house was opened as a hostel to any British servicemen going up to or coming back from the front line. In the garden, a carpenter's bench was found and for the rest of the war this bench became a makeshift altar in the chapel and was used throughout the war by Tubby Clayton. It remains *in situ* today.

Discipline in the house was kept not by cast-iron orders or army rules; rather, light-hearted suggestions such as 'IF YOU ARE IN THE HABIT OF SPITTING ON THE CARPET AT HOME, PLEASE SPIT HERE'.

Tubby Clayton was an officer, an army padre, but you wouldn't think he was a clergyman, not at first. He ran the place and was the life and soul of the party. He had a deep, almost bass, voice, and he could sing a good song and tell a good tale. He would sing any old chorus including, I remember, the Ivor Novello song 'Keep the Home Fires Burning'. The only time I heard that song in Belgium was Tubby singing it in Toc H.

The house was as homely as Tubby could make it, with flowers in vases, pictures on the walls, carpets and rugs on the floors, a piano and comfortable chairs to sit in, and open fires. You could have a cup of tea there and a bite to eat if you wanted. There were games going on, and you could join in, or, if you wanted to borrow a book, you could, and the price of a book was your cap, which was returned to you when you brought it back. I believe Toc H at one time was used as a grain store, and all the grain had been stored in the upstairs room. I take it the wheat was in the centre, as the middle was a bit dodgy and Tubby was afraid that the floor would collapse, so everyone used to sit around the edge on benches.

The room at the top was his chapel. Tubby upstairs became a different man from Tubby downstairs. He tried to reassure people in that room, to the best of his ability, that everything was all right. He knew damn well it wasn't. We took communion at the altar made from the carpenter's bench. He knew, as I think most of the people who went into that room knew, that there were people there who were about to go up to the front line and who would not come back. That time in particular was difficult, because we knew we were due to go into battle, and for some that communion would be their last supper. There was a lovely garden in the back, and I can remember going down there and in the middle there was a big shell hole, several feet deep. Today it is a lawn, with flowers. We looked upon Toc H as somewhere we could rest, but it wasn't safe; we were still well within shellfire.

That summer, the number of men visiting Talbot House reached its zenith, and cups of tea by the thousand were sold for a nominal price, and the seventeen staff, the largest number employed at the house, coped with these quantities of men pouring through the front door; these included Harry Patch and his Lewis gun team. In an attempt to assess the numbers using the hostel, a test tally was undertaken by the staff in 1917. The result: 117 men paid a visit in just one ten-minute period. 'And thus we lived through the summer,' wrote Tubby Clayton a year later, 'during which so many of our best friends died, and we came with set teeth to that unforgettable autumn when division after division went forward almost to drown, that those eternal slopes might at last be won, which, had the weather held, might have been ours in the first week of August. With the late autumn there came upon the spirit of the men a darkness hitherto unknown.' That 'unforgettable autumn' was the battle of Passchendaele, and Harry was about to play his part in the struggle.

5

PASSCHENDAELE, 1917

The third battle of Ypres, or the battle of Passchendaele as it is also known, was launched on 31 July 1917. Field Marshal Sir Douglas Haig, the British Expeditionary Force's Commander-in-Chief, was keen to press on with a new offensive in the belief that the German army was near to collapse after the attritional battles of the Somme and Arras. At the same time, British forces would break out of the salient to clear the enemy from the Belgian coast, as German U-boats were using it as a base for successful operations against the British merchant navy. Within senior Government circles, dire warnings had been given that unless the U-boat threat was broken, Britain would be so starved of essential supplies that she would not be able to prosecute the war in 1918.

War Cabinet approval for the summer offensive was given only on 20 July. Just eleven days later, after a ferocious preliminary bombardment, British and Commonwealth troops attacked and made, by the standards of the day, spectacular gains despite the onset of heavy drizzle. This turned to rain in the afternoon. The heavens opened and a battlefield which had proved passable just hours earlier became a veritable quagmire. For the most part, the captured ground was held, but the mud made it impossible for the artillery to move up to support the infantry, who were in places up to three miles east of their morning start line. The rain continued ceaselessly for the following three days, making further advances impossible. The offensive had temporarily ground to a halt.

The weather that August was exceptionally bad. The rain came down in torrents, twice as much as the seasonal average and five times more than in the two previous Augusts. Indeed, for the rest of the month there were only three days when rain did not fall.

For the next two weeks, both sides expended and traded an enormous volume of shellfire as each fought for battlefield supremacy. Vicious localized attacks continued on 10 August, before, on the 16th, the battle of Langemarck was launched in the morning darkness. Eight divisions were assigned the task of renewing the offensive on a wide front. Among the units to be sent into the ensuing mêlée was Harry's 20th Division.

The day before the attack, on 15 August, troops were thrown across a swollen stream known as the Steenbeek, attacking various positions to clear the ground for the forthcoming assault. Close to Langemarck, several pillboxes, including one large concrete fortification known as Au Bon Gîte, had been attacked. A number were knocked out, although Au Bon Gîte held firm, despite at one point being surrounded, British infantry even getting on to the roof of the pillbox. German counterattacks forced the infantry back, but nevertheless a vital foothold had been secured across the Steenbeek, and the next night infantry of the 60th and 61st Brigades would be able to cross and assemble within striking distance of the enemy.

Harry's brigade, the 61st, was given the task of attacking

three objectives known as the Blue, Green and Red lines. These were targets drawn on a map, at roughly 500, 1,000 and 1,500 yards from the jumping-off line. The Blue line would be taken by the first wave of assault troops, two companies of the 7th Somerset Light Infantry and the 7th King's Own Yorkshire Light Infantry. This line was defined as being the road bounding the western edge of the village of Langemarck. The men who reached this line would then pause for twenty minutes while the remaining two companies of each battalion would leapfrog their position and continue the attack to the Green line, clearing the village, on the far side of which they, in turn, would halt and dig in. During these initial attacks, the 12th King's Liverpool Regiment and the 7th Duke of Corn-wall's Light Infantry would be expected to make their way forward over the newly won ground, passing through the first waves, ready to continue the assault to the Red line, a complex of German trenches. The direction of the attack would be broadly north-east. A and C Companies of the DCLI would lead the way, A Company would attack on the right of C Company, in all launching two waves of infantry, each ap-proximately two hundred strong. Harry and his Lewis gun team would follow in the second wave to support the infantry by harassing any enemy troops they saw.

Supporting the infantry throughout the advance would be the artillery, firing a creeping barrage across no-man's-land. A creeping barrage consisted of a slowly moving curtain of fire and steel that fell just ahead of the infantry, obscuring their advance and pulverizing any enemy troops who might still be in position. The barrage would lift a hundred yards every five minutes, halting for a period in front of each objective before moving on over the open ground. This curtain of fire would continue until the Red line was taken, whereupon it would drop just 200 yards beyond the objective for an indefinite period, disrupting any possible German counterattacks while the troops dug in.

Throughout July, the 7th DCLI had been out at rest, preparing for the forthcoming offensive.

The third battle of Ypres was under way and we were to play our part in the general advance, that was obvious to see. We undertook intensive training through the early part of August in drizzly weather.

Before we went forward, all the men left their packs to be taken back by our transport into storage. We wouldn't see these again for the next few days. Some of the lads wrote home, and I may have done too; I know I made out my will. We understood what was going to happen in the morning and we had all those hours to sit down and think about it, so we tried to keep ourselves busy.

We were issued with two days' rations and ordered to see that our water bottles were full. Extra kit was issued to the men, shovels and more bombs, that sort of thing, while all the Lewis gun teams were ordered to carry further ammunition. Bob and I had to carry a full Lewis gun pannier in our haversacks, while nos 3, 4 and 5 carried not only one drum of ammunition in their haversacks but also special carriers which looped over the shoulder and in which it was possible to hold another four, all full of ammunition. It was no mean feat carrying all your equipment into action in dry weather, but over boggy, shell-pocked ground it would be hellish.

We were told that we were going over the top and what the objective was and that we were not to go beyond that, we mustn't go any further. Flares were issued to the infantry to signal when they had reached the German positions but in the event I don't recall any being used.

On the night of 15 August, the battalion fell in, single file, along the west bank of the Yser Canal, and at 11 p.m. crossed over, with C Company taking the lead. A gap of a hundred yards between each of the four companies was ordered but as they marched closer to the line, each company split into platoons, so as to minimize the casualties should a shell fall among them. At midnight, the battalion was halted and the men allowed to rest. At 1.45 a.m. the march continued by way of a trench board, and then a mule track constructed a few days before by the Divisional Royal Engineers. Soon after, the battalion crossed the Pilckem–Langemarck road. By keeping the disused Ypres–Staden railway track on their left, C Company arrived at the assembly position just west of the Steenbeek stream. It had been a tiring march, for it wasn't until 4.15 a.m. that the first men were in position.

In the darkness, the mud and occasional German shelling had caused several casualties and, in the confusion, half of A Company and both D and B Companies had become detached and were temporarily lost. One officer with C Company and two men were sent back to find the rest of the battalion and hurry them forward. As C Company waited in position, the Steenbeek was reconnoitred by the Commanding Officer and Adjutant for bridges and crossings.

The leading waves of Somersets and KOYLIs had to assemble on the far side of the Steenbeek in the dark, the men being ordered to advance as quietly as possible. In places, enemy posts were no more than eighty yards beyond the stream, and it was essential that they were not alerted to the forthcoming attack. Despite the 'normal' shelling and machine-gun fire, it became clear that the preparations were successful and that the men had crossed unnoticed.

At zero hour, 4.45 a.m., the advance began. As the KOYLIs and Somersets began to move to the attack, so C Company crossed the Steenbeek and formed up a hundred yards to the east of the river bank. The ground was appalling and in places men waded up to their knees in mud. Even so, progress was going as well as could be expected, for as C Company crossed the stream, the remainder of the battalion arrived just after zero hour, following the leading company over the water. At 5 a.m., the battalion was in position only a few minutes late.

It was now dawn, and soon the first British aeroplanes could be seen flying very low right along the line, observing the general advance. One of the two leading companies, A Company, by moving east of the river, had suffered some seventy casualties owing to machine-gun fire from the right, while C Company on the left was afforded some cover by the fall of the ground towards the disused railway line.

I'm told we attacked on 16 August, but the date doesn't mean much to me. I know it was some six weeks before I was wounded, so I suppose the middle of August is about right. I remember the names – Pilckem Ridge was one and the other was Langemarck – but it is such a long time ago that I can't quite connect them up in my head. How were we to know that a pile of rubble was this village or that, or that a gentle slope was a particular ridge, let alone what was going on across the front? You only knew what was right next to you, and even this was often obscured by smoke and fire. Strategy we left to those higher up. We were only warned to be quiet as we moved up, as this would be a surprise attack and the enemy was not to know that we were there.

A and C Companies were the assault companies so I assume B and D were in support. Ahead of us, two battalions in the division were to undertake the first advance and we would follow on. In the early hours of the morning we prepared to move off. I have a memory of crossing a flooded stream; it wasn't very wide, and I have since been told it was the Steenbeek. There were a number of trees there, like beanstalks, no leaves or branches, they were just smashed to pieces, or toppled into the stream. To my right, about thirty yards away, there was a little bridge that had been blown up, so instead the Royal Engineers had fixed up some canvas-covered pontoons, three or four feet wide. However, one of them broke loose and began floating away and there was a scramble to get it back and anchor it sufficiently so we could cross. We went over in single file, the pontoon rocking from side to side. I can see it now. Beside us, in the dawn light, the artillery was getting a couple of light field guns over, to shell the German support lines, I would guess.

Our guns' opening bombardment had begun with an almighty clap of thunder. You can't describe the noise, you can't, but it was enough to take your breath away; it was ferocious and much of it was dropping not that far ahead of us as the barrage crept forward with the infantry behind. There was an officer going down the line; I say a line: we were effectively in the open. He had his drawn revolver, and I got the distinct impression by the set look on his face that anybody that didn't 'go over' would be shot for cowardice where they stood.

On the far side of the flooded stream, we assembled. There was a look of apprehension in everyone's eyes, and horror in a few. There was white tape laid there so we knew where to stand and in which direction we were expected to go, otherwise we might wander off course, or fall into a shell hole; they were virtually lip to lip. I saw an officer at this time; he came along unravelling and putting down white tape. We saw him for about ten minutes before he moved on. He just laid it on the ground from one shell hole to another, it wasn't pinned down. We now waited for the whistle to blow.

The officer Harry saw was almost certainly Major Percy Norman, MC, of the 84th Field Company Royal Engineers. A mechanical engineer from Taunton, he enlisted in October 1914 and embarked for France when the 20th Division was sent overseas. He was commended in the Divisional War History for completing 'the very hazardous task of laying tapes under severe fire'. Norman and the men under his command laid 600 yards of tape, including 125 yards east of the Steenbeek from where the 7th DCLI commenced their advance. Harry was pleased to hear that Major Norman survived not only the attack but, indeed, the war.

During the initial fighting, German resistance had proved sporadic and confused. This was due, at least in part, to the fact that the exhausted garrison defending Langemarck was in the process of being relieved by fresh troops as the attack was launched. One large pillbox, in the ruins of an abandoned farm, held out for up to half an hour, long enough to threaten the pace of the advance, but this resistance too gave way and very soon streams of prisoners, as many as 150, were seen stumbling towards the waiting men of the DCLI. Fearing that they would disorganize his formation, the Commanding Officer pointed the prisoners in the direction of the railway, the banks of which would give some protection; 'they were only too ready to go and needed no escort,' wrote the CO after the battle.

The first objective was taken at 5.40 a.m., less than an hour after the attack commenced. Five minutes later, at 5.45, and now in broad daylight, the 7th DCLI was ordered forward, passing through the destroyed buildings of Langemarck to a position identified by a single poplar tree on the horizon.

It was just shell holes, and the team made its way forward in a line. It was absolutely sickening to see your own dead and wounded, some calling for stretcher-bearers, others semi-conscious and beyond all help, and the German wounded lying about too, and you couldn't stop to help them. I saw one German – I should think he'd been dead some time – well, a shell had hit him and all his side and his back were ripped up, and his stomach was out on the floor, a horrible sight. Others were just blown to pieces; it wasn't a case of seeing them with a nice bullet hole in their tunic, far from it, and there I was, only nineteen years old. I felt sick.

The ground remained sodden and cloying, with shell holes half full of putrid water. Keeping any formation was impossible and the men were allowed to proceed in any way they could. They crossed the first objective, coming across groups of KOYLIs digging in along the remains of a hedgerow. The KOYLIs' numbers were badly depleted but they had reached and secured the second objective, the Green line. It was now shortly after 6 a.m. and the DCLI halted among their comrades while the British artillery barrage pulverized the ground ahead for well over an hour. At 7.15 the barrage became intense, then, at 7.20, it began once more to creep over the German-held ground ahead. Company officers now ordered the two leading companies to move forward. C and A Companies of the DCLI passed through the KOYLIs, pressing the attack to the Red line in two waves, with another company, B, in support.

I can recall a large pond that we went round. Here and there, dotted around the landscape, there were concrete block houses, which had caused a lot of damage among the first waves but which had, for the most part, now been taken. As we pushed forward, we got mixed up with some Somersets, who had been attacking to our right and were busy mopping up any resistance. Some German prisoners were coming across; they had been pointed in our direction and I remember one was still carrying a Maxim machine gun, which I suppose he had been ordered to take with him, as no one else was armed that I can recall. They looked tired and dishevelled, what you'd expect men to look like after four days in the front. We didn't feel sorry for them. Why should we? They were out of it; we had to carry on.

We came across a lad from A Company. He was ripped open from his shoulder to his waist by shrapnel, and lying in a pool of blood. When we got to him, he looked at us and said, 'Shoot me.' He was beyond all human help, and before we could draw a revolver he was dead. And the final word he uttered was 'Mother!' I was with him in the last seconds of his life. It wasn't a cry of despair, it was a cry of surprise and joy. I think – although I wasn't allowed to see her, I am sure – his mother was in the next world to welcome him and he knew it. I was just allowed to see that much, and no more. Yet I'm positive that when he left this world, wherever he went, his mother was there, and from that day I've always remembered that cry and that death is not the end.

I remember that lad in particular. It is an image that has haunted me all my life, seared into my mind, but you saw plenty of people wounded, crying for help, but of course you daren't stop, for one you didn't have the medical knowledge to help them and for another you didn't have the time; your orders were to press on and support the infantry. Bob, our no. 1, was already forging ahead. I had wanted to go to the lad's tunic and find his identity disc, his name and his number. I would have written to his people, but Bob couldn't wait, and, with me having the spare parts to the Lewis gun, I had no option but to follow on.

The barrage held for a while, then after about half an hour it moved forward. We advanced behind it, hoping that no shell would drop short.

It was up to the DCLI to reach the final objective. Resistance was lighter than expected and as many Germans fell back or ran in confusion, the majority of casualties suffered from machine-gun fire; another eighty prisoners were taken. In little more than half an hour, the attacking waves reached the Red line. By 10.30 a.m., Brigade Headquarters had received reports by pigeon that the DCLI were consolidating the position and were in touch with the battalions on their flanks.

Any barbed wire had been flattened out by the terrific barrage, and by the time we reached the German first line it was clear, as was the second when we got there. We came down into a traverse from which two communication trenches led back to their reserve line where our lads were fighting. It was our job, if anything happened, to cover them with the Lewis gun. The fighting was hand-to-hand, but they were so mixed up that we couldn't use the Lewis gun; you'd have killed as many of your own as you would the Germans.

At one point I knew that Bob was flat on the ground, his hands employed with the Lewis gun. I would lie down on one side of him and, as he finished firing, the finger of my right hand would be on the receptor. As I pressed it in, releasing the empty pannier, I lifted it off just as my left hand pressed a new pannier on. I would then pass the empty pannier back to no. 3 and he would pass it back to no. 4 and no. 5, and they would reload it and pass it up to me, to my left hand. It was a cyclical action between all five of us, and all the time as the machine gun fired it got hotter and hotter to the point when it became difficult to hold.

I'd just changed a magazine on it, and Bob was looking elsewhere in the support line when two or three Germans came out of a trench and one of them spotted the machine gun and came straight for us with rifle and bayonet. Now we were all lying down, under cover – behind a dead German, to tell you the truth – and he must have seen us because he came towards us with a fixed bayonet. He couldn't have had any ammunition in the rifle, otherwise he would have shot us. My right hand was free; I'd just changed a magazine. I drew my revolver and I shot him in the right shoulder. He dropped his rifle but he came stumbling on, no doubt to kick the gun in the mud and us to pieces if he could – it would have taken us half an hour to get it working again if he had.

I had four seconds to make my mind up. I had three rounds in that revolver. I could have killed him with my first; I was a crack shot. What should I do? Four seconds to make my mind up. That Cornishman's 'Mother' was ringing in my ears and I thought, 'No, I can't kill him', and I gave him his life. I shot him above the ankle, and above the knee. I brought him down. He called out something to me in German, I don't suppose it was complimentary, but for him the war was over. He would be picked up by stretcher-bearers, interrogated, passed back to a prisoner-of-war camp, and at the end of the war he would rejoin his family. Perhaps he was married; perhaps he had children.

I've often wondered since if any of those three shots made him lose an arm or a leg. And I've often wondered whether he realized that I gave him his life. He was no more than fifteen yards away when I shot him. I couldn't miss, not with a Webley service revolver, not at that range.

Bob had picked up the gun and we were on our way again. Things had more or less calmed down when we caught up with the front line, getting tangled up in barbed wire as we went. Of course the barrage had blown the wire all over the place and we had to find our way through it. If you came across a piece of barbed wire that was probably obstructing your way forward, you would cut it with a machine gun and push it on one side.

The trench was a mess. There were dozens of German stick grenades lying about, but, though they looked all right, we wouldn't touch them in case they were booby-trapped. In the past I'd seen our own bombers throw a Mills bomb over with the pin still in, and if a German was fool enough to pick it up and pull the pin out, bang, he'd had it. The bomb was already fitted with an instantaneous fuse, and directly that lever flew off, it exploded. It was a trick our bombers did and I had no reason to believe the Germans' own bombers weren't just as crafty. In the same vein, there were any number of little dugouts in the enemy trench we could have gone into, but we daren't in case they were booby-trapped; we had been strictly warned beforehand about this. The bombers used to clear them and they had their own methods. They would go along to a dugout that looked innocent enough, and throw a hand grenade down there. The explosion of the grenade might detonate whatever was in there, or, if there was a German lurking in there, probably kill him too. As a rule, I never touched anything on the battlefield. No souvenirs: you took souvenirs at your peril.

While the bombers cleared the dugouts, we got busy reversing the trench, using our entrenching tools to move the firestep from one side of the trench to the other. As machine gunners, we were usually excused such duties, but not now. We worked as hard as everyone else, moving the sandbags from one side of the German parapet to the other, piling them up with an aperture for the Lewis gun in between, where we could sweep in case there was a counter-attack, because we were certainly expecting one. Where we were, the Germans had found some timber, put it across the trench and covered it with corrugated iron and earth. We set about piling sandbags on top. We hunted round. There were a number of our dead lying about and we took their groundsheets from their haversacks to place on top of our little shelter to make it waterproof. It made a shelter of sorts. We had one man looking out and the rest of us tried to get what rest we could. In front of us there was a pond and what looked like the remains of an orchard and the ruins of a farmhouse, a perfect place for a sniper, but we didn't get any trouble from there.

Some time later a few men were ordered to search the dugouts, looking for anything of interest, documents and letters which could be sent back to headquarters for examination. The battle had been over by mid-morning and so we waited all that afternoon for an attack that never came. We were sitting among a sea of shell holes, you can't imagine how many, craters lip to lip. They were half-full of water and one, just at the back of where we were, well, the stench was terrible, a half-rotting body was in there, no doubt about it. Right across the battlefield, the bodies of the wounded who were dying, or those who had died, would sink out of sight in the morass. They would never be buried. In places we were up to our knees in mud, gluey, sticky mud. The water came oozing through the earth, you couldn't stop it. The trench was boarded up to keep the sides back, otherwise it would have collapsed.

As night approached and the firing subsided, you could hear the moans of the wounded and the cries for help in both languages. We stayed put all through that long night before we were relieved the next day, exhausted but intact. The only casualty was one of our ammunition carriers who found that his overcoat had a bullet hole through the tail, straight through one flap, and out the other, without him being touched. He was lucky.

The wounded were in a bad way. Those who were walking made their own way back as best they could. The battalions' stretcher-bearers were assisted by two hundred infantrymen detailed to help. They had been given just a week's rudimentary training in first aid and the application of field dressings. Their job was to scour the ground and evacuate the wounded as hastily as possible, but there was no such thing as haste in the swamp that engulfed them. One hundred stretchers had been made available, two men to carry each one, but often four men were needed over the most difficult ground.

The wounded had to be carried across the newly won terrain, and back across the Steenbeek. The first rudimentary medical treatment was available at one of two Regimental Aid Posts (see map on page xiii), yet these were over three-quarters of a mile from the swollen stream. From there, the journey continued to Gallwitz Farm, where four steel-and-sandbagged shelters had been constructed on the eve of battle. The farm was a Forward Advanced Dressing Station, another three-quarters of a mile trudge for the stretcher-bearers. It was only here, if the casualty hadn't already died through loss of blood and shock, that he could be removed on either a horse-drawn ambulance or a trolley that ran along a light railway.

Any casualty badly wounded forward of Langemarck on the 16th had to be carried at least two miles across a polluted battlefield before they could be properly evacuated. It might take several hours for two stretcher-bearers to make even one round trip, by which time they would be exhausted.

After the fighting had died down, the battlefield had taken on an eerie silence as both sides needed time to work out and adjust to their new positions. Three or four contact planes of the Royal Flying Corps flew over the lines to clarify the position on the ground. They were engaged by enemy aircraft which brought down one plane, driving the others off. Four more enemy aircraft appeared, flying up and down the newly won ground at a low altitude, as if photographing. These planes intermittently opened up with their machine guns, spattering the ground close to the men who were working hard to dig in. Lewis guns returned fire.

The Germans were unlikely simply to accept the loss of territory and, as Harry surmised, would almost certainly attempt to muster forces to make a counterattack against what they would calculate was a tired and depleted opposition. At about 5 p.m. a force about one battalion strong was seen massing in front of the DCLI, who were ordered to open rapid fire with rifles and Lewis guns. As an extra precaution, a green-coloured SOS rocket was fired in order to bring down accurate artillery fire on the enemy, forcing the Germans to disperse. A second German attack was launched just as the sun set at 7.30 p.m. and got to within 200 yards of the Red line before that too was broken up, and withdrew before darkness fell. Patrols were sent out to reconnoitre no-man's-land, capturing two Germans in the process, but otherwise the night remained quiet.

In the morning rations and water were sent up to the men holding the new line, while periodically the Germans shelled the village of Langemarck. In the evening of the second night, a small attack was launched on a short section of trench that the Germans had reoccupied to the DCLI's right, and this was retaken without much opposition. These would be the last casualties that the 7th DCLI suffered in the operation, for at 1 a.m. on the morning of 18 August they were withdrawn. They arrived back into their bivouac camp at 6 a.m., exhausted.

For the scale of the attack, the 7th DCLI's casualties were relatively light. Two officers and forty-one other ranks were killed or died of wounds, while a further 140 others were wounded. Of the seven battalions closest to the DCLI, the average loss was fifty-four dead, a low casualty return in the context of the Great War.

The 20th Division's attack opposite Langemarck had been a success. The advance had taken the men 1,500 yards east of the Steenbeek, and a large number of casualties had been inflicted on the enemy; twenty officers and four hundred other rank prisoners had been taken. A section of enemy 4.2-inch howitzers and one 77-mm field gun were captured, as well as twenty or thirty machine guns. A number of concrete pillboxes had also been put out of action.

As a result of its success, the division was also awarded two Victoria Crosses. Private Wilfred Edwards of the 7th King's Own Yorkshire Light Infantry won his VC just ahead of Harry's battalion, while Sergeant Edward Cooper of the 12th King's Royal Rifle Corps won his VC to the right of the DCLI. Both medals were awarded for successfully neutralizing German block-houses. Two more Victoria Crosses were won by men of the 29th Division, who attacked just to the left of the DCLI, on the other side of the Ypres–Staden railway line.

Victoria Crosses were predominantly awarded for success and not for failure and overall the day was an almost unmitigated failure. To the south of the DCLI the results of the fighting were nothing short of a disaster and around 15,000 men were lost for little advantage. Among all the other divisions that fought that day only one other Victoria Cross was awarded, and that to a stretcher-bearer. It was symptomatic of the day's effort. The one gain was the village of Langemarck, after which the battle was named, and it was the 20th Division, including Harry's Duke of Cornwall's Light Infantry, that won the plaudits for this.

I am often asked what I thought of our Commander-in-Chief, as if I must have an opinion. All I can say is that sometimes Haig's intelligence was good, other times it was rotten. But we didn't talk about him among ourselves, in the trenches or out at rest. I know people think that we must have spoken about him, but I can't remember ever doing so. We were there to do a job, and we did it. We weren't there to criticize; we knew when they'd gone wrong.

The weather was fine and the men were described as being in 'fine fettle'; while exhausted, they were no doubt elated at having come through such an ordeal. Their battalion's ranks were greatly thinned, and, at no more than 330 strong, their numbers must have seemed shockingly low to the men from the transport who met them at Proven camp. The following day, a voluntary church parade was held, after which the men cleaned their equipment and indents were made out to replace lost items. Twenty recommendations for awards were submitted and two weeks later, on 3 September, the battalion paraded as medal ribbons were presented by the Divisional Commander, and the Divisional Band played. New drafts were sent to the battalion in late August, making good the numbers lost on the 16th, but not the experience.

For the rest of the month, new drafts underwent further instruction and training, and working parties were sent out under the direction of the Royal Engineers. In early September, the Lewis gun teams were sent to the ranges, and battalion sports and football competitions were organized for the men. Photographs were taken of various groups and companies, before the battalion's inevitable return to the front, and to a position close to Langemarck. Here the men were ordered to undertake battlefield salvage, collecting some 250 rifles and two Lewis guns, many lost by their comrades such a short time before.

Only on the evening of 9 September was the battalion deemed fit and ready to return to the trenches, where once again a tour of duty brought its commensurate number of casualties, both killed and wounded.

The period out of the line, after the fighting, is something of a blank for me now. I've been shown pages of the War Diary, but for the most part it's hard to relate to the record. Going over the top, as I did, overshadowed much of the mundane, ordinary life that we lived out of the line. In the Diary, I see we were reviewed on one occasion by a senior officer. I thought it was the King, but I must be wrong. I remember being reviewed only because the officers and NCOs had a hell of a job to get us out to cheer him. We were too damned tired.

*

In billets or in trenches we lived with rats and mice. The rats, in particular, were frequently huge, some say as big as cats; well, I don't know, but getting on that way. They would pinch your rations and gnaw at your leather equipment and they would have a go at your bootlaces if you stood there long enough. When you went to sleep, you would cover your face with a blanket and feel the damn things run over you. They were quite tame and they certainly weren't afraid of you; most rats will scamper away from you, but not those in the salient.

Roaming around the destroyed villages were not just rats but cats, dogs, mice; you name it, we had it. Stray cats would come into the line, and a stray dog occasionally, and, as a rule, they'd be as vicious as hell. After the war, I worked with a builder who had a terrier that had been born in the trenches. How he had got the animal home is anyone's guess. However, if you were in the same room as the dog, the only way you could get out was if you had a saw in your hand and you showed him the teeth. He was fierce. It was the way they had to live. They survived on what was dead, thrown away or abandoned.

There were times when you'd look out into no-man's-land between the firing points, and all you could see were a couple of stray dogs looking for something to eat to keep alive. These ordinary, domestic dogs had lost their homes and their owners were long gone. Having nowhere else to go, they used to come into our trench, and no doubt they visited the Germans, too. I watched them on many occasions and I thought about their struggles to survive. If they found a biscuit to eat – which was probably ripped from a dead man's tunic pocket – they would start to fight over who should have a bite. And I thought, 'Well, what are we doing that's really any different? Two civilized nations, British and German, fighting for our lives, just the same.'

As a Lewis gun team, we took our orders from the officers, but when we were in the trenches we were just that little body alone, and we shared everything. Now, my mother used to deal with a big grocer just outside Bath, and every fortnight he used to send out a parcel to me in a cardboard box, with an ounce of Royal Seal tobacco, two packets of twenty BDV cigarettes, some sweets or chocolate, if the grocer could scrounge them, and a couple of cakes. Number 4 on the Lewis gun and I were pipe smokers, so the ounce of tobacco was cut in half; half was mine and half was his. The forty cigarettes were divided among the other three, thirteen each, and they used to take it in turns who should have the odd one. Cakes, chocolates, anything else, were all divided. If you had a pair of clean socks and a fellow had socks with holes in, he'd have the clean socks and threw the others away. And that was the spirit that was within that team. There was no question of sharing with anyone else; like the bombers, they must look after themselves.

I remember Bob had a good thick sweater came out one time, and whoever was on lookout that night had that sweater to put on.

You talked to your mates in the Lewis gun team. There was always a certain amount of emotional chatter, nerves. Shall we get through tomorrow or shall we get a packet? I am going up the line tonight and am I coming back? It's getting dark, OK, everything may be quiet, but are you going to see the sun come up in the morning? That was why the comradeship was so important.

Anyone who tells you that in the trenches they weren't scared, he's a damned liar: you were scared all the time. We constantly reminded each other, 'Keep your head down, don't look up.' If you didn't duck low enough behind the parapet, or if you were fool enough to look to see where the German lines were, then death could be instant. There's a sniper ready every time, see a tin hat, bang. There was an officer in C Company and out of the line he was very fond of seeing that your buttons were polished and shined. Of course this was the worse thing you could do in the front line as any reflection, any unnecessary glint, would attract attention, so whenever we were going up the line we used to smear them with mud.

There was a routine to staying alive. To calm nerves almost all men smoked, and if they could get enough cigarettes they would chain-smoke. To hide any glow from the pipe I smoked I turned it upside down, placing my thumb over the tobacco so it didn't fall out. During the day I could always get under a groundsheet with a cigarette or pipe so no telltale smoke rose above the parapet.

Front-line service wore the men down. I would get a butterfly in my stomach and my hands would shake, so for a moment or two I would have a job to coordinate my nerves to do anything. You couldn't deal with the fear and apprehension we had about being hit by shrapnel. It was there and it always would be. I know the first time I went to the line we were scared; we were all scared. We lived hour by hour, we never knew the future. You saw the sun rise, hopefully you'd see it set. If you saw it set, you hoped you'd see it rise. Some men would, some wouldn't.

The shelling was ferocious at times; you'd feel the vibration of the ground, you couldn't help but tremble, mild shellshock. There were those, the least noise, anything like a shell bursting, would send them into hysterics practically, and they would be taken down the line because they had nothing but an adverse effect on the other men. They were a danger to everybody, you'd no knowing what they might do; you couldn't trust them. Word would come down, perhaps one of your mates had been wounded or killed, and the news that so and so had had his chips. That always made you think, 'How long is it before I get hit?' Not if, but when.

6

WOUNDED

For Harry, 22 September is the day he remembers as the day he lost his machine-gun team and he was badly wounded by shrapnel. Given the passage of nearly ninety years and the effect of his wound, the actual events are now a little opaque. The battalion was relieved from the line on the 19th and proceeded to a place known as Soult Farm. Owing to heavy fighting at the front line, the battalion stood to at 5.40 a.m. on the 20th, and throughout the day they were ordered to be ready to move at fifteen minutes' notice. On the 21st the battalion remained on alert but once more they were not required. On the 22nd the weather was fine, and enemy Gotha bombers were seen in the neighbourhood of the camp. On two occasions, bombs were dropped near the DCLI and the battalion suffered about twenty casualties. The following day, the 23rd, the bombers returned in the afternoon and more bombs were dropped, with no loss of life. The battalion was ordered to parade, and in the evening, around 7 p.m., they left the camp to return to the line, relieving battalions of the Somerset Light Infantry and the King's Royal Rifle Corps. From 10 p.m., a thick mist fell over the battle area, hindering the relief. However, the mist hid them from enemy observation and the War Diary notes that there was very little shelling. The only casualties were one officer who was slightly gassed and three other ranks killed and four wounded. It is quite possible that Harry's Lewis gun team were among those killed or wounded that evening.

We were returning from the line, going back into reserve. It was a quiet night, with very little shellfire at all, if any, that I can recall. Nevertheless, as a matter of course we walked in single file, about ten feet apart, to lessen the chance of the team being hit. It was always important to stick to communication trenches where you could, but, if there weren't any, then you just went over the top in the open and took a chance. We'd stopped briefly as Bob was attending to the call of nature in a slight traverse, causing us to bunch up a little as we waited.

Heavy shells make a 'whump' sound, but the light shells, the whizz-bangs, they used to come over so quickly with a 'zuppppp, bang, flash', and I guess it was a whizz-bang that got us. The only thing I saw was a flash; I can't recall any noise at all, but I certainly felt the concussion of that shell bursting, because I was taken off my feet and thrown to the ground. For a couple of minutes I couldn't move; the explosion seemed to paralyze the nervous system, and I lay there, conscious but incapable of anything. Two or three minutes later, movement gradually returned. I didn't even know I was hit at first, but a growing pain told me otherwise. I looked down and saw my tunic was torn away, and there was blood oozing out from the area of my stomach. Under the corner of my tunic was a field dressing and I applied it to my wound. After that, I must have passed out. I don't remember how long I lay there – it may have been ten minutes, it may have been half an hour – but stretcher-bearers came along and I was picked up. I was taken by a Red Cross motor van along a bumpy road as the ambulance hit divots or rocked from one side to another. There were four of us in there lying on stretchers, one man above me moaning.

I don't recall anything else until I found myself in a tented encampment, a casualty clearing station where there were nurses and where a doctor cleaned the wound of congealed blood and lice and put a clean white bandage on. The metal fragment in my body had been scorching hot and I guess that is what deadens the feeling, but now that it had cooled an intense pain took hold.

There were a lot of seriously wounded there, so I had to wait for the rest of the night and all through the next day. I just lay on a stretcher with a blanket over me, surrounded by wounded men. You read in the Bible about the Tower of Babel, and you had it there, wounded all over the place, calling for help, in German, French and English.

The next evening, the doctor came. As shrapnel wounds went, mine was serious but not as serious as others'. He could see the shrapnel in my stomach and asked me, 'Shall I take it out? Before you answer yes, we've no anaesthetic in the can, it's all been used on more seriously wounded than you and we've had no more to replace it.' I thought for a moment. The pain from it was terrific, and I felt that perhaps a couple of minutes' more intense pain might be worth it, so I said, 'All right, carry on.' The surgeon called for some help. Four people caught hold of me, one each leg, one each arm, and the doctor got busy. I'd asked him how long he'd be and he'd said, 'Two minutes', and in those two minutes I could have damned well killed him. Sweat poured off me. He cut around and then got hold of the shrapnel with tweezers, and dragged it out. He dressed the wound and put a couple of stitches in and as the pain began to subside he showed me the shrapnel. It was two inches long, about half an inch thick, with a jagged edge. 'Do you want it as a souvenir?' he asked. 'I've had the bloody stuff too long already,' I told him and with that he threw it away. The doctor went over to the table and the fellow in the next bed said to me, 'If he writes anything in the green book at the desk, you're for Blighty', soldiers' slang for home. Sure enough, the doctor took his pen and wrote in the book, and I thought, 'Well, that's it then, I'm going home.' I was lucky, very lucky indeed, for the word Blighty meant everything to a soldier.

I didn't know what had happened to the others in the Lewis gun team at first until Bob wrote and told me when I was back in England. I had lost three good mates. The Lewis gun team was a little band together and the last three, the ammunition carriers, had, I understood, been blown to pieces. My reaction was terrible; it was losing a part of my life. I'd taken an absolute liking to the men in the team, you could say almost love. You could talk to them about anything and everything. I mean, those boys were with you night and day, you shared everything with them and you talked about everything. We each knew where the others came from, and what their lives had been, even where they were educated. You were one of them; we belonged to each other, if you understand. It is a difficult thing to describe, the friendship between us. I never met any of their people or any of their parents but I knew all about them and they knew all about me. There was nothing that cropped up – doesn't matter what it was – that you couldn't discuss with them in one way or another. If you had anything pinched, you could talk to them, and if you scrounged something, you shared it with them. You could confide everything to them. When they got letters from home, any trouble, they would discuss it with you.

I couldn't really believe I was going home until a few hours later when my name and number were called out. Hospital orderlies then came and took me to the railway station, from where I was taken to Rouen with hundreds of other wounded men. Rouen was a massive base camp, but we weren't taken to hospital, rather to a warehouse. Here we were stripped, shirt, trousers, pants, tunic, everything went. Nurses put a waterproof dressing on my injury and gave all of us a hot bath and shampooed our hair. What was in the water, I don't know; we used Harrison's Pomade to kill lice up the line, but the water killed them and when we got out of the bath, you could have shovelled them out. We got into another bath where the water was clean, and then they put us each in a suit of sterilized hospital blue. What they did with our clothing I don't know, but my clothes were ridden with lice and blood so they may well have been burnt. They then made us ready to be taken down to the quayside to embark on hospital ships that would take us back over the Channel.

Once on board, the more serious cases were taken below while those who were stronger, like myself, were placed on the top deck, still lying on a stretcher. We didn't sail that night. There were submarines in the Channel, so we sailed the next night, no lights, and landed at Southampton on a typically foggy autumnal morning. We were laid out on the dockside under

Harry's parents, William and Elizabeth (née Morris) Patch. Longevity is in the family: Elizabeth lived until she was ninety-four, dying at Fonthill in 1951.

The 1901 Census return, taken in March that year, records that Henry J. Patch, son of William and Elizabeth Patch, was aged just two (*last entry under 'Fonthill'*).

Harry's father outside Fonthill *c*.1905. Harry's bedroom window (*top right*) has an ornate metal guard which his father put in place to stop his young son falling out.

'Greetings from Combe Down': a multi-image postcard of the village, including the church where Harry sang in the choir.

The Avenue, Combe Down. This photograph, taken *c*.1905, shows two of Harry's contemporaries on the right.

Pulteney Bridge and the weir. Harry, and school friends Leslie Lush and Charlie Wherrett, frequently 'shot' the weir, despite anxious warnings from tourists near by.

The spirit typical of Kitchener's Army. The sergeant leading these men over the hedge would later take them to France.

Leaving for the front. Soldiers line the deck to wave an emotional and optimistic goodbye to family and friends.

A Lewis Gun team cleans the machine gun's magazine and the cartridge guide. Such tasks were undertaken daily to ensure that guns did not jam in action. The man nearest the camera has his left hand in the spare-parts bag and may be the No.2, Harry's position on the team. Note the unlit cigarettes, almost certainly handed out by the photographer in exchange for the men's co-operation.

'Ration parties would bring water up in petrol cans which were rarely washed out. There was a standing joke that if you were out there long enough you could tell the difference in taste as to whether the water came in a British Petroleum or a Shell can.'

Unidentified soldiers make their way across the shell-torn ground on Pilckem Ridge. They are heading towards the front line to take part in the fighting around Langemarck, 16 August 1917.

Pioneers laying white tape across the Ypres battlefield. Harry and his comrades lined up along such tape before going into action.

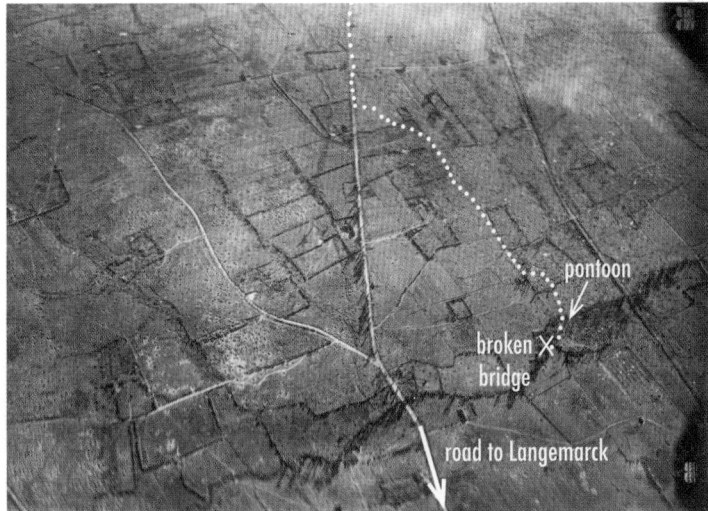

A German aerial photograph of the land behind the Steenbeek, taken shortly before the Allied offensive began. The 7th DCLI crossed these fields prior to the attack on Langemarck. The route up to the front line, the broken bridge and the position of the pontoon over which Harry crossed the Steenbeek are indicated.

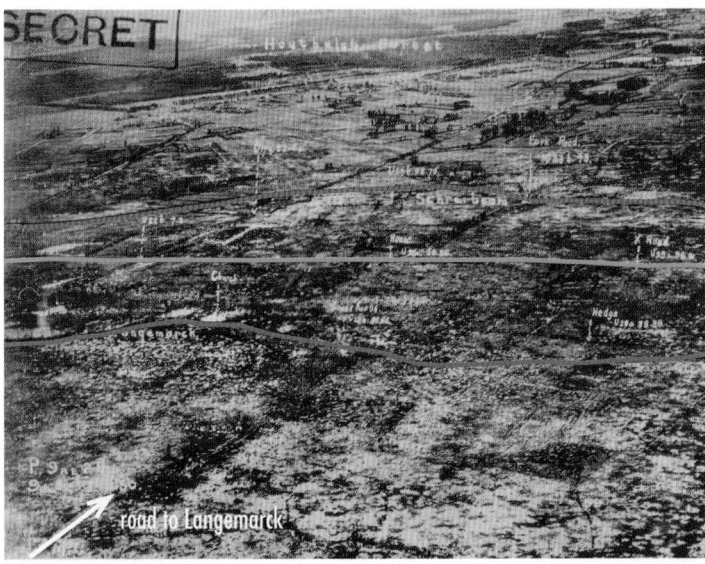

A British aerial photograph of the land to the east of the Steenbeek just after the attack on the 16th. The complete devastation of the land, in contrast to the German photograph, suggests the ferocity of the fighting in the first weeks of the third battle of Ypres. The three objectives, the blue, green and red lines, are shown.

Artillerymen stop to watch the progress of the battle. They would be called into action soon afterwards to bombard the enemy's trenches behind Langemarck.

A shell explodes close to a British forward battery during the attack.

The Steenbeek, pictured shortly after the fighting. The flooded stream had made the crossing hazardous; the trees lining the banks were smashed and the felled trunks were sometimes used to cross the water.

Battle casualties receiving treatment on 18 August. These wounded men are in an advanced dressing station, possibly 'Fusilier ADS' (see map on page x), near the village of Boesinghe. They are directly behind the old front line from where the 7th DCLI attacked, and so may well be soldiers from Harry's battalion.

Summer 1918. Home, wounded and recuperating, Harry, in uniform (*fourth from right*), attends the wedding of his brother George to Lilian Shore. Harry's cousin George Morris (*centre*), also in uniform, survived the war.

PRIVATE S. J. FORD
R. FRANCIS
E. W. GRANT
V. G. HEAL
H. HILLIER
E. G. HISCOCK
L. E. LUSH
F. J. MACEY
S. O. MILLER
W. E. MILSOM
L. R. MORRIS
SAPPER H. NEATE
PRIVATE C. H. NAISH
RFN. W. J. PAINTER

PRIVATE F. A. PATCH
A. E. PEARCE
C. PEARCE, M.M.
S. G. PEARCE
A. G. SALTER
F. TOOZER
SAPPER S. G. TOOZER
PRIVATE C. H. WHERRETT
R. WHITAKER
E. G. WHITE
GUNNER V. E. WILKINSON
PRIVATE E. G. WILLIAMS
H. G. WINDELL
W. G. YOUNG

Combe Down War Memorial, which Harry attended the unveiling of in 1921. On it are inscribed the names of many of his childhood friends, as well as that of his cousin Fred Patch.

The topping-out parade at the Wills Memorial Building, Bristol, 1926. Harry Patch (*pictured front left, sitting, with a mop of hair*) joins other workers to celebrate the completion of the sixty-six-metre university tower.

Looking up Park Street, Bristol. This picture was taken just after the tower was unveiled by King George V and shows how the building dominates the city's skyline.

The Great Hall where Harry, standing at the back, listened to King George V as he officially opened the new building.

The wooden scaffolding that Harry and his colleagues climbed each day during the construction of the Wills Memorial Tower. In high winds the men could be trapped at the top of the tower.

The countdown to war: Harry (*centre*) joins the Auxiliary Fire Service. Too old to fight again, he chose instead to use his knowledge of plumbing and Bath's water supply to tackle the fires caused by German bombs.

April 1942. After two years of relative peace in Bath, the German bombers attacked. They targeted cities of architectural beauty, in revenge for the RAF's attack on Rostock and Lübeck.

A house in Bath with its walls blown out. Almost 19,000 buildings were damaged and 401 people killed in Bath during several nights of bombing.

Bear Flat, Bath, the morning after a raid. It was here that Harry spent most of the night dousing flames at the National Provincial Bank. One of the pipes he used to tackle the blaze can be seen snaking across the ground. Until daylight, Harry had no idea that his pump was parked across an unexploded bomb.

Harry with Ada, the love of his life. They are pictured in the early 1970s, shortly before Ada died. Their marriage lasted nearly sixty years.

In the caves below Combe Down. In 1990, aged ninety-two, Harry was asked by geologists from Bristol University to help explore the tunnels, using the knowledge he retained from his childhood.

After once vowing never to return to Ypres, Harry agreed to go back in 2004. He returned to Pilckem Ridge and laid a wreath to his fallen comrades in an emotional ceremony.

Harry shares a seat with the late Doris Whitaker, his close companion and soul mate for the last six years.

Harry holds out his Légion d'Honneur. This highly prestigious medal was awarded by France to all surviving British veterans nine years ago; of the 350 medals awarded in 1998, only three are now held by living recipients.

Harry spots the author taking a clandestine picture and raises a salute not typical of former soldiers.

Harry in 2007. Above his medals is the cap badge of the Duke of Cornwall's Light Infantry.

blankets to keep us warm. I don't care to admit it, but I was a little tearful, after what I'd been through. The Salvation Army were bringing along hot cups of tea, while members of the YMCA took postcards round, already stamped, on which it was written that we had landed back in England, slightly or badly wounded or sick, whichever it was; all they required was your name and address and they would post them. At the same time, the Red Cross were coming along, saying, 'Where's your nearest military hospital?' Well, the Royal United in Bath was at that time a military hospital so I said, 'Bath', and I thought, 'This is it, I'm not just home, but I'll be among my own people, where my parents can visit me.' For a while I was semi-conscious and half-asleep, and I hardly remember the train journey, but it was interminable, and I thought, 'Well, damn it, this train's a long time reaching Bath.' Eventually we pulled into a station and I could see a glass roof. It obviously wasn't Bath, so I said to the orderly when he unloaded us, 'Where are we?' and he said, 'This is Lime Street station, Liverpool.' So much for Bath!

Outside the station a fleet of ambulances was waiting to take us to hospital, the Hahnemann Hospital in Hope Street, a grand-looking red-brick building, a civilian hospital, part or all of which must have been requisitioned for use by the military. The injury to my stomach was treated on a daily basis with Lysol to clean the wound, and fresh bandages. I was fortunate that no operation was required. As well as the shrapnel injury, I had a badly sprained foot and had torn some ligaments in my chest. When the shell exploded, I was carrying on my left shoulder the machine gun's spare parts in a canvas bag.

I surmised that when I was flung to the ground, I had landed on the parts and they had dug into my side and ripped these ligaments or muscles, which made breathing and laughing difficult. This was unfortunate as in the bed next to me was an Australian I called Digger, although I must once have known his name because right from the start we got on famously. He was a real wag.

Digger and I slept in a big ward, a mixed ward, ladies at one end, then halfway down it went to men. Between the two sexes was a desk where the ward sister sat all the time; there was also a trained nurse about and if you woke up the nurse would attend to you and would report back to the ward sister who would come if it was important. Digger and I were the only two who were out on a veranda. The veranda had at one time been open-air, but perhaps because of war emergencies they had boarded both ends and glassed the front. There were two cast-iron radiators behind our beds to keep us warm and other extra beds which were not in use. I was quite jumpy for a while. The least noise and I wanted to dive for cover – you couldn't help it – but that feeling began to subside.

Because we were on our own, we had plenty of time to talk, which quickly led to fun. I always remember the nurse coming to Digger one day. She was bringing each of us a cup of tea on a tray, tea which was a bit thick, a bit strong. As she handed him the cup of tea, she looked out of the window and said, 'It looks like rain, Digger.' 'Yes,' he replied, looking at the tea, 'looks like rain, got the colour of cocoa, tastes like toffee, but I suppose it is tea.' It took the nurse a moment for the penny to drop, but I was already laughing, difficult though it was.

Digger came from a family of horse breeders down under,

working with his brother, but his brother had lost a leg in the war, and indeed Digger's injuries were caused by shrapnel in his legs. We got on so well that he asked me to go down there and join him after the war, but I told him I'm a plumber, not a horseman.

By November, both of us were up and around, and to speed our recovery we were given permission to go out of the hospital and take light exercise. Down the road from us was a cinema, free to any soldiers in hospital blue; you could just walk in. One afternoon we were watching a serial film there called *The Grey Ghost*, with the latest episodes being shown on Monday and Friday. For dramatic effect, every episode finished just as something exciting was about to happen. One episode ended as the villain was about to shoot the heroine, and as you witnessed the hammer going back on the revolver, 'Continued on Friday' came up on the screen. So on Friday a group of us went to see what would happen; we sat down and the trailer came on, but what we didn't know was that Digger had taken a paper bag with him. He had blown it up and directly the hammer went back, he banged it. I think everybody in the cinema screamed, we got thrown out and we never got to see the resolution of *The Grey Ghost*. It was an interesting film, not least because it was the first time sound was ever put on a silent film.

Sleeping out on the veranda was enjoyable, with one small reservation. Old Digger had a habit of grinding his teeth at night, and it was a horrible noise. Of course he wasn't aware of this and he used to get a bit fed up when the sister came down and gave him a shot of cold water from the end of a syringe, waking him up. He decided to get even, went down town and bought a pound packet of flour. Just for fun, I helped him rig it up on some twigs above the ward door that led out on to the veranda. Digger got into bed and baited the sister by grinding his teeth. Presently we heard her coming down the ward to give Digger a shot, but Digger was not asleep, and unfortunately it wasn't the sister, but the matron. She caught the flour fair and square on the head. There was no argument as to who had done it, and playing such a trick demonstrated that neither of us was that 'ill' any more. Within days, Digger was sent back to Calshot, his regimental depot, and soon after that I was discharged too, to a convalescent camp.

I was sad to see Digger go. We had got on famously and he had done me the world of good with his humour and his mischievous fun. We exchanged addresses and corresponded for a while; I even wrote once after the war when he was back in Australia but we never met again. I never considered for one moment going to Australia. My home was Somerset.

As it was, just about Christmas I was given leave and I returned home before being sent to Birmingham, and then Sutton Coldfield, No. 2 Convalescent Camp. All those who had just left hospital were given a green badge to wear on their khaki epaulettes. This colour would change as health improved, first to yellow and finally red. Red meant that you were A1 and ready to return to your unit for training, but I was still a while away from that.

My time at Sutton Coldfield was unremarkable. I still received minor medical attention, but most of the time the men slept or sat around and played cards, while our overall health improved. I wasn't inclined just to waste the time doing nothing, and while I was recuperating I was allowed to study. Before I left Sutton Coldfield I took and passed the

London Examination to become a sanitary engineer. It was a correspondence course, letters from London, and I had to answer a large number of questions.

The time at Sutton Coldfield was most notable for one thing: I met my future wife, Ada Billington.

I actually met her when I accidentally knocked her down. Three of us were hurrying for a bus to save ourselves a three-mile walk from Erdington to Sutton Park. Once a month, we got a pass out of the camp. It was valid from Friday night to Sunday night, back in by midnight. It wasn't long enough to go to Bath, so we used to book a couple of nights at the YMCA in Birmingham, and get back for Roll Call on Sunday. As we went round the corner, Ada and her friends were coming down the steps from a cinema and I bumped into her. I picked her up, dusted her off, and, as it turned out they were going for the same bus as us, I took her home and the next night we agreed to meet and we went for a walk, and on Sunday we met again.

It was a drizzly February night in 1918, and I was waiting on the street corner for her outside her home. An old chappie came up to the gate, and said in a North Country accent, 'You waiting for the maid, laddie?' 'Yes.' 'Well, don't wait out here. Come inside.' He took me into the house. Ada was staying with her aunt, and the old man was her grandfather. I can't remember the conversation, but you can bet they were quizzing me, finding out what they could about me, who I was and my intentions. 'What are you going to do on a night like this?' her aunt asked, so I said that I thought we would go up town somewhere, find a show. 'Why don't you stay here? Nasty night,' so we stayed there by the fire. Her aunt and uncle found something in the dairy to do – they had a dairy business on the Chester Road – while Ada's sister Maud, who was living there too, made herself scarce and Granddad went to bed early. When Ada's aunt and uncle came back in about ten o'clock, they made a cup of cocoa and asked if I would like to come down and spend the weekend with them, so that's what I did and that's when Ada's and my friendship developed into something deeper. At Sutton Coldfield I'd noticed that there would be lots of girls who would hang round the camp and go out with any soldier, but Ada was different, and it dawned on me that I had found a girl here who didn't chase after everything in uniform.

In time I was introduced to all her family. She was the daughter of a wire drawer who worked for Sankeys, a large Midlands steel business. He had a skilled job in a foundry, rolling steel back and forwards until it came out as thick as your finger. Ada was about three years older than me and was born and raised in Shropshire, in a village near Wellington called Trench Crossings, the fourth of six children. During the war one of her brothers, Tom, had served in munitions and another, Bill, won the Military Medal and was badly wounded serving in the Machine Gun Corps, suffering an experience not dissimilar to mine. His team had all been killed, except for Bill who had been left for dead, next to his machine gun. A stretcher-bearer had seen him twitch and he was picked up and sent home. What the extent of his injuries was I never knew but his face was very badly scarred. While he was in hospital he studied for chartered accountancy in Birmingham, and later emigrated to America to start his own business.

In July 1918 I was given a week's leave. I travelled south with two fellows from Bath with whom I had struck up a friendship while convalescing. Their names were Titch Harding and Bill Taylor, both privates in the 5th Somerset Light Infantry. We had spent a lot of time together, in fact I had been with them both the evening I had met Ada outside the cinema.

Titch Harding was a proper comedian. As we were going on leave together, Bill and I gave Titch our travel warrants to go and pick up the train tickets. Titch got the tickets, and we got on the train at New Street, Birmingham, to Bristol. We had got so far on the way when Titch felt in his pocket and said, 'I've only got two tickets. I wonder where the other one has gone; it must have gone through the lining. What are we going to do?' So he pulled out three matches and struck one and said, 'Whoever draws the burnt match must go under the seat. We'll put our kit bags down and hide him. It'll be all right.' Bill lost. When the ticket collector came in, Titch pulled out and gave the man all three tickets. 'Where's your mate?' the ticket collector asked. 'Gone to the toilet or something?' 'No,' Titch said, 'he's a bit rocky "upstairs",' pointing to his head. 'He suffers from shellshock. When he heard you banging the door, and a loud noise, he dived for cover. He's under the seat!' When we arrived at Bristol, the guard got out and found a Red Cap, a military policeman, and told him about Bill. The policeman led us to his sergeant. 'Hello, what's the matter with these three? Travelling without passes?' the sergeant asked. 'No, passes are all right, but this one's a bit dodgy; he suffers from shellshock.' 'All right, get back on duty,' said the sergeant, whereupon he took over and accompanied us on to the train to Bath, where we were met by our families. A week later, Bill, Titch and I were all travelling together and we got off at Bristol to change trains, and who should be there but the old Red Cap sergeant. 'You again? Have you enjoyed your leave? You going back? Good, now come along with me,' and he took us over and put us on the train to Birmingham. The sergeant called the guard over. 'Give them a packet of sandwiches and a cup of tea and charge it to me. When you get to New Street station there should be a van to take them to Sutton Coldfield. Find a Red Cap there and hand them over.' The guard took us to a first-class coach where he locked the door, allowing us to travel back in style. It was one of the few advantages of being a wounded soldier in wartime.

In early August I left Sutton Coldfield. I returned to the regimental depot at Bodmin and Titch Harding and Bill Taylor returned to their depot at Taunton. From Bodmin, I would be sent away for training, a prospect that filled me with dread. Ada and I were committed to one another and it had been difficult to leave Birmingham, unsure when we would be able to meet again.

It must have been a few days later when I travelled to Perham Downs, near Tidworth, to join up with other men who were returning to training. News from France was increasingly good: the Germans had been turned and were retreating, but we'd heard of retreats before and we didn't think that this might be the beginning of the end. Most of the men at Perham were pretty much back to full fitness, as least as far as the army were concerned. These lads were not fresh recruits by anyone's imagination, and were far less willing to be ordered about by time-served sergeants, or NCOs the men suspected had never seen the front. They would accept orders, of course, but there was a limit. On the notice board one morning was a note that the company would go on parade for bayonet practice. A number of the men objected and said, 'No.' 'We've had the real thing,' they said. 'We are not going to stick our bayonets into a bag of straw.' Some had no doubt been wounded by a bayonet. In truth, they were absolutely fed up with being told to right turn, left turn, about turn, being told to jump through hoops! These men had gone over the top and they'd used the bayonet, damn it, they didn't want bayonet practice! Treating them like raw recruits! I was quite in sympathy with the rest of the crowd but I was about to find out that I wouldn't have to join them.

Directly I put my equipment back on again, I got a pain in my chest precisely where I had landed on the machine gun's spare parts, so I went sick and got a week's excused duty. The following day there was a company officers' parade and, of course, I didn't go on, being excused duty, and they put me on a charge for it. Instead of going in front of the company officer the next day, I went sick again. The doctor said to me, 'I thought I gave you a week's excused duty yesterday?' I said, 'You did, sir,' and told him what had happened. 'When I give you excused duty, that means everything. I'll have a word with your company officer about it. You'll have to go in front of him tomorrow. Who put you on a charge?' 'Sergeant Major Smithers,' I replied. Now, he had served in France but by 1918 he was training the men back home, and nobody liked him. Even the officers didn't like him. He said, 'You can tell Sergeant Major Smithers, from me, he can stick his crime sheet . . .' and he was very explicit as to where he could stick it. Next morning I went before the company officer. Sergeant Major

Smithers was there, too. The doctor had a quiet word with the company officer and the charge was immediately dismissed. It was noted that I had been excused duty by the doctor. Then the officer said, 'Is that *all* the doctor told you?' I said, 'Yes, sir.' He said, 'He didn't give you a message for anybody?' 'Well,' I said, 'he did. He gave me a message for Sergeant Major Smithers but I don't care to repeat it. There are ladies in the office,' I said, pointing towards the WAACs. He said, 'Don't trouble about them, they know all your slang. If you have a message, you'll give it, and that's an order.' Of course the sergeant major was standing there fuming as I told him what the doctor had said – that he could stick his crime sheet up his arse and set fire to it. I added, too, that the doctor had hoped it might burn some sense into his rear end because there was none up top. It was clear that the officers wanted to take Smithers down a couple of notches, he was so overbearing in his manner. I didn't say anything, but that incident was all round the camp in half an hour, and my life wasn't worth living after that. All the dirty jobs were mine, courtesy of Sergeant Major Smithers.

About a fortnight later I went on parade in full kit and I got the pain in my chest again and I just couldn't stick it. I went to the sick bay and an officer examined me, and fetched the senior medical officer and had a probe and asked a few questions. They had a powwow and the senior officer came back and told me to go back to my hut, and pack my kit bag and report to the company office at two o'clock; I was going to hospital. When I went back, the sergeant major came into the hut. 'What have you got now, more excused duty?' I said, 'No, Sergeant Major, I am going to pack my kit, report, and the ambulance will pick me up and take me to Handsworth Hospital.' He seemed surprised. 'Oh,' he said, 'what's the matter with you?' I suggested he went and asked the medical officer. There was nothing he could do now; I was away from that camp, thank goodness. The luck at being sent to Handsworth was almost too good to be true, and as soon as I got to hospital I spoke to one of the nurses. 'Can you ring this number?' It was Dunlops' business number, where Ada was working. 'Whoever answers it, tell them to pass a message on to Ada Billington. Tell them I am in Handsworth Hospital. I don't think we can meet tonight, but tell them what ward I'm in.' Anyway, come six o'clock that night she was there to visit me, and promised to come back every day.

My injury was diagnosed as ligament damage and it was treated three times a day with massage. Ointment was rubbed into my chest, then a small rubber disc was held against me. This disc was attached to something that looked like a drill, from which an electrical cord ran down to a generator which made a low rumbling sound, vibrating the disc which was run up and down my chest.

Ada was working in Aston, as an inspector of gas masks. She worked alternate weeks, one week on night duty, then day duty the next. When she was on night duty, she used to come off at 6 a.m., go home to bed, and then get up about 3 p.m. to make some sandwiches and come over to Handsworth. She would sit with me until 6 p.m. when visiting hours were over, then leave to go off down to the factory, sitting in the canteen until it was time to go on shift.

This had been going on a week or two when one of the nurses asked me one day, 'That lady who comes to visit you, is she a relative?' I told her that she was my girlfriend and she said, 'Oh, we can't have that.' She told the ward sister and the ward sister told the commandant, and the next time Ada came in, they took her to one side. 'Don't you bring any sandwiches again, you'll come in here and you'll have dinner with your friend in the tea room and you can stay here until 7 p.m. and then you can go down to the factory.' And that's what happened. When I was able to get out, they gave me a late pass to get back by 8 p.m., the same time as Ada booked on.

I imagine I was at Handsworth no more than a few weeks when the doctors passed me as fit and I was given instructions to report to the Isle of Wight. When the time came for me to leave, the nurse, the ward sister and the commandant all came to see me off and they said, 'You know our address and we know your girl's address. Now keep in touch with us and if we are in England and you come through all right, we'll come to your wedding.' We weren't even engaged at the time but, when we did marry two years later, all three nurses were invited to attend. Sadly, they were serving with the Army of Occupation in Cologne, so none could come, but Ada and I not only stayed in touch with all three, but when they got leave they all visited us and we kept in touch with them by letter until they all died. The nurse came from Handsworth, the commandant from Nuneaton and the ward sister from Aston.

Ada and I corresponded almost every day at this time. Whenever I was off duty I would write her a letter; I remember one was twenty-four pages long. I knew she was the girl for me, and when I was due to return to France once again I asked her if we might get engaged. 'No,' came her reply. So I asked, 'Shall we get married?' 'No.' She wouldn't get engaged and she wouldn't get married. 'I'll wait for you until the war is over, Harry,' she told me. A lot of girls didn't want to marry when their loved ones were returning to France. Perhaps they felt it was bad luck; perhaps the heartbreak would be too much if they were killed. Ada didn't say anything. She would wait until I came home, that was all I knew. It was several years later that I found out why. Just before the war, in 1913, she had been very close to a boy from her own town, Wellington in Shropshire. His name was Harold Thomas, and he was in the Territorial Army. In 1914 he was called up straightaway, but before he left they had got engaged, and he was killed. She never wore the engagement ring after that, and she swore she would never get engaged again until the fighting ended. She didn't want to be a war widow. Harold Thomas' engagement ring sat on our dressing table for years after Ada and I were married. It might have bothered some men, but it never bothered me at all. Much later, Dennis, my elder son, took it and got it resized and he wore it in remembrance of that dead soldier. It was only after the war, over Christmas 1918, that Ada accepted my proposal of marriage and we got engaged.

There was, perhaps, another reason for Ada's hesitation. Ada worked at Dunlops' with her sister Maud. Maud had met and gone out with a sergeant of the Royal Artillery. She got pregnant, but before they could marry he was called up to go to France. The marriage was arranged, but before he could get leave he too was killed. Their shared tragedy must have made them very wary about any other commitments. Maud, however, found herself in a far greater predicament than Ada. She had a son, Reginald, who was brought up by his paternal grandmother, such was the feeling against unmarried mothers back then. Then Maud met a New Zealander from Auckland, Ernie Hurst. She married, settling in New Zealand, where she had a daughter, but even though her marriage to Ernie did not survive, she never returned home.

7

MUTINY

The injury in my chest may well have saved my life. Had I not had the problem there, and it was a mild injury by any measure, I would undoubtedly have been back in France by the late summer of 1918. As it was, in early November I was in billets at Golden Hill Fort. The Fort was a huge Victorian building, hexagonal in design, built to defend the Isle of Wight, and so had superb views over the Solent. In the centre was a parade ground, and heaven help anyone the sergeant major caught walking across that hallowed gravel; you had to double across every time. Hundreds of men were billeted in barrack rooms inside the Fort, but there were so many people training there that the overflow was billeted just outside the Fort's main entrance, in huts.

By this time I was marked down as A1, and had been placed on the next draft to go back and rejoin the regiment in Belgium. It was common knowledge that the Germans were being pushed back all along the line, but we didn't dare believe that the war might actually end, but end it did. On the morning of 11 November we were on the firing range and were told that, if a ceasefire was signed, they'd send up a rocket. We watched for the rocket and about eleven o'clock we saw it go up and we all cheered. I remember the feelings of joy to think that I would not have to go back and relief that the war was over. We were using a lot of spare ammunition, so the officer said, 'Get rid of it, fire it out to sea, we don't want to carry it back.' The fellow next to me had started blazing away when I noticed that his rifle was pointing across mine and I said, 'What the hell are you firing at?' He said, 'That bloody hut up there.' I said, 'That's where the markers are!' The markers registered our shots on the targets, but at that moment they were inside, taking refuge on the floor as this lad pumped ammunition through their hut. Far from being the last casualties of the war, they were inches away from being the first victims of the peace.

The sergeant got us together and we marched back to camp, and, while still carrying our rifles, we went to church for a service of thanksgiving, after which we were told we would not be allowed out of camp. The men didn't like this, and later that day they chased this same sergeant along the long pier at Yarmouth, and when he got to the end they chucked him into the sea, and that night we had hell's delight, a real party. At the Fort there was Hurst Castle Lighthouse on one side of us and the Needles on the other, and that evening, on the night of the Armistice, the lighthouse sounded its fog horns for the first time in four years in celebration.

Within days of the Armistice being signed, an order came through that anyone who had seen active service wouldn't have to go back to France. There were a large number of men who fitted that description and so they formed an E Company, all light infantry blokes, Duke of Cornwalls,

Somersets and Green Howards. Furthermore, if you could produce a letter from your employer indicating that you had a job to go to, then you were given what was called priority demobilization, but, for all the promises, that simply didn't happen, not in my case, and not in many others either. It had taken three days to get me into uniform but it would be five months before I got out of khaki and out of the army, and this was to cause a lot of resentment.

We were a very mixed bunch in E Company. In barracks, in the bed next to me, was a man by the name of Perkins, an interesting fellow if ever there was one. He was a Londoner from what would be called today the wrong side of the tracks. Nevertheless, you couldn't help liking him. The pair of us were on guard duty one night, and an officer came down from paying the troops. There were so many men coming out of hospital to join E Company that, rather than being about 260 strong, we had grown to well over a thousand, so he must have had a considerable amount of money at one point. Anyhow, whatever he had left over, he brought down to the office where I was on guard and put the money in a safe in the wall and left.

Perkins had only just come back from the canteen with the orderly sergeant, and both had come back a bit merry. Perkins had just come on guard with me when he saw this officer place the money in the safe. Speaking to the orderly sergeant, Perkins offered him a wager that he could open the safe within half an hour, get the money out on the floor and then put it back in the safe and lock it. The sergeant took him on for a small sum, ten shillings I think it was. There were a few people about, so Perkins asked everybody to be quiet and he sat down on the floor next to the safe, twiddling the dial this way and that, in deep concentration. You could hear these clicks, until presently there was a click that must have sounded a little bit different, for he then wrote a number down. In twenty minutes he had done it. He showed the sergeant the money and won the bet. The next day the officer came down, took the money out and back to the bank, and was none the wiser.

Some time after this, one of the filing cabinets in the office went wrong and this sergeant remembered Perkins and said to the officer in charge, 'There's a man here who can open anything. He'll open it for you', and Perkins was sent for. However, he refused to open it, maintaining that if anything was missing he might, for some reason I didn't understand, get the blame. Eventually they persuaded him to open it and Perkins went back on parade, but the officer was interested in him. On the next parade, he spoke to him. 'What are you by trade in civilian life, Perkins, a lock-smith?' 'No, sir.' 'Well, what are you?' No answer. He said, 'What are you in civilian life? I want to know and that is an order.' Perkins said, 'Sir, if you want to know, I'm a London cracksman.' The officer asked if he intended going back to his job after the war and Perkins didn't know. 'It rather depends how many of the gang come through the war, sir.' 'Well,' said the officer, 'if you go back to it, don't pay me a visit.' 'Where do you live, sir?' The officer told him the London district. 'You're OK, sir,' replied Perkins. 'We only go where there is stuff worth pinching.'

Perkins was a character. If we were anything short on kit parade, tell Perkins, and within half an hour I bet you had it; he'd thieve it from somewhere. We never went hungry. The cookhouse door was nothing to him. He was a bright lad as well. He had a set of loaded dice and if he found anybody playing Crown and Anchor, he'd join in. The game consisted of a mat made up of six squares in each of which was one of six symbols: the crown and anchor, and the four suits in a pack of cards, spades, hearts, clubs and diamonds. It was normally a game of chance and no skill. Men placed money on one or more of the squares, and the dice, with the six symbols on the sides, were rolled. The banker paid out on the money placed on the winning symbols shown on the dice, before scooping the rest. The banker rarely came off worst, but they didn't count on Perkins. He used brilliant sleight of hand. You wouldn't see him put his loaded dice down but he did, switching his with the banker's, and when he'd won enough money he'd switch them back. Then he was gone, leaving the banker a little poorer than when he started, which made a nice change.

To stop the men getting bored, the army used to keep us busy with one thing and another, physical training and marching, as well as firing on the ranges. They also had a Lewis gun there, and we went up eighteen men at a time. There were six targets, two sets each at 200, 400 and 600 yards, for us to have a go at. The first time we went up there, a sergeant got us in a circle and said, 'Right, any of you fellows know anything about Lewis guns?' I said, 'Well, yes, I was a number two in a team at Ypres.' So he said, 'Can you show us how it works?' I said, 'Yes, I think so, though it's been twelve months since I handled one.' He told me to take it apart but I asked, before I touched the gun, was the magazine loaded or empty, as we didn't want any accidents. He said it was empty so I put my thumb into it and took the magazine off and straightaway told him the gun was useless. He asked what I meant. 'There is a part missing with two poles on it; one opens the magazine and throws out the round that's been fired, the other drops a live round in, then the piston will come back against the recoil spring, and if you keep the trigger pulled it will fire until you release it. Anyway, that part is missing.' He put his hand in his pocket and said, 'Is this it?' 'That's it.' 'You know your Lewis gun, don't you?' he said.

I don't know what he was trying to do or to prove. Anyway, I told him that if I had had that gun in France, I would have been on a crime sheet. It was filthy, so we cleaned it up and I showed them how it worked.

Before we finished, the sergeant said, 'We've got a live magazine', and asked if I would like to use it. I was to fire at number six target, and see what I could do with it. I lay down, and decided to have a little fun. I fired downwards, then came across once and down once, and put an H on one side of the bull's-eye. I went across the other side and I went up and round to form the letter 'P', and said, 'There you are.' I'd put my initials on the target. Shortly after, I was called into the company office and there was a major there and he said, 'I understand that you are leaving the army?' I replied, 'Yes, sir. I've got a job to go to.' 'That's a pity. I hear you did some fancy firing on the range.' I said that I was told I could use the magazine as I liked. 'Yes, I know,' he acknowledged. At that time the army was offering cash, quite a bit of money, too, to try to persuade men to sign on and stay in the services, but most men weren't interested. Almost all of us in E Company had a job to return to, and why the army was refusing to demob us, I don't know. Only those without a trade were tempted to re-enlist.

This officer was impressed with my shooting, and had been tempted into a little bet with my sergeant. 'I've bet your sergeant a pound at five to one that at six hundred yards you couldn't take the bull's-eye out of the target with one magazine.' That distance was too far, but I said I would do it at four hundred. 'No,' he said, 'six hundred.' We agreed on five hundred.

We went up on the range, six of them round me, and I asked for a practice shot. I was then given the magazine, forty-nine shots, and I went not on the bull's-eye but the inner ring, and I started at the bottom and worked my way around. The sergeant at the target phoned back to the major and said, 'The bugger's done it, sir.' I knew it already, for I could see the grass behind the bull's-eye. I had cut the bull's-eye clean out with three rounds left. The officer repeated that he thought it was a pity I was leaving the army. 'I would have backed you against anybody that would have challenged you, whether with a Lewis gun or a rifle. I've never seen anybody fire like that.' In those days I had good eyesight and a steady hand.

There was a lot of small-time gambling going on to help alleviate the boredom, but in the end there was trouble and it was inevitable. We had an officer, a captain, a peacetime officer risen from the ranks, and he took E Company out for a route march. I was on fatigue duties at the time, peeling spuds in the cookhouse, and it was only later that I heard what happened. This officer was at the head of the men and he started them at the double – well, half the company went at the double – but four Birmingham boys said they weren't going to double for him, and they stayed marching, and the rest of the company behind them followed suit. The officer didn't know what to do. He managed to get the company back to camp, where the men got together and decided that they'd had enough of this officer and wouldn't parade again.

The officer's authority had been well and truly challenged, and he was not the sort of man who was going to put up with it. He ordered the sergeant major to come down to our huts and rouse us. The first door he opened, he shouted, 'On parade, E Company!' He got his answer. Somebody threw a boot at him and he reported it to the officer. So the officer came down. 'On parade, E Company!' 'We are not going,' came the reply. Back to the company office he went.

Things began to get nasty. A group of men went up to the officers' mess and asked for this officer. After they'd spoken their mind, the officer pulled his revolver out and you could hear the click, click, as the hammer went back. Whether it was loaded or not, I don't know. I only heard what the others told me. Nobody said anything; they all dispersed and simply went back to their huts. Some of the men had been on the firing range and so they rounded up what ammunition they could find, sorted it out between them and went back and asked for him again. This time I was with them. He came out, click, click, went the hammer on his revolver, and crash, crash, went back about thirty rifle bolts, mine included, before someone shouted, 'Now, you shoot, you bugger, if you dare.' Had he not backed down, he would have been shot, there's no doubt about it. All those rifles were loaded, one round each. Anyway, down went the revolver and he scarpered back into the mess.

We had mutinied, and so a brigadier with a chestful of medal ribbons was brought from the mainland to sort out the problem. He immediately set about finding what had happened and then he asked for the men and addressed them. He said, 'I've heard the officer's version of events and now I want to know your side, but I don't want to identify you. We'll have a canvas screen put up between the huts, you'll go behind the screen and tell me your grievances.' He interviewed perhaps thirty men from E Company in all, each talking from behind this screen so that they could speak freely without fear of intimidation. One of the lads said what we all felt: 'It's three months since the war ended, we've each got a job to go to, yet we're still in the army. When we joined up, it was for the duration of the war; that was what we were told, so why are we still serving?'

The brigadier listened and gave his verdict. E Company was to undertake fatigues only, no more parades, and the officer was to be taken right away from the Fort, so I suppose we were in a way exonerated. From then on, we picked up the fag ends, scrap paper and litter around the camp, just keeping the place tidy, that's all, until we were demobbed. The army was keen to get shot of us. Most of us were down for immediate demobilization and we had decided ourselves that we were more or less civilians, and that army rules no longer applied to us.

Soon enough we got our orders to leave the Isle of Wight and we were taken to board a ship for Gosport, where we were to stay one night. It was a wintry March evening when we got there, to be greeted by the news that we would have no blankets that night. The boys were not having that: we weren't going to sleep without anything to cover us up, and we started to create about it. The sergeant in charge said, 'Well, where are you from, anyway?' We told him, 'We're the Duke of Cornwall's from the Isle of Wight.' 'All right,' he said, 'we don't want any trouble, we'll get some.' I suppose he must have heard about the incident. So they issued each of us with four pure white blankets from the stores. We noticed straightaway that none had the distinctive Government stamp on them and so, by the time we left the following day, I should think everybody in Gosport had a white blanket; we sold the lot. There were plenty of girls around the camp; well, to put it in plain English, they were prostitutes, so I can't say that all of the blankets were sold for money.

From Gosport we went to Fovant on Salisbury Plain, and that's where I got my demob papers. We were sent to the quartermaster's store and given our civilian clothes, all the same and ill-fitting, or, rather, it would be more accurate to say they fitted where they touched. We were then handed a travel warrant and set free. There was a light railway going from Fovant to Salisbury, from where we took a main line to wherever we were going. I headed for Bath and home.

8

BACK TO WORK

By the time I was demobbed I was thoroughly disillusioned. I could never understand why my country could call me from a peacetime job and train me to go out to France and try to kill a man I never knew. Why did we fight? I asked myself that, many times. At the end of the war, the peace was settled round a table, so why the hell couldn't they do that at the start, without losing millions of men? I left the army with my faith in the Church of England shattered. When I came home, I joined Combe Down church choir to try to get the faith back, but in the end I went because I enjoyed the music and had friends there, but the belief? It didn't come. Armistice Day parade – no. Cassock and surplice – no. I felt shattered, absolutely, and I didn't discuss the war with anyone from then on, and nobody brought it up if they could help it.

The one thing I could look forward to was my marriage to Ada. With the war over, she left Dunlops' and got a job as a lady's maid in Manchester while I returned to work again in Bath. We soon decided that Manchester and Bath were too far apart and so we set a date for our wedding,

13 September 1919, when we could be married and live as husband and wife in the house that Dad had promised as a wedding present, no. 5 Gladstone Place. Six months later, we married at a little place called Hadley, just the other side of Wellington in Shropshire, with Tom, Ada's brother, acting as best man. It was a very quiet wedding; my parents were getting too old to travel to Shropshire, so only Ada, her sister Wyn and her husband were there. Our honeymoon was in Shropshire, Church Stretton, where the Welsh mountains start, and for a week we walked the countryside and climbed some of the hills and talked about our future.

Marriage came as a welcome break from work. I had sought to return to my job with Jacob Long and Sons in April 1919, but, rather than paying me properly as a fully registered plumber, Mr Amor, the foreman and office manager, insisted that I finish my apprenticeship. That would have taken another two years and pay of just ten shillings a week, and I wasn't having that, not when I was going to be married. I had been an apprentice for three years from the age of fifteen, and you can accept that sort of wage then, but not at twenty-one. I was effectively being penalized for serving my country.

The upshot was that I dug my feet in and refused to go back to work. I told them that, rather than go back at their rate of pay, I would sign on again in the army if need be. It was a bluff. The last thing I wanted to do was go back into the forces, so I returned to Combe Down and over the next few months undertook several odd jobs and some private work to keep myself ticking over while I looked round for alternatives.

Every so often I used to take the train into Bath and called in at J. Long and Sons, ostensibly to see my brother, who worked there as a carpenter. Mr Amor used to see me; he would say, 'We've got nothing to offer you', and I would retort, 'Don't worry, I'm not coming back.' Nevertheless, there was one thing I wanted: I wanted my indentures signed. I asked on several occasions that the firm sign them to signal formally the end of my apprenticeship, and at first they refused.

I pursued the matter again after speaking with my father's solicitor, and what he told me was interesting. In his opinion, not only had the contract been broken when I was called up, but on joining the army I had agreed to serve only for the duration of the war. By March 1919 the war had been over five months and yet I was still in the army. 'Your apprenticeship was a legal contract, stamped and signed by Jacob Long, your father, by me as your solicitor, and finally by you. By failing to release you in 1918, the Government has broken the contract; you are free.' Because I felt that it wasn't me who had broken the contract I wanted the indentures signed, not because I couldn't work without them, but because it was a matter of pride.

The question was what to do in the meantime. I flirted with the idea of joining the Somerset County Police. There were so many demobilized men, and, with unemployment rising, one of the most sought-after careers was with the police force because it was a guaranteed weekly income and for men with families this was important. I applied to join. It was critical to have an exemplary conduct record on your demobilization papers; anything that hinted at second-rate service, convictions for drunkenness or being absent without leave, and they wouldn't look at you. Fortunately mine were fine, and I was invited for a medical at Taunton. There was one problem: my height. I knew I was five feet eight, and that was one inch too short. At the medical I passed everything, and I thought, 'When he checks my height, it'll be all right. I'll stand on my toes, get the inch that way,' but the doctor must have been used to the trick as he told me to lean back and stand on my heels; that did it: no police service for me. To tell you the truth I had no ambition to be a policeman; I thought joining would be a soft option.

For the time being, I worked for next to nothing. I lived with my parents at Rosemount but money was still tight and I did several small private jobs, helping out at home, doing odd bits and pieces such as plumbing in a sink for my mother. The water company was bringing mains water to each house on Combe Down and they asked if I could dig the holes to a terrace of ten houses so that each could have its own separate water supply. There was some haggling over the work. The water company wanted to pay one fixed price for the excavation but I told them I wanted the price of ten excavations, or tappings as they were called, and in the end they agreed to pay.

Yet this was no way to carry on. It was frustrating not seeing Ada, and prospects were not good. Nationally, there wasn't a flat rate in the building trade for plumbing work and the rates in Bath were among the lowest paid anywhere. Ada was keen to move closer to her mum, or at least not to remain in Manchester on her own. I had a think, and decided to find work away from Bath, so I wrote to the plumbers' trade union secretaries at Birmingham, Shrewsbury and Manchester to see if there was any chance of a job. These secretaries would know if there was anything going and, as I was a member of the union, they would help if they could. It was possible in those days to be a freelance plumber without belonging to a union, but you would never get on to the books of a big firm without being a member of the Plumbing and Heating Engineers Union.

Neither Birmingham nor Manchester could give me a job but there was an offer from Shrewsbury for a guaranteed nine months at a housing scheme under development at Gobowen. The rate was half-a-crown an hour and I took it. The following week I went into Long's office in Bath and insisted once again that they signed my indentures. This time I told them about my job offer, whereupon they abruptly decided that they would take me on at the full rate of pay for a plumber. 'You're too late; I've telegraphed to say I am taking the job and I'm going, but I want these indentures signed.' They could see that I wouldn't let the matter rest and reluctantly they signed, just to get me out of their hair.

At Gobowen I lived among a Welsh-speaking community, lodging with another plumber called Parker. Our place was a short walk away in a village called Chirk, where we slept in a miner's cottage. A couple of months after I arrived at Gobowen, Ada and I married. Ada had given up her job in Manchester and moved to live with her brother Tom in Hadley, in Shropshire, and at weekends I used to go over to see her. It wasn't a perfect arrangement by any means but it was far better than we had previously.

I worked for nine months on the housing scheme, just ordinary plumbing jobs, much of it hot-water work, putting in the pipework to the baths and boilers. Ada was pregnant and shortly after the end of my work at Gobowen, in June 1920, our first son, Dennis, was born. He was actually born at my mother-in-law's house at Trench Crossings, just outside Wellington, and I can recall the joy at racing over to see them, getting home in time for his birth.

After I finished at Gobowen, we moved in with Tom and his wife and I took a job with a small firm in Ludlow that specialized in private work. One of the houses I visited was Petton Park, a beautiful mansion house owned by an old lady. The grounds were extensive, with huge flowerbeds, and were occasionally opened to the public.

A considerable amount of work had been undertaken there, with new electrical cables and plumbing installed. On one occasion when I arrived, her ladyship wasn't up, so I wasn't allowed in. I waited until about 11.30 when I said to the butler, 'Look, if I can't get in, I'm going,' as I had a list of other calls to make. A few minutes later I was told her ladyship wanted to see me. I entered a large, imposing room, and there she was, sitting, two dogs either side, looking like Queen Victoria.

'Do you know the water service here?' she asked. I said, 'Yes, I've attended to it on a couple of occasions.' 'Well,' she said, 'I've lost a thousand gallons of water since Thursday. I want you to find the leak.' So I went and found the butler and told him what she'd said. 'Then you will want the keys to the tank room,' he said. The tank was in one of the battlement towers. 'Don't be silly,' I told him. 'If you've lost a thousand gallons of water in the tank room, you won't need me to find it; the place will be flooded.' The house was not on any mains system but had its own private water supply with a pump house called Round Towers, which drew the supply from very deep bore holes. I asked for the keys, went to the house and examined the pumps. They were electric and worked so soundlessly that the only way to tell whether they were working was by looking at the amp meter. I tried both pumps, and they worked all right, so I spent the next two hours hunting round for a leak all over the park, looking for the taps used for watering the flower-beds: nothing doing. I went back and the butler asked what I'd found. When I told him that I'd found nothing, he suggested that I'd better go in and tell her.

Her ladyship was waiting. The only explanation I could come up with was that someone had left a tap running. 'I've had that idea myself, but the staff are as close as devils in hell; I shall never find out.' As the pumps were working perfectly well, I had refilled the tanks for her. With nothing else to do, I prepared to leave when the butler took me to one side. 'I'll tell you the truth now,' he said. The upshot was that the lady's maid was just getting ready to go out. It was her evening off and her boyfriend would be calling in his car. She was running a bath when a message came that her ladyship wanted her. She left the bath with the tap running but now, being short of time, she'd simply changed and forgotten all about the bath. 'That's where your thousand gallons went, down the plughole.' The maid's error, as the butler explained, had compounded another failing, also hidden from her ladyship. It was the gardener's job to switch the pumps on each Monday and Thursday to fill the tanks. However, his wife had been taken ill with a burst appendix, and, in his urgency to go to Oswestry, where she was in hospital, the tanks had not been topped up and so by Thursday the maid had run them dry.

The secret was safe with me but I told the butler that her ladyship would still get a bill for two hours' work, adding, 'But why on earth didn't you tell me this story before I spent two hours looking for a leak?' 'If you hadn't gone round looking for the problem,' replied the butler, 'she would have smelt a rat.' He was protecting the maid and the gardener, while her ladyship was right: the staff did look after their own.

There were several grand houses in the area, owned by long-standing families with influence. Twelve miles from Petton Park was Schotten Park, owned by Lady Mary Cambridge. I went to her house on three or four occasions, taking the train to Whitchurch in Shropshire. On one of these visits, all I was required to do was replace some guttering above and around a dormer window, an easy job, and in a couple of hours I was finished. A coachman and trap usually took me back to the train station, but, as it was such a lovely hot summer's day, I chose to walk. Next to the railway line was a field where I ate some lunch and went to sleep. The next thing I heard was the whistle of my train leaving the platform so I sauntered down to the booking office and asked when the next train to Shrewsbury might arrive. One was due in at 5 p.m. that afternoon so I began to walk away when the stationmaster came tearing after me and told me to come back. An express train was running ten minutes early, so the signal had been put against it. 'You can get in the guard's van and get out at Shrewsbury,' I was told. That train had been halted for me. And why? Because the stationmaster knew I had been working at Lady Mary Cambridge's house, and that still counted for a lot in those days.

In early 1921 we left Ludlow and moved back to Combe Down and into no. 5 Gladstone Place, finally getting a house of our own. Although the house was a wedding present from my father, it had, at the time of our marriage, been occupied by a gardener. He worked for Angels, the millionaire antiques dealers in Combe Down, and, owing to a legal restriction, he could occupy the house until alternative accommodation was found. This was a wartime measure which had remained in force to protect key workers from eviction. Fortunately, in the intervening time between our marriage and my return to Combe Down, Angels had generously built Long Wood, a house on the North Road, and given it to their gardener. It meant that, as he moved out, we were able to move in.

In one sense it was good to have the family together again. It had been nearly ten years since we had all lived in the village, and I'm sure my parents were pleased to see us. I got on well with George, my eldest brother. As well as working at J. Long and Sons as a carpenter, he had made his own furniture out of mahogany, all beautifully inlaid. I recall that he made a fire screen in three sections and each section was made of one thousand individual pieces linked together to create the most intricate honeycomb pattern. The patience that took was incredible and I couldn't help admiring his work. William, my middle brother, had come back to no. 4 Gladstone Place after he was demobbed. He also worked at J. Long and Sons, picking up his trade again as a bricklayer, but later left to take a job as an overseer at the RAF station at Cullern, just outside Bath. In the army he'd risen to the rank of sergeant major and, as the saying goes, 'Once a sergeant major always a sergeant major', and you knew it. After I came back to Combe Down he had a tendency to order me about, silly little jobs really, but he would expect me to do them, and that didn't go down too well with me. No job could ever be done to his expectations, so did we get on? Well, passably!

After the war there were repeated strikes and reports in

the press of riots and a general unease in society. There was still a coalition of the main political parties but it was increasingly in difficulty and under strain. In 1918, there was an election and the number of people who could vote increased dramatically, in part because they could hardly withhold the right to vote from soldiers who had fought for their country.

Up to that point, you could vote if you owned property, so only my father, in our family, had taken part in a poll. With the new law [The Representation of the People Act, 1918], suddenly all men over the age of twenty-one and women over thirty could vote, which included my mother for the first time. Unfortunately for me, the election was held just weeks after the Armistice, which meant that I couldn't vote as I was still six months short of twenty-one.

So it wasn't until November 1922 that I first voted, for a man called Sir John Barlow, a Quaker who had been opposed to conscription in the war. He was a long-standing Liberal MP in Bath – the Frome Division – and I supported him because my parents did. I can't say I took much interest in politics.

The company for which I worked in Ludlow was owned by a man whose brother was managing director of a well-known firm in Bristol called Sculls. This had given me the idea of applying for a job back home. I wrote and had an interview, not with Arthur Scull, the senior partner of the firm, but his son Anthony, who had, I believe, enlisted under age in the Great War. He asked me if I had served in the army, and had I done an apprenticeship? I explained the situation, that the war had interrupted my work but that I was a qualified plumber. He seemed to like me and told me to bring my kit down on Monday morning. 'We will meet you at Temple Meads train station and take you to your job.' As I was leaving the office, I said, 'I've got a letter of recommendation here from your uncle in Shrewsbury.' 'Why on earth didn't you mention it?' he asked me. I told him it was a matter of professional pride. 'I didn't want any influence. I wanted to get the job on merit.' He took the letter and read it, and said, 'Your job's the University Tower.'

The Wills Memorial Tower was a very prestigious development in Bristol. It had been commissioned about the time war broke out and work had been halted in 1916 and was only restarted in 1919. It was situated at the top of Park Street, and when I joined the project it was already well on the way to reaching its full sixty-six-metre height. It was built as a memorial to one of the Wills tobacco empire, and was just part of a huge scheme that included a great hall, library and various other chambers and lecture theatres that would form the core of Bristol University. It was faced with Bath stone and cost over half a million pounds, an enormous sum of money. When I began to work there the following Monday, I little knew that I would work on this site for the next four years, a wonderful project and just the sort of long-term employment that I needed.

I tried to put the war to the back of my mind, although for a long time I remembered the mates that I had lost and used to get very bad dreams about it. The war might have been over but the effects were never far away. Well into the 1920s, those who fought continued to be affected by loud noises. A car backfiring might make a civilian jump but old soldiers were more inclined to duck. I'd see a man duck, and I would know that he'd served in the war; you didn't have to ask. I, too, was affected. A loud noise could bring things back in a flash, and there were more tangible reminders, too. All around the country, every community held ceremonies, unveiling war memorials to their dead. In 1921 a huge congregation turned out in Combe Down to honour those from the village who had not returned. I attended, not least because I sang in the choir; I was a baritone, and the vicar and the choir would naturally lead the commemoration.

Combe Down's memorial was built on the Firs Field, a piece of land given to the residents of Combe Down by two spinster sisters called Stennard, well known to fight each other like cat and dog but very generous to the community. They had owned the field for as long as anyone could remember but nothing had been built there, and the field had remained just rough ground for local children to play on. The sisters instructed their lawyers to draw up the deeds which stated that the land must never be built on, and it remains the community's land to this day.

The unveiling began with a service at the church, after which the choir walked fully robed to the memorial. All those who had served wore their medals. The church, always the focal point for much of the community, had lost so many of its members. The Reverend Richardson's son, Alfred, had been killed serving in Palestine in 1917 with the Somerset Light Infantry. He had at one time served on Gallipoli, I believe. Captain Daubeny, who often read the lessons in church, lost his only son, Charles, who died of wounds in France in the same year. Kendrick Frankling, who stood opposite me in the choir, a bass, he was killed, and the losses didn't end with the Armistice. Eric Grant, a young tenor, died in 1919 while still in uniform, as well as

Victor Wilkinson, a policeman, a member of the congregation and my parents' next-door neighbour.

There was a big crowd there that day, a beautiful late-summer day. Railings surrounded the site which stood in the centre of the field, a large stone cross with brass plaques adorning the plinth, inscribed on which were the names of the fallen. The names of my close friends are on those plaques: Lionel Morris, Stanley Pearce, Charlie Wherrett, Harold Chivers, and my cousin Fred Patch, too, and dozens of others I knew at school, or who were no more than acquaintances around the village, people whose families I spoke to – the butcher, the chimney sweep, a farmer, a carpenter. They had all lost sons in the war, most in their teens or early twenties.

We sang 'O Valiant Hearts', all seven verses; you can imagine how hard it was to sing.

> O valiant hearts who to your glory came
> Through dust of conflict and through battle flame;
> Tranquil you lie, your knightly virtue proved,
> Your memory hallowed in the land you loved.

There was a large Union Jack over the cross, which was pulled down after the appropriate words were spoken. I can't recall who unveiled the memorial – some big noise in uniform, covered in medal ribbons, or scrambled egg as the soldiers liked to call them. Prayers were said, and wreaths laid at the base of the memorial before the service ended and people were left to their own private thoughts.

After I had been working on the tower for six weeks, the foreman came and spoke to me. 'The boss wants to see you tomorrow morning, ten o'clock at the office.' He didn't often see anybody, so the foreman wondered what I had been up to, and I wasn't sure myself. Sculls had a works in Redcliffe Street in Bristol and the next morning I went to see the old man, Arthur Scull. I was called into his office and he told me to sit down in the chair opposite his desk. 'I've been to see my brother in Shrewsbury last week, and I hear you've got the plumbers' certificate and the certificate of the Institute of Sanitary Engineers. Why the devil didn't you tell me?' I said that I didn't think he would be interested. 'You don't intend staying a plumber all your life?' he asked. I told him, 'No.' 'Then what sort of job do you fancy?' I said a building instructor or sanitary engineer. I can remember now, he looked at me over his thick glasses. 'How old are you?' 'Twenty-five, sir.' He shook his head. 'You'll never get a job like that; they'll look at you and say, "Too young, no experience". They'll pass you by. Your qualifications are not good enough. You want the MRSI' [Member of the Royal Sanitary Institute]. I said, 'That's the top exam, I'll never pass it.' 'Have you ever tried? Try. Talk it over with your wife.' I appreciated that he had taken an interest in my career and I took him up on his suggestion, studied for the next three years, took the exam, but failed. The day after I got the result, I went to see him. 'You've failed. Take it again.' 'I can't,' I told him. 'You'll be a fool if you don't,' he replied. By this time I had a wife and two children to support and I couldn't afford the expense. Arthur Scull persisted. 'Take it. I'll pay your expenses, and, if you pass, pay me back out of your wages; if you fail, it's a gamble I've lost.' I studied hard, took the exam again and passed, and in time I paid him back. Arthur Scull was good to me.

On all four sides of the Wills Tower was wooden scaffolding, held together by chains, although none of the scaffolding was actually attached to the building. There were no cranes to haul the materials up to the top, so as well as climbing ladders to the roof level we carried everything else up with us, from the huge tool bags of our trade, full of everything you might need, to the great slabs of lead we used for flashings or for the heavy pipes. We had to carry it all up, which was exhausting, and at the end of the day, at least as far as our plumbing kit was concerned, we had to carry it back down again to be stored away. A plumber's kit cost about £50, several months' wages, so our tool bags were always locked away at night.

Everything on that memorial, all the cornices, was covered in lead that was cast in our workshops, eleven pounds to the square foot. It took some working when the lead was half an inch thick. It was all burnt together by melting the lead to make the joints watertight; it wasn't soldered. The expansion of solder was much greater than that of lead, and the first hot summer it would have split. It was a skilled job, and I was taught the art of lead burning there from a chap called Tommy Smith, fusing the metal together with little drops of lead all the way down. The skill was to get the oxyacetylene flame just right, otherwise the flame would simply melt the lead. It was a very useful and marketable skill.

There was one electric lift that went as high as the belfry, which was used to take bricks up. It was worked externally by one of the men. If the boss came on site to see us or check what we were doing, the man who worked the lift would always take him one floor above us, then let him drop back down fast to where we were, just to shake him up a little; it got him every time. It was also a useful ploy to give any of them who were not working at that moment enough warning to be hard at it when the boss arrived.

The bell for the memorial tower arrived and had to be placed into position. At that time, it was the third largest bell in England, set a half-tone higher but slightly smaller than Big Ben and smaller, too, than Great Tom that hangs in Christ Church, Oxford. Bristol's bell was known as Great George, and it weighed eight tons, heavy enough that when the engineers lifted it a foot off the floor in the Great Hall, the tackle broke. The only solution was to go to Wolverhampton where the bell had been cast, to borrow specialist equipment. They cut a hole in the belfry roof and lifted the bell, placing it in a reinforced-concrete carriage.

The foreman on the job, a Welshman, had a notice printed stating that the bell belonged to Bristol and that nobody must ring it until the tower was officially opened by King George V. It was the worst thing he could have done, because everyone with a hammer, spanner or mallet used to give it a good rap as they passed, and if they didn't have anything to hand, they'd kick it. If he'd said or done nothing and had left the bell alone, nobody would have taken any notice. As it was, the bell was rung all day long.

The work on the tower and the surrounding buildings was impressive and the men worked hard in all weather conditions, keeping the project on track and on budget. Nevertheless, in bad weather work was forced to stop and there was sometimes a risky scramble down the freestanding timber scaffolding. If the wind picked up too much, we could find ourselves trapped up in the tower until it had abated. It was not that the wooden scaffolding was likely to fall, but that the planks were only nailed down, and it was perfectly possible that sudden gusts could rip a plank or two off, injuring anyone still on the scaffolding or indeed down below.

Heavy thunderstorms were also a danger. The top of the tower was shaped like an eight-sided lantern with windows, none of which had glass in them. I was working up there covering the cornices with lead when the sky darkened and a thunderstorm broke. Two of us, myself and the foreman plumber, got under cover out of the rain, and the foreman was standing in one of the windows, a steel knife in his hand. Suddenly there was a terrific bang. Lightning had struck the tower, hitting the bell which had acted as a conductor. Fortunately, the bell was connected to earth by a big copper band. However, the foreman standing in the window had the knife ripped out of his hand. He was thrown to the floor and was incapable of using the arm that had held the knife for three weeks afterwards. The strike must have burnt all the oxygen out of the air, for there was a distinct reek of sulphur, then a second or two later you could feel a gust of air coming back into the tower.

On top of the tower, directly above the bell, was a trap door. One of my jobs was to cover the door with thick sheet lead. The job on the Wills Tower was coming to an end, and so before I placed the lead over the trap door I drilled two holes the depth and width of a penny, and the lad I was working with and I both signed our names in the woodwork underneath and placed two new pennies, each dated 1925, into the bored holes before sealing the door with the lead. I am quite sure the pennies are still there today, although our names would surely have gone by now; must have done.

When the tower was finally finished, we held what was called the topping-out parade, when the last stone was set into position. Very often some money is placed under the stone, just as it is under the foundation stone; it's all for good luck. In our case, a cameraman was there to take a picture, in which I appear clearly identifiable with my thick mop of hair.

All that was left was for King George V and Queen Mary to come and open the building, which they did in June 1925. It was a fine day, crowds of people. I don't remember much. I know the King gave a speech in the Great Hall because we were somewhere near the back, but I can't say I was that interested.

It was at the end of my spell on the Wills Tower that I retook the MRSI exam and passed. Within days of the result being known, Arthur Scull had appointed me manager of his Clifton branch, a significant promotion which acknowledged the efforts I had made. As I lived in Combe Down, I travelled each day to Bristol on a workman's ticket, which cost a shilling return. Each morning I left on the 7 a.m. train to open the shop at eight o'clock, closing at 5 p.m., and then went home. I was very settled at this time, for I had a steady and good income and by this time I also had a second son, Roy, who had been born at the back end of 1924.

Unemployment was rising sharply and the economic outlook was poor. I knew how lucky I was to be with a big plumbing firm, in charge of the branch shop. Sculls employed a number of plumbers and hot water fitters; the boss managed the hot water side of the business, me the plumbing, and we made sure that there was enough work coming in to keep us going. It was all too common to see unemployed men, still in their old army greatcoats, who came in asking for jobs we just didn't have. It kept us all on our toes. With Sculls, to be honest, you had to be a very good plumber to stay there; if you didn't pull your weight, you were out.

When the General Strike hit in 1926, there was no question of missing work and I cycled the twelve miles from Bath to Bristol each day to open the shop. Other than the lack of transport during the strike, we remained fairly unaffected but we certainly felt the effects of the general depression when trade was very bad. There was a lot of gloom and despondency at the time, and business could be quite cut-throat. At the height of the Depression a number of workers who commuted from Bath to Bristol to work were thrown out of their jobs, and Bristol people took their places, while the Bath workers returned home to find a job if they could. It wasn't pleasant.

One big advantage that Sculls had was that the business was related by marriage to another firm in Bristol, which looked after, renovated or sold a lot of property in the area. This relationship was useful, as we received a lot of work through this other company. If they were about to sell a house and they wanted a bathroom put in, then it was my job to undertake the work. Nevertheless, there was a problem. The foreman builder at this other firm was a man by the name of Williams, and I came to discover, quite by chance, that he was pulling a fast one on Sculls.

At the time all orders used to come down from the other company and, because of the volume of work, they had the first call on me. The work was one of two types: contract work, which was subcontracted and charged at a lower level, and day work, which was set at a higher price. Williams would tell me which type of job it was, and more often than not he would add, 'This one's contract, keep your price down', and so I did. My boss at Sculls would only get a certain percentage of the total price, much lower than if it was a day rate. If a client was being charged at the day rate but we understood it was contract work, then there was a considerable excess, and this profit was going to this other firm. I wasn't losing anything; I still got my plumber's rate, but my employers were losing money, and I had a much greater allegiance to Arthur Scull than I ever did to the other firm.

One of the other firm's painters let something slip that roused my suspicions and I followed it up. I knew that all orders were signed and countersigned by a confidential secretary, Phyllis Kay. She was a Sunday school teacher and a friend of mine from church, and I told her what was happening. She agreed to help me out. From then on, if I got an order signed Phyllis Kay, it meant that it was all right and I was to go ahead and do the job, because it was day work. If it was just signed PK, it would mean it was contract. From then on, if Williams tried to pass off something as contract work, I would tell him it was day work and I would undertake the job only if it was paid as such. Williams never found out how I knew the difference. At one point he wouldn't let me go into the office and collect the orders – he'd bring them to me himself – but still I knew and he couldn't fathom how. Sculls never found out that this scam was going on. They were being ripped off, but as there were family connections between the firms there might have been awful ructions if I had said anything.

In the end, the manager of the other firm wanted me moved from Clifton back to be an ordinary plumber at Redcliffe Street. I already had ideas of my own to start a small business. I had ten years' experience so I politely declined, and instead resigned. Whether Anthony Scull ever asked any questions – because they were very much out of pocket – I don't know. I already had enough small jobs to start on my own and I had made good contacts within the building business, people who trusted me and would put work my way. One of them was a well-known architect, Mowbray Green, who got me a lot of business because I could lead burn.

When I was finally going it alone I decided to splash out on my first car, an Austin Seven. I had been taught to drive in the 1920s by a grocer's son, Reg Ings, who was serving in the cavalry. He used to take me out into Bath to get used to the traffic, what there was in those days. Back then, I only needed to apply to the County Council for a driving licence as there were no actual tests; they didn't come in until the mid-1930s, I believe. Unfortunately, the Austin Seven was troublesome. The magneto-ignition, which gave the spark to start the engine, was always failing, so we swapped it for a Ford Eight. This car had been owned by two army officers: one had been drafted abroad and the other didn't want a car and put it on the market. It was practically a new car and served two useful purposes: as a family car that took us on day trips to such places as Weston-super-Mare, and as a works car that was insured to carry my plumbing tools for the new business.

Despite my contacts, running my own firm and choosing my work hardly removed me from the world of sharp practice. There were too many contractors from whom it was difficult to get money owed, and that made me wary. One such man was a chap called Clifford. He had been working on Midford Castle near Combe Down. The roof needed considerable work, and in principle I was happy to take on the job. The Castle had interested me from my boyhood as it had been built by a man who had once been a society gambler. The Castle was designed in the shape of the ace of clubs, the card he had won a huge pot of money on during one of his games. In all my childhood, I never saw the owner, who was a recluse and married to one of Captain Daubeny's daughters. After he died, the Castle went to the Daubeny family, and it was indirectly for them that I was asked to help put the roof back in perfect order. The place was a time warp: no gas, electricity, just torches and candles. Mowbray Green asked me to work at the Castle but I told him that, as the builder was a hell's delight to get any money from, I couldn't do it. Mowbray reassured me that every time I'd spent £200 in wages and expenses, I was to let him know and he would see that I got it.

During the 1930s, I expanded my company as the effects of the Depression gradually faded and work picked up. Most was very local but I would travel frequently to Radstock and Midsomer Norton, and occasionally further afield to Exeter and Exmouth. The boys were growing up fast, and while Ada was bringing them up I worked very hard to make sure that we had a comfortable life. I gradually took on three other registered plumbers, Jack Bath, who lived next door to us, Leslie Duckett and George Taylor, both of whom I'd known for years. Working locally meant that one of us could be called out at all hours on some emergency or another. A number of houses had large tanks under the roof to collect the rainwater. Water was metered and people were often quite conscious of keeping their bills down to a minimum. The rainwater would be used for domestic purposes, such as washing and the toilets. Drinking water by this time came from the mains. However, with so many tanks in the roofs, there were always small problems, flooding being one of them.

One of my clients was a Miss Davies, a Welsh speaker, and because of my time at Gobowen I could converse a little with her in Welsh. Miss Davies had a recurring anxiety. She had built several houses in Monkton Combe, and in all of them there were problems with the water pressure that made the washers in the taps constantly split, wasting large quantities of water. The water in Combe Down and Monkton Combe was supplied by a private company, the Combe Down Water Company, and the inspector was Vernon Bishop. We had never been friends since school, and the incident when he had kicked the headmaster had always stuck in my mind as being fairly typical of his behaviour. Twenty-five years later, he was in the process of taking over his father's business, which included contract work with the Combe Down Water Company. Owing to the water problems in Monkton Combe, Vernon had been called in and he'd told Miss Davies that she would have to change all the bathroom taps as they were not up to standard.

Now I had changed the washers on these taps on various occasions because the pressure was too high. The taps themselves were fine, indeed, Vernon's father had passed them as being fit. Nevertheless, Vernon's father had written to Miss Davies to tell her I wasn't doing my job properly. He advised Miss Davies to let his son take over from me, blatantly trying to take my business and give it to his son. The problem was that Vernon didn't have either my qualifications or experience.

Miss Davies showed me the letter and I gave it to my solicitor. I said, 'Get Vernon Bishop to come round and you choose any tap in any bathroom you like and he can take it apart.' We had a meeting. Miss Davies' solicitor was present, as well as an independent plumber. I knew damn well that all the taps were stamped JCSWR, a stamp of quality and approval. They chose the tap on the bath, and he dismantled it. The stamp was there and the independent plumber confirmed it was perfectly adequate for the job.

I sat and listened as Vernon claimed that it was critical to keep the pressure in Monkton Combe to force the water up the hill to the village of Windsley, and that he couldn't do anything about it. What he meant was that he didn't want to be seen spending the money to cure a problem that was of the water company's making. However, I had already told Miss Davies that there were solutions. It was possible to build a little reservoir about forty feet up the hill. I said that if Monkton was connected to that, the pressure would automatically be lowered. Alternatively, a pressure-reducing valve could be fitted, a more expensive option that would cost a few hundred pounds. The water pressure hadn't just affected Miss Davies' house but Monkton Combe School's pipes were always bursting too, and a solution had to be found. Once it had been shown that the problem was nothing to do with my work, Miss Davies turned on Vernon. 'You either put that reservoir in, or I will make sure that you are sued for damages.' She was a formidable lady with plenty of money. A reservoir was dug, and Vernon and I remained not the best of friends.

With competition, fair or unfair, there was always pressure to ensure the work came in, but as I could turn my hand to most things, odd jobs were always available if business was quiet. My father had taught me how to lay bricks, so if a wall needed building, I was able to manage.

For anyone working in the plumbing trade, there was exposure to dangerous or noxious substances that would simply not be allowed today. Handling old-fashioned lead piping or lifting any lead flap after a few years would expose the plumber to a white powder underneath, sulphate of lead, which was highly poisonous. You must not breathe it in, otherwise it would cause headaches and nausea. Handling the powder with bare hands would, in time, cause lead poisoning, turning not only the fingernails blue but hands, too. Yet no plumbers wore face masks, and men handled this powder all the time, just as long as they remembered to wash their hands thoroughly.

For many years I mended a lot of guttering using asbestos while lead-burning so as to keep the heat off the woodwork fascia. I mixed up buckets and buckets of asbestos powder with water to coat boilers, smoothing it over to create a good finish. It seems strange, but I don't recall any of us suffering any ill effects.

By the late 1930s, both my boys had left school. Roy followed me into the building trade while Dennis studied for accountancy. In 1939, Dennis was about to take his last accountancy exam and, if war hadn't broken out, he was going to emigrate to America, to Chicago, where Ada's brother Bill now had an accountancy business. Unbeknown to the rest of the family, Ada and I had decided that we would go and start a new life over there too. I never told my parents we were going; of course I would have told them sooner or later, but as the eventuality never arose, they never knew. War had once again intervened to change the passage of my life.

9

WORLD WAR II

It was difficult to watch as Europe slowly slid back into war. Hitler wanted more and more space for a new Germany, a Germany which was re-arming at a frightening rate. I remember watching the newsreel of Chamberlain stepping out of his plane, waving his piece of paper in the air. He had flown back from his visit to Germany, and he told us it was peace in our time, and you hoped it was true, but I was sceptical.

In Britain, Oswald Mosley and his British Union of Fascists were in the news, but this was Quaker country. Clarks, the shoe people, were down here, and they were Quakers; Morlands, the coat company, they were Quakers, and their influence was strong and no one I knew was even interested in his organization, never mind joining it.

In the event of war, I would probably be too old for combat, at least initially, but I felt I needed to do something. About the time of Chamberlain's trip to Munich, the Auxiliary Fire Service (AFS) was set up to equip and train civilian firefighters should the deteriorating European situation lead to war. It made sense to join. To start with, I knew about water, and I knew where all the hydrants were on Combe Down. There were two water mains in the village: one was just ordinary pressure, about ten pounds per square inch, and the other was high pressure, and I knew one from the other, so I, along with one or two local ex-Great War men, joined the AFS Combe Down in one of three teams.

Preparing for war was difficult. For those of us who had been through the 1914–18 war, the idea that we were going to go through it all again was difficult to accept, let alone contemplate, not least because my own sons were teenagers and just about the same age as I had been in 1914.

I was forty-one in September 1939 when Hitler invaded Poland and war was declared. I was indeed just outside military age [18–40] to be called up for national service. Dennis, however, was nineteen and studying for chartered accountancy; he only had his final exam to pass. Dennis didn't want to join the army so he went to Portsmouth, took a test, and joined the navy as a writer, which meant he dealt with the captain's administration, mail and correspondence. He signed on not just for the duration of the war but for twelve years.

For the first few months nothing much happened. It was known as the phoney war. In 1914, Germany had invaded France almost from day one, but in the second war we dispatched an expeditionary force for the Continent, but it would be the best part of nine months before Germany invaded France and all that meant for the troops and their retreat to Dunkirk.

In Bath, preparations were made, with air-raid shelters being built, wardens given rattles and whistles, and sirens erected, but I don't think we heard a siren for real for the best part of a year. In Combe Down, a lot of iron railings and four gates from around the church were taken away to be melted down for the war effort. They took some railings from in front of our house, but there was no point in protesting; you couldn't argue with government directives. Besides, how unpatriotic would you look if the railings from your neighbours' homes were taken away and yours remained intact? No, we were all in the war together, as a community, and you were willing to do your bit. I believe that most of the railings were of such poor quality that they were fit for nothing, and the idea of collecting the iron was as much to do with keeping up local morale as anything else.

With the threat of invasion very real, a system consisting of three lines of defence was established to protect Britain. The first line of defence was still the navy, the second line was troops under training, including, I believe, the Dad's Army which would occupy, among other things, the concrete pillboxes you can still see today. At the end of the war I saw a map which showed every pillbox from the Wash to South Wales, and there were hundreds of them. As a member of the AFS, I was to be part of the third line of defence along with those who manned searchlight batteries. Because I had served on a Lewis gun, I was given particular training on the belt-fed Vickers machine gun, a much better piece of equipment than the Lewis gun.

While there were searchlights round about Bath, there was little or no protection, no anti-aircraft guns, and right up until 1942, when we were bombed, Bath was an undefended city; I don't think anyone imagined we would be a target. We all had blackout curtains in our houses, and some people taped up the windows against the risk of a blast shattering the glass, but we didn't bother. We also made some curtains for Combe Down church. You had to watch it: the first glimmer of light and you were in trouble. At one point, a policeman threatened to report me because he said the curtains showed light through them. I told him to carry on. I also told him the material had been officially supplied by Somerset County Council. I heard no more about it.

Everyone could do something. Dad, although he was nearly eighty, took a job as a firewatcher, while others in the village, such as my great friend George Atkins, were air-raid wardens. As part of the AFS, our crew was regularly training. We used to go out on a Sunday morning, the whole crew, having a practice, sometimes with Bath Fire Brigade, sometimes on our own. We were very competent but we also had a lot of fun. We went out one morning to a very tall building on Combe Down. We ran the hose out, started the pump, put the ladder up, and the no. 1 on the crew, called Williams, went up. The idea was to rescue a dummy from a notionally burning house and bring the dummy back down the ladder. As it happened, Williams couldn't get the window open. Chief Officer Gibbs, who was watching him fumbling around, called out, 'Go on, Williams, make it realistic', so Williams pulled his axe out and smashed the window to pieces. When he got the dummy and brought it down, Gibbs was unimpressed. 'You bloody fool, that window was already unlatched.'

We often used to practise with the professional crews of Bath Fire Brigade, but on Sunday mornings we were usually on our own and we would operate in front of crowds of local people. We would compete with the other AFS crews: no. 1 crew would run so many lengths of hose out in such and such time, and our crew, no. 2 crew, had to see if we could beat it. Sometimes we would actually use the pump. The hosepipe was rolled in a coil and was coupled to the pump, while the suction pipe was placed in water, in the canal, a canvas reservoir or perhaps the Midford Brook. We had to be very careful. The pump turned the water into high pressure, and if the hosepipe was folded or twisted and they turned the water on, it would throw you down, you couldn't hold it.

Most public displays weren't designed simply for entertainment. They were essentially instructive, showing what civilians could do in the event of a raid, or how to handle small incidents. The vicar of Claverton proposed to give a public demonstration of how best to tackle an incendiary bomb. It was to be held at the vicarage, and he thought it would be interesting to see how long it would take us, from an initial call, to drive from Combe Down to Claverton. It was supposed to be a dry practice. We would arrive, smartly jump into action, and run a hosepipe out, but with no water. The call was taken and we raced to Claverton, two miles in four minutes, only to find the vicar's demonstration had gone totally wrong. Somehow, during his efforts, he had managed to set fire to a lot of undergrowth in a wood, and so the dry run became a wet one.

The field was very steep, and we left the car at the top end and pushed the petrol-driven pump down to the fire. The nearest water was the canal, so we uncoupled the suction and delivery hoses and put the fire out. By this time the ground had got a bit slippery, so we asked if a few of the civilians would help push the pump back up the hill to the car. There were five of us on the team, two on one side, two on the other, and me at the back. A number of civilians helped us, but, as we started, we got too close to the canal edge. One of the team slipped on the canal side and, grabbing at his pal, took him with him into the water.

At Combe Down we had three crews; no. 1 crew would go to the fire, no. 2, which might be ours, would stand by, and the third crew would be resting. In a proper raid, all three were called out. We kept our Bewick fire engine in an old stable attached to the vicarage; we had the stable downstairs for the car and the pump, while upstairs was a hayloft. One of the firemen built a fireplace in there, and we had four beds and a telephone. We were told by telephone which fire we should go to. The Chief Officer, Gibbs, lived a short distance from us. He would take a call, then he would come to our front door. If it was night, he pressed a button which activated a buzzer under my pillow; it was like an electric front-door bell without the bell, and was just enough to wake me up. It was my idea, actually, to help wake me up, and I would depress a button to let him know I'd received it. I'd then get up and dressed and run down to the stable while he'd go round four more houses and shake them up. Ten minutes, and we had a crew out.

We had to know the roads well. The rule governing illumination included vehicles as well as houses, and we drove with masked headlights and just a thin strip of light showing. In the dark, you never knew what you might come across.

In 1940, the first heavy raids on Bristol took place, which meant that the professional Bath fire crews went to give help and the AFS were left to tackle any emergencies. One concerned the train station at Monkton Combe. The railway ran through the old disused coal canal and the station was actually built in the bed of the canal. Right opposite, there was a factory belonging to a family called Freeman. They used to tear up rags, making them into flock for stuffing furniture and mattresses. Anything metallic was meant to have been removed, but evidently a button or something similar had gone through the machines in the rag mill and caused a spark. For a time the material must have smouldered. The rags had been bundled up and loaded on a railway truck which burst into flames. We were called, and as the material was thrown out of the wagon it was our job to damp it down. The suction was from a nearby brook so we had plenty of water. As we damped down the flames, I climbed into the carriage. It was dark, and with the truck doors open on each side, I pointed the hose outside until I was alerted by somebody running along the station platform shouting and waving his arms furiously. 'What the hell are you doing?' I didn't know, but in the gloom it seems that the power of the water had smashed the window of the ladies waiting room and completely flooded it.

The raids on Bath in 1942 came as a direct response to the Allied attacks on German cities of culture, notably Rostock and Lübeck. There had been unbridled anger at the Allied raids, and it was quickly concluded that Germany would retaliate by working its way through the Baedeker tourist guide, bombing historic towns in Britain. Thumbing through the guide, they decided to hit those picturesque towns given three stars or more, notably Exeter, Bath, Norwich, York and Canterbury, all of which were hit between late April and early May.

The raids came just as German attacks on Britain's major cities had begun to wane. By 1942, Germany was heavily engaged in fighting in Russia, and was committing vast forces to new spring offensives after the initial invasion the previous year. Britain's key industrial cities and ports were better prepared and defended, so that softer targets such as Bath were, in reality, the only available option.

Although air-raid sirens sounded in Bath on average one in three days throughout the war, the vast majority of alarms were purely precautionary, as German bombers, picking up the Avon, had followed the river to Bristol, or swung round in a wide arc to attack towns and cities in the Midlands, dropping their bombs as they continued onwards for home. This time would be different. On the nights of 25 and 26 April, eighty Junkers and Dornier bombers took off in eight waves from airfields in northern France and headed for sleepy Somerset. Such was the dire shortage of men and machines that the Luftwaffe was forced to scrape together every airworthy aircraft.

Using both crews in training and their instructors to pilot the planes, the Junkers and Dorniers set off for Bath, crossing the cliffs of Dorset before picking up the river that would take them directly over Combe Down.

I was at home when we were called out. I remember it as a clear, moonlit evening and as we left the house the first German aircraft began to circle around the city. Aircraft engines droned above us as numerous flares were dropped, lighting the whole area up. My wife commented how beautiful it looked. I couldn't see the beauty myself, and told her to get inside quick. We didn't have an Anderson or a Morrison shelter as we had never expected Bath to be raided; it was an open city, no guns, nothing at all, just a few searchlights. The only thing Ada could do was to go next door and get under the stairs with my sister-in-law, as I went on duty. My brother, William, like my father, was a firewatcher and he was already out that evening.

We got news that the Germans had dropped a large number of bombs on Wells Way, a steep hill that led indirectly from Combe Down on to what was known as the Bear Flat, before descending into Bath proper. The National Provincial Bank on the corner of Wells Way and Shakespeare Avenue was reportedly on fire, and our engine was directed to go and put it out. We raced to take the pump down, parked it along the road and tried to deal with the fire, which was already very extensive. My job was to couple the sections of hosepipe on to the pump and put the suction hose wherever we had water, but by this time many of the water mains were fractured and the water flooded uselessly away. Bath had prepared for such eventualities and had erected static canvas tanks around the city, and it was on a corner where two roads met on Wells Way that we drew our water to tackle the blaze. Although these tanks held thousands of gallons of water, the pump's water pressure damn soon sucked up every last drop. The bank was ruined and all we could do was damp it down and save what papers were left in the cellar.

All the time we could hear aircraft overhead. We could tell by the sound of the engines which was a British plane and which was German. Anyway, at about 11 p.m. one of their damn bombers went out, turned round and came back up, dropping flares as he went. He was no more than fifty feet – in fact he was so low he seemed to skim the roof tops – and as he came back down the Wells Road, over the Devonshire Arms pub, he opened up, machine guns blazing. In the darkness he must have seen us clearly illuminated by the firelight. I dived under the pump as bullets spattered all down the road, ping, ping, ping.

We dealt with fires all night as best we could, until about 9 a.m. We were just damping down smouldering houses when a warden came along and said that we'd parked our pump across an unexploded bomb. We had no idea. When we bent down, we could see the bomb lying on the road; in the dark we'd almost driven right over the top of it. We tentatively shifted the pump, but it was a close shave.

For all the crashes and reverberations that each bomb made, the Germans had pretty much failed to hit their targets. The railway had been missed altogether and famous sites such as the Royal Crescent and Circus were hardly touched at all. Even so, the damage to the town was extensive and lots of roads were closed off to everyone but the emergency services. One place that was destroyed was my old firm, J. Long and Sons. Their offices were close to the railway, and, in missing the station, the German bombers had a direct hit on my old plumbing and building firm, and all the machinery was destroyed. Another site to take a hammering was the gas-works in the Lower Bristol Road. This was hit by several bombs. A huge gas-fuelled flame shot skywards and the gas-holders quickly deflated, cutting all supplies to the town for the next three days. Williams, a Combe Down member of the AFS, was already there. His father, George, had been in the fire service before the Great War and was on HMS *Hampshire* when it was sunk in 1916 with Lord Kitchener aboard. His son had always been a very keen member of the AFS, and when little happened in the first years of the war, he'd moan about how he wished he could get some action. Well, he got his action at the gas-works that night, and he got it in the neck from us too. 'So what about it now, Williams? Keen for more action?' He'd been bloody scared out of his wits, and didn't fancy action after that, although we never quite let him forget it: 'Keen for more action yet, Williams?'

The second night, the German bombers came back again and we were called once more to the Bear Flat. Part of our immediate problem was that the Germans were targeting the railway station and the track, both of which lay in the dip just below the steep ridge on top of which sat the Bear Flat and Wells Way. The enemy aircraft chose to attack over the top of Combe Down and the Flat because all other routes into Bath were protected by a tremendous number of anti-aircraft positions, not protecting the town itself, but strategic sites of importance further away such as the Cullern fighter/bomber base, and to the north and to the west, those guns defending Bristol and the docks. The one undefended route into Bath was from the south, over the Bear Flat. In failing to hit the station, they were bound to hit the buildings where we were working.

On both nights the Germans dropped sticks of incendiaries as well as bombs, and once again houses burnt across the city, and roofs and walls gave way, filling the streets with debris. After nearly seventy years, it's hard now to distinguish much between the raids; all I can recall is putting out a fire in a residential house. The flames had been extinguished but, as we turned the pump off, a chair in the dining room suddenly burst into flames. We were in the process of leaving the house when we sent the message to turn the water on again, not noticing that we had twisted the hosepipe. Two of us were holding the pipe but we lost it. The nozzle flew off, hit the wall and bounced back, the water pressure driving it across the room, where it flew off again in a different direction. By the time we had chased it all round and caught it, both of us were wet through.

In the morning the full extent of the damage was evident. Those houses not badly damaged had all their glass smashed and front doors blown off their hinges. Elsewhere, homes had been reduced to near-dereliction, and, among the debris, our hosepipes snaked through the halls and living rooms of homes opened up to the world. It was like looking into a large doll's house, with pictures or mirrors still hanging on the wallpaper-covered walls, fire-places intact even if the floor had gone. The risk of collapse was severe, and roof tiles frequently slipped, causing a small avalanche into the street below. Many streets were closed off, and a chequered flag marked the spot where an unexploded bomb lay awaiting the bomb disposal squad.

A German propaganda picture came to light after the war, marked 'a badly bombed area'. It showed Bath, but it was actually that part of the city that had undergone slum clearance and was waiting to be rebuilt; they thought it was bomb damage, but it wasn't.

The clear-up operation was immense. Teams of men began digging in the rubble, removing bodies, while families made homeless sifted through what was left of their houses to see what they could salvage, pulling out personal possessions and looking for any useful timber. Neighbouring towns such as Bristol sent down vans to serve mugs of Oxo and tea to civilians and those in the services, and mobile kitchens dispensed vegetable soup. Meals were served in municipal buildings that had escaped damage. There were some houses along Clevedon Road, all of which suffered at least some damage, but Jerry had dropped a bomb and blown one of these homes out. I knew this street well because the houses had been built after the First War by the family of my friend Titch Harding. He had got in with Bath City Council, and, as his people also ran a decorating business, they had built these houses from start to finish. In all honesty, they weren't built to the highest specification, and as I walked by I couldn't help but smile. Some wag in the know had stuck a notice out on the rubble in the morning: 'Jerry built and Jerry bombed.'

After the raid was over, all the small firms went together to put things right. As a plumber, I had been issued with a builder's licence which meant I could get access to plumbing supplies at cost price from a place called Memories in Bath. I went back to Shakespeare Avenue and met an electrician there who was going from house to house trying to get the electricity working again, while I went in to trace the plumbing and the gas. In one house I told the lady that the electrician who was following me was a bit deaf and that she should shout at him to make herself heard. I then popped out and spoke to the electrician, and mentioned that the owner was a bit deaf and that he needed to shout. Anyway, we watched as the two of them shouted at each other, until they rumbled that we were pulling their leg.

The raids on Bath were the worst I was called to deal with. The damage on the Bear Flat was truly awful. Off Wells Way there are a number of streets all named after poets, Shakespeare Avenue, Wordsworth Avenue, Milton Avenue, Chaucer Avenue, and so on. They all suffered damage, but Wordsworth Avenue got the worst of it – it was destroyed. Combe Down was relatively untouched. Clevedale Road had a hit, and the road to Purbeck College had a crater, but there were no casualties. After the raids on Bath, most people used the caves for shelter when the sirens sounded, and there you were guaranteed to be safe. As for the three teams in the Combe Down AFS, no casualties were suffered either night, although I understood that two lady messengers were killed.

In all, I went through four raids, one in Bath, two in Bristol and one in Weston-super-Mare, but nothing was as bad as those two nights. Did the bombs remind me of Ypres? Of course they did; I was going through it again, and it was tough. One thought did flash across my mind, though. When that German plane machine-gunned our team, I couldn't help thinking that if I'd had my Lewis gun I could have downed him easily, he was that low.

The Baedeker Raids, as these attacks became known, were highly destructive. In all, 401 people were killed in Bath and 875 people wounded, 360 of them seriously. The final death toll was the highest among the towns hit during the Baedeker Raids and reputedly higher than any single raid on Coventry. Nor was the attack on Harry's AFS crew an isolated incident. As the raid was designed as a reprisal, firemen, policemen and ambulance crews were targeted.

Despite the precautions taken since the outbreak of war, including the construction of forty-three municipal air-raid shelters, no one expected any raids. The best-laid plans went quickly awry as buildings which had been set aside for casualties were hit and put out of action, and people fled into the surrounding countryside.

In all, some 19,000 buildings were damaged, including the famous Assembly Rooms. They had just been refurbished at great expense and were completely burnt out. However, Bath was not quite the benign city of culture and tourism it appeared to be. Elements of the British Admiralty had relocated from London to Bath, while an engineering works in the city was designing torpedoes for the navy, and at Kingswood School the famous

Mulberry Harbour was being planned. Sporadic, largely oppor-tunistic, raids continued for the next two years; indeed, it was not until three months after D-Day, in September 1944, that the Government gave the all-clear to the West Country.

Because I had my own business in Bath, I found myself in the same position in the Second World War as the company to which I had been apprenticed in the First, namely that all the people I had working for me – and I had three plumbers – were called up. I struggled on, trying to cope, but I couldn't do four men's work, it was impossible; so towards the end of 1942 I sold the business to a fellow in Holloway in Bath and looked around for a new opportunity.

In one of the trade papers, I noticed that the Ministry of Works was advertising for a civilian garrison engineer to come to Wells to look after the plumbing and sanitation at a number of military camps at Glastonbury and Street. The applicant had to be over military age; well, I was forty-four by then, so that was all right. I had the qualifications and I sent them through to the Colonel-in-Chief at Houndstan who interviewed me and offered me the job as a sanitary engineer. I was glad to go and soon after we moved to a pretty little village outside Yeovil called Compton Dun-don, where I would live for the next ten years.

The job itself was money for old rope, really. I had to sign the Official Secrets Act because by the nature of my work I would see all the troop movements. If a regiment was coming in, I knew where it was coming from, and if a regiment was going out, I knew where it was going to, because of sending barrack-room damages after them.

From 1942 the Americans had begun to arrive in increasing numbers and all the camps gradually filled until they were absolutely bursting at the seams, with bell tents erected between the huts. One thing I noticed straightaway was that none of the black and white GIs shared a tent. Nor would they walk down the street together. It was very marked that the whites couldn't stand the blacks. I didn't know why. I was surprised at the antagonism; in fact, I got on very well with the black troops, not least because I found them better behaved. I couldn't get on with the white GIs. The black soldiers' accommodation was just as good as that of the whites, but the segregation was seemingly accepted. At one camp, the black GIs were billeted in what was the old Glastonbury railway station. They had their own cookhouse there, and as part of my job I went to see that everything was all right, repairing the brick ranges where they made their food. The black GIs had a way of cooking that was different from the English. Instead of cooking Brussels sprouts and cabbage and such like, they used to stew up prunes and raisins and sultanas, and it made quite a decent variation on what I was used to. I made a point of visiting them quite a lot during meal times, because I would be invited to sit down and have lunch with them.

There were several incidents between white and black GIs that caused quite a bit of ongoing friction. One incident occurred at a wedding reception in Glastonbury. It was being held at a pub, the First and the Last – today it is the Pike and Musket. Anyway, the marriage was between two local people, but invited to the reception were several black GIs and some of the whites didn't like it, so they went down with the intention of disrupting the party. In Glastonbury, there was a policeman known as 'Ginger' Rogers, an amateur boxer, and when he heard about the disruption he went down and restored order by laying six of the white GIs out.

As well as dealing with the fresh water and sanitary arrangements in the camps, I was given a similar role for a group of four searchlights that were permanently manned just outside Yeovil. One of the group was far more powerful than the rest and was known as the Master Light. This shone an incredibly powerful beam into the night sky, and, if it picked up an enemy aircraft, then one of the other three searchlights would join the fray, holding the plane in the glare of the crossbeam. This helped in calculating, by triangulation, the height of the plane so that the anti-aircraft fire could be aimed more accurately.

The men working the Master Light lived in an underground bunker. I was never allowed beyond this bunker or to approach the Master Light too closely for reasons of security. Nevertheless, I did watch the crews light up the bulb which was powered from a large generator. It worked when two carbons in the centre of the light were brought together, creating a spark that lit the beam. The heat was intense, and for twenty feet in front of the searchlight the grass would be scorched.

During a raid, these beams would search the sky trying to pick out an enemy plane which, when caught in the searchlight, often tried to dive down the beam in order to fire at the crew and knock out the light. At the same time, night-fighter Spitfires would scramble from nearby Yeovilton, flying above the enemy aircraft. Directly a Spitfire was about to attack, the beam was switched off. The sudden darkness blinded the enemy pilot who, until this point, had been swathed in brilliant light. As it took a few seconds for his eyes to adjust, he was momentarily vulnerable as he couldn't see what he was doing. On a number of occasions, we saw German bombers caught in the beam and brought down under heavy fire, while we looked out for the crash and telltale flames on the ground. One German bomber came down just outside Street, and, after the war, five crosses could be seen, marking the place where the crew of a Dornier or Junkers was buried. Only after D-Day, when there was no further threat from German air raids, were these searchlights no longer manned.

Throughout 1943 enormous preparations were being made by the Allies for an invasion of France. American forces were continuing to pour into Somerset, and everywhere there were secret dumps of ammunition in the woods, while along the roads long convoys of lorries were often seen. Heaven help you if you got caught behind one because it was impossible to get past.

One of the best kept secrets during this period was the Allied decision to build a secure oil pipeline across southern England that would, in time, stretch across the Channel to Europe and would help resupply the vehicles and tanks of any landing force there. The pipeline was called PLUTO [Pipe-Lines Under The Ocean] and during my work around Yeovil I had come to hear of its existence. The Germans could bomb as many army lorries as they liked, but they wouldn't be able to break the supply of fuel unless they knew where PLUTO was, and this was secret. Sometime in late 1943 or early 1944 I happened to stumble across it.

I was in Combe Down on my way to a cottage in Monkton Combe when I saw three men in khaki on private land belonging to the Reverend Warrington, and as far as I knew they had no business to be there. I wandered across and asked them what they were up to and they told me they were laying a three-inch gas pipeline. 'Who are you kidding?' I laughed. 'I'm a plumber and I know a gas main is identified by a continuous red mark painted along its side.' Marking identified every type of pipe. If the red line was dotted, it was domestic hot water. A blue line meant mains drinking water, a dotted blue line meant water fed to domestic tanks for sinks and lavatories, and not to be drunk. The pipe they were laying was a natural colour with no markings. That is the pipeline under the ocean, 'Pluto'. The pipeline began in South Wales and ended at Fawley Oil Refinery, and at various points this fuel could be tapped for use in military lorries. They also had one line that went to the RAF station at Yeovilton to refuel the aircraft there. After that I don't know where it went. The men told me that I would have to sign the Official Secrets Act, but I already had. In fact they were not laying the line at all but were checking it for obstructions. One of the men was walking along the route of the pipeline with a little instrument. As long as the instrument was ticking the line was all right. If it stopped ticking, it meant there was an obstruction and they dug down to the pipe to see what the problem was and that was what I had seen.

In the weeks before D-Day, the camps became utterly choked with American soldiers. As I've said, I knew the time and date of all movements in and out of every camp in this area, except for one, and that was D-Day. We knew that a major assault on Europe was planned, for there was an extraordinary number of men and huge quantities of ammunition, trucks and tanks, too many for there to be any other explanation. I knew all about the ammunition dumps in the woods around Street; these woods were army property, and sentries were always around, warning off kids. I can only be thankful that the town was never bombed! But that day, 6 June 1944, was kept secret by everyone. I went away one night, everything was normal, camps full of Americans, everything as it should be. Came back in the morning, and not a soldier was to be seen, they were gone. It was quite eerie. Fires in the camps' ranges were still burning. There were urns of cocoa, coffee, tea, all hot. Cheese, butter, bacon, it was all there, in the dining room, with half-consumed meals on the tables. It came as a complete surprise to me to hear that D-Day had happened.

After the troops had gone, a number of men, including me, were given the job of dismantling some of the camps and giving them back to the owners. There was a prisoner-of-war camp at the foot of Bristol Hill, Sobury Park, and the clerk of works would obtain permission to borrow prisoners to help dismantle the various sites around Street. We were never particularly friendly with these prisoners, but we treated them as we would expect to be treated, and they responded likewise. I understood that these prisoners were well looked after, almost too well, for as far as I know none ever tried to escape. They were all clearly identifiable and wore clothes with large bluish cloth patches on their backs. All these men seemed content to see out the war in relative safety. Who could blame them?

We were instructed that, once a hut was dismantled, the POWs would load all the corrugated iron on to a lorry which would go to a returns depot at Shepton Mallet. However, the very first time we did this the lorry returned fully loaded, with a message, 'We don't want this. This is American.' We then tried a depot at Taunton but the same thing happened. They wouldn't accept anything. In no time, we had a hut full of corrugated iron sheets that no one wanted, so in the end we sold them to the farmers at two shillings a sheet. And not just corrugated iron. All sorts of things littered the camps, and we packed up and sold spirit levels, saws, carpenters' tools, gardening tools to anyone happy to buy. We gave some of the proceeds to police funds, always a wise thing to do, and the rest? Well, don't ask!

One of the camps we cleared is where St Dunstan's car park in Glastonbury is today, right in the main street. At this camp there were four petrol pumps. All of them had been more or less wilfully damaged by the GIs before they left, ensuring they couldn't deliver petrol. Any fuel was more or less liquid gold during the war, so I said to the clerk of works, 'I wonder if the whites have left any petrol in the tanks?' He didn't know, but we soon found out, borrowing a dipstick from a garage. The first tank we found to be empty, but to our great surprise two of the four underground tanks were full and the third about half full. We had with us what was known as a semi-rotary pump, and we pumped the petrol out into anything that would hold fuel. Given my profession, I could get hold of a number of hot-water cylinders which I plugged to seal them. Each took about fifty gallons of petrol and I filled to the brim just as many as I could get hold of. We then drove the cylinders to Street, where the clerk of works had some Nissen huts on a site which, ironically, was being used as part of a camp for petty criminals. The clerk had sole access to some of these huts, so we stored the cylinders there under lock and key. There would be no shortage of petrol for us, and for the rest of the war I was able to travel around, often visiting my parents in Combe Down. Indeed, there was too much fuel for just the clerk and myself, so we sold petrol to anyone who wanted it, or rather to those who were 'in the know' and could be trusted. Do you know who our biggest client was? It was the chief superintendent of Glastonbury police, who had his own car. In the end, we cleared the lot. The pumps were repaired and then handed back to the owner, a firm based in Shepton Mallet.

The job of repairing damage, as well as clearing the camps, took many months. The American troops had certainly left their fair share of problems, having been accommodated in buildings right across Somerset. A large number of soldiers were housed in Prior Park, which had been standing empty for about eleven years. It had been a Roman Catholic school before the Americans arrived. Despite all the talk of how much they got paid, some at least obviously felt that this was not enough. They stripped all the lead from the huge porch in front of the main entrance and sold it to some scrap-metal merchants at the bottom of the hill. These merchants had a business under one of the viaduct arches and were happy to buy whatever the soldiers could get hold of. After the war the site went back to being a Roman Catholic school and I was given the job of re-covering that porch with lead.

Another site I dealt with was a big house in Glastonbury called The Populars, which had housed a number of GIs. In their spare time, these men started to build a brick swimming pool at the back but, for whatever reason, it was never filled. Instead, they built a cookhouse in the bottom. I went to inspect the site prior to pulling it down. I took a team of men to the cookhouse and we looked around. I had one lad with me, very inquisitive, and he opened the door on the range and looked inside. Sitting in the middle of the range

were two boxes of Mills bombs, all live, with their deto-
nators in. What possessed them to put them in the oven,
I've no idea. We had no option but to call the bomb squad
in and they destroyed them.

With so many camps empty, a lot of squatters began to
move in. Some were young people with children who just
wanted a home; some were people who got married and
wanted a house; others were much older people. Few, if any,
had money to buy coal, so wardrobes or any other furniture
that was left behind was gradually broken up for firewood.
On the Somerton Road, just by Millfield School, there had
been a large tank camp, No. 1 Camp, and squatters had
moved in almost straightaway and established themselves
to the degree that they set up their own committees, and
held residents' meetings which I would attend in my
official capacity as Garrison Camp Engineer. There were
always disputes about who would pay for the electricity,
and a man from the electric light people would be there and
try to sort out the issues. The problem was that the
electricity was communal; it wasn't metered for individual
huts. On one occasion, he told the squatters that unless an
electricity bill was paid they would be cut off. I remember
one old lady moaning that some other lady in the next-door
hut was using an electric machine to make gloves and was
therefore consuming far more than she was, but the man
held firm. 'Unless it's paid, I shall cut you all off.' It all got
rather heated. 'All the switches and fuses are in my hut. I
shan't let you in,' she said firmly. 'Don't worry about that,'
he said. 'I shall climb the bloody pole and cut you off.' On
another occasion, I was given the order to turn the water
hydrant off to stop them from having water but at the last
moment that was rescinded, so these squatters had a

sympathetic ear somewhere on the council. I must say that most of the squatters were very nice, with the exception of one or two, and in the end the council allowed them to stay for years.

War or not, Somerset always had its fair share of people on the move. Many were itinerant workers looking for casual employment. Gypsy caravans were a frequent sight around Glastonbury and Yeovil, while roaming the country were a large number of vagrants and tramps who lived off the land and did odd jobs to stay alive. I remember, as a child, that there was once an old workhouse near Bath, what is now St Martin's Hospital, at the top of Wells Way. There was a rough dry-stone wall surrounding the building. The nearest workhouse to Bath was Frome and tramps used to walk to Bath, have a night there and then be on their way again. Some of them had a regular round. They daren't enter the workhouse with any money, so if they had any coins on them they used to find a suitable fissure and press their money in to hide it in the wall. Of course they would be looking around to see that no one was watching. We knew that money was hidden in the wall and so we used to go along and search, looking carefully into every gap, and pinch what we could find. Of course, there were times when we would see the tramps looking along the wall, trying to recall where they had left their money. It seems heartless, looking back, but as kids you didn't always think.

During the war, and for many years afterwards, there used to be an old white-haired tramp who was different from most. He used to come through Wincanton, work his way round through Castle Carey, come through Compton into Street working his way round Street and back to Wincanton again. He had an old bike, and he used to cuss like a trooper if he got a puncture. I often used to walk up Compton Hill with him and, if I saw him anywhere round Castle Carey, I'd go and say hello. He was often down a little side road, making his tea for breakfast, and I would go and have a cup and a chat. He was always neat and tidy, clean-shaven; you would hardly think he was a tramp. One day a policeman from Castle Carey asked, 'You don't know who he is?' I said, 'No, but I often meet him.' He said, 'I won't tell you his name, but we always know where to find him. In the winter he sleeps under the racecourse grandstand at Wincanton and, wherever he goes, the local police always tell us. During the First World War he was an admiral of the fleet, and he lost his only son, and since then he's just gone as a tramp.' This man never spoke about the war, he just talked about ordinary things, where he'd been and the people he'd met, but you could tell he was well educated. Local people would keep a friendly eye on him.

When I moved down to Compton Dundon, I remained in the Auxiliary Fire Service but nothing was happening, and in effect I was responsible for fires that were small enough for me to deal with almost on my own. There had been no more alarms for a long time, no sirens that put us on guard in case of a raid, and when I realized Hitler was no longer a threat I left the AFS for good and returned to civilian work.

Victory in Europe Day (VE Day) soon followed, and at Compton Dundon there were enthusiastic celebrations on Street Hill. I went along and watched as fires were lit at the top of the hill, at a place called Marshall's Elm. People sang and danced, but as I'd never learnt to dance I watched and had a drink. It was impossible to get excited. My oldest brother, George, and his wife, Lilian, had two children, May and Bob. At the outbreak of war, Bob had come back from

Canada where he had gained his 'wings', and met a man called Reginald Hughes, the son of a chemist. Hughes had come back to Britain from training in South Africa and they teamed up as bomber pilots but were transferred and flew as test pilots on the new jet engine. In November 1943, Bob had a flying accident and was killed. He was just twenty-three, the same age as my own elder son. Bob was buried at Haycombe Cemetery, Bath. He lies close to Reginald Hughes, who had been killed back in June 1943 in another flying accident, while testing the same engine. The saddest part of the story was that Hughes was engaged to my niece, May. They were real soul mates. So May lost her fiancé and her younger brother, and my brother and sister-in-law lost their only son. The shock of his death caused Lilian to have a heart attack; she could only watch Bob being taken through the house for the funeral, and she died soon after. May did not marry until she was fifty-eight, and has no children. Yet again, war had cost my family dear.

IO

GROWING OLDER

Harry turned forty-seven the month after the war in Europe finally came to an end in May 1945. With the cessation of fighting, the Government no longer needed Harry's services and he returned to purely civilian work, joining E. R. Carter's as a plumber, and staying with them until he retired. In due course, he moved once more, leaving the village of Compton Dundon where he had lived since 1943, and going to Yeovil. Here he remained until well after retirement.

After the war, Harry's two sons returned from fighting over-seas. Dennis eventually chose to sign on for further service, remaining with the navy for the next seventeen years, finishing with the Admiralty in Bath. Roy left the Royal Army Service Corps, taking a job with Morlands, a sheepskin factory in Street. In 1946, he married a local girl he met through work; she had settled with her family in Somerset after leaving the East End of London as an evacuee during the Blitz.

By 1945 Harry was sick of war and its terrible consequences.

I felt then, as I feel now, that the politicians who took us to war should have been given the guns and told to settle their differences themselves, instead of organizing nothing better than legalized mass murder. I had no interest in what happened to the Nazi war criminals. Another war was over, and once again both I and my family had paid a price that was always too high. Fortunately for me, both my sons had come back; Dennis was on HMS *Sheffield*, a light cruiser. This was the ship that took part in the sinking of the *Bismarck* and later the *Scharnhorst*, but I didn't discover that from Dennis. He never spoke about his war, and I never wanted to ask.

Just after Christmas 1945, Harry's father, William, died at the age of eighty-two. He and his wife, Elizabeth, had returned in the late 1930s to their former home, Fonthill, selling Rosemount, which had become too big for them. For the next six years, Elizabeth continued to live at the family home, looked after by various members of the family including May Patch, eldest daughter of Harry's brother, George, who frequently popped in to see how Elizabeth was, right up until her grandmother's death in May 1951 at the age of ninety-four.

Throughout the late 1940s and early 1950s, Harry remained with Ada at Compton Dundon, living in an idyllic thatched cottage. In many ways, these were some of his happiest times. Like his father, he had a large vegetable plot, and also reared pigs and chickens. In the extensive gardens, there was an orchard with valuable cider apples, more valuable than Harry realized. For a while, he grew and sold the apples, ignorant of their true worth as a rare variety of cider apple, a mistake he soon corrected! As his father had done, he cultivated as much land as he could, while continuing to hold down his full-time job. Harry even found time, and space, to build his own caravan. 'It was made out of hardboard. It had two single beds, a table, no washing facilities but a two-ring cooker that was heated by oil. The tyres were the front wheels off a Morris car and it was towed behind one of the company vehicles that I was occasionally permitted to borrow.' Throughout the 1950s, Harry holidayed frequently on the south coast in the caravan, meeting up with relations as well as with his best friend, George Atkins. George's wife had moved to Chickerell, close to Weymouth, during the war, but as chief air-raid warden in Combe Down, George remained behind, only joining his wife after VE Day, when he took a job at the Portland Dockyard, taking supplies to naval vessels in the harbour. After the war, Harry and Ada spent much of their free time in Weymouth.

Increasingly, Harry looked towards a time when he could enjoy life. His love of history had already drawn him into public speaking about Bath and its Roman history, a subject about which he had enormous hands-on experience from his work at the Roman baths, as well as his knowledge of the local countryside. However, it was his love of one book in particular that drew him into a ten-year-hobby-cum-quest, to find the truth behind a story he had read as a boy.

That book was *Moonfleet*, written by the popular writer J. Meade Falkner. Falkner had written two other adventure stories for boys, but *Moonfleet*, his classic yarn of smuggling and murder, in the same tradition as *Treasure Island* or *Kidnapped*, won popular acclaim among Edwardian boys brought up on the *Boy's Own* comics and books that extolled heroism and daring adventures. George's move to Chickerell was significant because it was less than half a mile from the tiny hamlet of Moonfleet, so small, indeed, that it does not even appear on motoring atlases.

As children, both Harry and George had read *Moonfleet*. It tells the story of a fifteen-year-old boy, John, who by chance discovers a secret passage under the church at Moonfleet. The tunnel is being used by smugglers with whom John becomes entangled. Inevitably in stories of its time the villains die and John returns to a peaceful life. However, rumours that the tunnel actually existed led Harry and George to set about their own part-time search.

Falkner's story was based, at least in part, on truth. Smugglers had used a secret passageway to the church's crypt, where they had stored kegs of rum. The church, located just behind Chesil Beach, was a useful staging post for the illicit smuggling ring. One evening, as the congregation was singing, a violent storm blew up during which the sea broke through the beach and into the crypt. The sound of strange, unearthly noises emanating from beneath their feet terrified the worshippers. They fled, unaware that, rather than the knocking of the dead, the noise was in fact the floating kegs bumping against the crypt ceiling.

The smugglers' tunnel was believed to have been dug close to a gravestone, and any search required permission from the Bishop of Salisbury. We went to Moonfleet and read as much as we could about the history of the church. The hamlet was originally called Moenfleet, Moen meaning west, and this was gradually changed to Moonfleet.

In the second chapter of the book, there is a storm, that is true, but there was supposed to be an underground passage going from the church down to Fleet Water, but we could never make out how this was possible. According to George's compass – he had a non-magnetic compass – it was going into Chesil Beach but we couldn't find anything for a long time.

George was in the habit of having a walk around, and he climbed the hill opposite the church. It was a hot summer and that night he wrote me a letter. 'Come down for the weekend.' He'd noticed a difference in the grass behind a tombstone. He said, 'I've got some pegs; I'll get on the hill and tell you which way to move and drive a peg in.' We had a spade and took the turf off, and underneath we found two big stones. We lifted them, and there was the passage. George wanted to go down, but I insisted on testing the air first, and we put a candle down. It was all right, and we went in. The tunnel was two feet four inches wide and less than four feet high. It was the right one but it was not a smugglers' tunnel. Now George, before he died, met a fellow from Charleston, well over ninety, and as a boy he had seen the crypt opened in the 1870s, and he told us what it was like. There were six coffins inside. The kegs bumping about under the chancel floor had smashed all the coffins to pieces. The parson gathered up the bones and the brass plates and put them in a space in the vault and it was sealed again. We'd noticed that the tunnel we found led towards the vault but that it ended in solid masonry. The book tells you there's an entrance; well, there isn't.

In 1963, I retired at the age of sixty-five. The owner of the firm said to me, 'You've got your health and strength, Harry, why don't you carry on?' But I told him, 'I've got my health and strength, and that's the time to enjoy life. I've had fifty years in the building trade and that's enough for me.' The boss had four daughters but no son to carry on the business, so in time the company itself closed.

For the next decade, Harry and Ada lived quietly in Yeovil. Then, in 1976, Ada had a stroke which incapacitated her.

It was a massive stroke after a period of ill health. She was in hospital in Wells but in the end they felt she was well enough to be discharged home again. One afternoon, Dennis took us for a drive round Wedmore and back; she seemed all right then. That evening we were sitting upstairs and I said to Dennis, 'She's not with us.' We called the doctor and she was taken to hospital straightaway. Dennis and I stayed with her until late evening when we came home. When we went back up next morning she was dead.

Harry was devastated. Ada was eighty-one years old, and their marriage had lasted over half a century. She was cremated and her ashes interred at Haycombe Cemetery in Bath. The following year, George Atkins also died, and a close friendship that had lasted seventy-four years was also broken.

The late 1970s were difficult years for Harry. Dennis had been very close to his mother and her death hit him particularly hard. Within a year, he had turned to drink, financed by a generous naval pension and supplemented not only by further income from his subsequent civilian career as an accountant for Clarks Shoes, but also by a state pension. By this time Harry had left Yeovil and moved back to live with Dennis in Wells, but life in his new home became increasingly intolerable. 'Dennis would come home, have the tea which I prepared for him, shower, change, and go to the pub with his friends. He soon turned alcoholic, whisky and brandy, never beer, and that destroyed him.' Dennis grew progressively difficult to live with. He began to sell off family heirlooms, including Harry's own Great War medals. 'Eventually he sold everything that he could lay his hands on, all the silver, so he could drink whisky with his friends.'

In 1980, Harry met a widow called Jean and soon afterwards they were married, moving to Valley Close in Wells. Harry married partly, as he himself admits, to escape life at home. 'To be honest, I married to get out of my son's way; you couldn't live with him.' Jean was about Harry's age, and had moved from rather poor accommodation in Wells to sheltered housing, close to where Harry had been living.

It was shortly after Harry and Jean married that a chance conversation with a friend took Harry abroad for the first time since the Great War. He returned to France, not to the battlefields of his youth but to those of World War II.

A friend of mine in Street, who was part-owner of a coach company, phoned me one night and said, 'We've had a cancellation for two people who were going to Normandy to see the beaches. Would you like to take it up?' After much thought I said that we would, and my wife and I went to France. I didn't really give it enough thought and what I saw made me regret going. The experience was more than enough for me, and I was shocked at my reaction. The tour took us to see the beaches where the men had landed, and the Mulberry Harbour which had been built to supply the troops. We saw the German dugouts and the gun emplacements, some of which had been blown to pieces by our fleet out at sea, but it was the cemeteries that I found too much to bear.

We went to one American cemetery, above Omaha Beach. I met an attendant looking after the graves and he told me there were 9,500 Americans buried there. I surveyed the scene and I thought how I must have known some of them. I stood in the pathway, gravestones on each side of me, but I could not bring myself to walk down among the graves. I stood and I cried, and some people helped me up the steps to a pavilion with more names, those of the missing, all round. Those GIs that I had known, none of them by name of course, but their names were all round me, no doubt about it, and I sat there as the people from the coach trip went off, walking through the cemetery. I looked at those tombstones; they didn't die a normal death, they were shot, bayoneted or torn to pieces with shrapnel. Many must have died a terrible death, and those tombstones took on an entirely different light to me. At that moment I felt there could not be a god, and I became an agnostic. Those 9,500 men must have prayed that they would go home safe, and their families prayed as well, but it was decided that they should not live. I thought, too, of the differences between the blacks and the whites in Somerset, and the problems between them, but they must have been as one when they landed in France to fight, and they were certainly as one in this cemetery; no distinctions here.

It was doubly hard to see such wasted life. My own son at home had served in the navy throughout the war and had been fortunate enough to come through when others hadn't, but he was drinking his life away. I was glad to get out and go back home, and I swore that I would never go abroad again.

Shortly afterwards, back in Wells, Dennis came round to our house. He was in a bad way. He pulled his trousers up, and I could see his legs were very badly swollen. We picked up the phone and got the doctor to see him. I was approached by one of Dennis' boozing friends and he told me Dennis had sclerosis of the liver. My son had never told me anything. We spoke to a doctor and decided to get him to London to see a specialist. I asked what would happen if they couldn't do anything for him; then what? The doctor said, 'I'll give him a fortnight to live.' He went to King's Cross Hospital and he lived eight days. He was sixty-one.

After Dennis died, I told my solicitor I didn't want any money from my son's estate and it was passed to Roy, including the house Dennis had bought. The car went to one of his boozing friends.

The death of Harry's elder son was compounded soon after by the death of his second wife. His marriage lasted just four years before Jean died of cancer. The distress over Dennis had led to a confrontation between Harry and his other son, Roy. A rift developed between them that was never healed, and for the last twenty years of Roy's life they never spoke. Roy died of cancer in 2002.

By the mid-1980s, Harry was on his own once again, though he continued to be supported by long-term as well as new friends. His neighbours in Wells, Fred and Betty Isaacs, were particularly close, and they helped Harry through many of the dark days. When Fred eventually died in 1988, Harry returned the kindness he had been shown and cared for Betty. 'They had two bedrooms in their house and if Betty was ever ill I used to go and stay in their spare bedroom. Fred had asked me before he died, if anything happened to him, to look after Betty. I promised I would. I said, "For what you've done for me since my wife died, yes, I will", never expecting to live as long as I have.'

By the mid-1980s, interest in the Great War had begun to grow, as people became aware that the number of veterans was diminishing rapidly. The seventieth anniversaries of the battles of the Somme and of Passchendaele were commemorated widely in the press and on television, but Harry was not interested.

I didn't meet any old comrades from the regiment after the war and I made a point not to watch war films. Anything to do with war on television, and I turned it off straightaway.

Even when I finally appeared on television talking about the war in 1998, well, to be honest, I slept through most of it. I didn't even like the old wartime songs, because they brought back too many memories, and Passchendaele was about as deeply buried at the back of my mind as I could possibly make it.

While Harry's war experiences remained dormant in his mind, his vast knowledge of Somerset and particularly the now-closed quarries was increasingly in demand. In 1990, aged ninety-two, he helped geologists from Bath University explore the ground under Combe Down. Council interest in the quarries and their potential danger to the village was growing. In the Firs Field, where the war memorial stands and where local children played, a light hole or ventilation shaft was exposed by the fall of a beech tree during a storm. It revealed the floor of a quarry just twenty feet below the surface. Immediate action was needed. Harry, wearing hard hat and dungarees, was taken underground. It was the first time he had been down there in seventy years, and he was featured in the local press for the first time. 'Henry (aged 92) shows the way' the local paper trumpeted, and reported that Harry not only helped check the underground workings for Bath City Council, but showed them a quarry that no one else knew even existed. The trip revealed several roof falls, including one that Harry judged to be below the important road junction of Richardson Avenue and The Avenue. Urgent repairs were undertaken, including a concrete cap to seal the light hole in the Firs Field, and Harry's opinion was frequently sought. It was the first time that Harry's age was significant, for few people still alive had such a thorough knowledge of the quarries, most of which had been sealed to prevent access for more than sixty years.

Despite much private sadness, Harry remained resolutely positive, and with Betty he began once more to travel around the United Kingdom and Ireland. They travelled by coach tours organized by a company in Shepton Mallet.

Locally, we went to Ilfracombe, Bodmin, Westward Ho! We also went to places as different as London and Llandudno. Later, we travelled to Cork, then all round the Ring of Kerry, while another trip took us as far as Fort William in Scotland. Eventually, Betty became too frail to tour and in time the doctor told her that she should give up her independence. She must go where somebody would look after her around the clock, and that's why we came here to the residential home, over ten years ago now, and here I am today.

I I

LIFE BEGINS AT 100

They say life begins at forty, don't they? Well, for me it began again at 100. On that day, back in 1998, the home had a big party for my birthday, and it was after that, that I suddenly started being contacted by newspapers and television, and it hasn't really stopped since.

People talk to me about that war. I find it easier to talk about it now, having talked since 1998, but until that birthday I wouldn't mention it. I didn't mention the war even to my first wife and we were together for fifty-seven years. I don't think she had any idea about my service, and never brought it up. Now it is usually all people want to talk about, and I'm tired of talking about it. I appreciate the fact that people want to write to me about that time, but it's too much: photographs, autographs, letters asking for an interview, you get fed up. I'm not available!

I've been told that I'm the last survivor of the trenches, the last fighting Tommy; I like that title. Henry Allingham, who is a couple of years older than me, was air force, so I think I am the only one left who actually lived and served in the trenches. My entire generation fought that war and

I've turned out to be the last, and it does make you wonder. I read that one woman who died recently was 116. I shan't make that, but 109 – fingers crossed.

Going back to France was nothing I ever thought I would do, and certainly not at 105 years old. I was asked on many occasions whether I would consider going back and I said, 'Never', but in the end, I don't know why, I decided to go and I'm pleased that I did. Seeing Ypres again and the battlefields was very emotional. I've been back by coach with Genesta, a battlefield group, and when I first went back I travelled with two other veterans, Jack Davis and Arthur Halestrap. Jack was Duke of Cornwall's Light Infantry as well, and we formed a bond. We visited the cemeteries, and the places where the effects of war can still be seen, and I have returned to Pilckem Ridge. The first time I went back there, we drove to my Divisional Memorial, the 20th Division. I was on a coach and we parked opposite, and the idea was that I would lay a wreath to the memory of my dead friends, but I couldn't. I looked from the window and the memories flooded back and I wept, and the wreath was laid on my behalf.

I've also been to Toc H in Poperinge, visiting the chapel at the top of the building where Tubby Clayton held his services. I don't know if either Jack or Arthur ever went there during the war. Now they are both gone, and I've had no desire to go back again, and it's harder to go, physically, in any case.

I'm aware that it's the ninetieth anniversary of Passchendaele in 2007 and I don't know whether I will be able or willing to go, although no doubt someone will suggest a trip. I never thought I would return to the Ypres salient in the first place, and each time I have returned I have said and accepted that it would be my last visit. I don't feel the need to go. I know that Arthur Halestrap always felt it was his duty to go until the end, but I don't know, we shall have to see. Each visit has been that much more exhausting and, coming towards 109 years of age, perhaps it will be just too much.

My last visit was in late 2004. The BBC were making their series about the last Tommies and I was asked if I would meet a German veteran, Charles Kuentz. My first reaction was 'no' but I came round to the idea. Charles was conscripted just like myself and fought for the Kaiser as I had fought for the King, relations, of course, cousins, so it was a family affair. It shows you how stupid war is.

I shall never forget the German cemetery at Langemarck and the British cemetery at Tyne Cot. I went with Charles and I put a wreath of poppies on one of the German graves. He couldn't speak English; his father was born French but he lived in Alsace, and Charles was conscripted into the German army, and he fought against me. We had an interpreter, and we exchanged presents: I gave him a bottle of Somerset cider and he gave me a tin of Alsatian biscuits. I was glad I met him before he died, a few months later.

War is organized murder and nothing else. Charles told me that he was ordered to fire his artillery gun; it was nothing personal, he said. He couldn't see what he was firing at, and it was just done by coordinates. I told him that we fired at the legs and didn't aim to kill, and that was the truth. I enjoyed the meeting; we had lunch together on Kemmel Hill where he had served at one time, and toasted each other and shook hands. I was very happy to shake his hand. Later that evening, we went together and sat under the Menin Gate in Ypres, side by side, during the 8 p.m.

ceremony there. I never felt sorry for the Germans during the war, but I did for Charles. I felt sorry for what he had to go through; no one deserved to go through that war.

Each evening under the Menin Gate they play the Last Post, and when I was there they asked me to say the oration, 'They shall grow not old, as we that are left grow old . . .' But that is not what Tubby Clayton taught us. He used to say, 'With proud thanksgiving let us remember our brethren who fell', and then he would say, 'They shall grow not old . . .' They always miss that line out and I don't know why. That was the prayer we always used to finish those meetings with at Toc H, and they always leave out that little bit under the Gate, and I think that is wrong, so I've made a point of saying it.

It always amazes me how much interest there is in the Great War. You only have to see all those people standing under the Gate when they sound the Last Post to see what I mean. I also know there are issues that still stir up much controversy. Was Field Marshal Haig any good? I've given my view on that subject. One thing I will say is that I'm glad to see they are pardoning those men who were shot at dawn, but that's just a personal opinion. There was a veterans' day held at No. 10 Downing Street recently and I spoke to the Prime Minister. I said the people who were shot at dawn as cowards, they were no cowards. I said you get a shell and the concussion robs you of all powers of movement for two or three minutes. Since then I've read in the papers that the sentences had been repealed because of a court ruling over one family's father. They should never have been shot. What about the relatives left behind? We say on Remembrance Day, 'They shall grow not old, age shall not weary them . . .' All right, remember the dead, but I also remember the people left behind, mourning.

For me, 11 November is just show business. Take the Armistice Day celebrations that night on television; it is nothing but a show of military force, that's all. I don't think there is any actual remembrance except for those who have lost someone they really cared for in either war. That day, the day I lost my pals, 22 September 1917 – that is my Remembrance Day, not Armistice Day. I'm always very, very quiet on that day and I don't want anybody talking to me, really.

From 1918 until he died in the 1970s, I kept in touch with the no. 1 on our Lewis gun, Bob Haynes. On the Somme, in the last months of the war, he had been injured in the shoulder and had come back to England. After the war he worked on industrial electrical engines, settling down in Henley-on-Thames before eventually moving to London. We never met again but we occasionally wrote. We both kept faith with our understanding that we would never write and tell the families of those who died in our team exactly what had happened. I mean, there was nothing left, nothing left to bury, and I don't think they would have wanted to know that.

When I received the Légion d'Honneur, in 1999, I received it not for my own good. I received it in memory of the three friends I lost, and that's why I wear it. My friends earned it more than me. We had a little ceremony here at the home, and Major Watson from the British Legion came and pinned on the decoration. It is a very prestigious honour, I know. I was also told by someone that when I wear it I am entitled to free public transport in France, and one or two other things besides, but I don't know if that's true or not.

I don't know what they intend to do in France, but there is an idea about giving a state funeral to the last veteran in Britain. The newspapers came and asked me what I thought, telling me it would be something like Churchill's, but then he was a great Prime Minister. I said that the honour must be given to a veteran who had seen action on the Western Front, not to anyone who happened to be in uniform when the war ended. Overall, the idea was all right, I suppose, wanting to honour the generation who fought, but I wasn't interested. I don't know what Henry Allingham thinks. He wants his body left to medical science, does he? Well, there you are then. It's not for me. I want to be buried in Monkton Combe alongside my family in the churchyard. I've been back there recently. As you walk along the path, you pass on the left the grave of William John and Elizabeth Patch, my parents, who were also married in the church. A little further along, there is George, my eldest brother, and his wife Lilian, and also my middle brother, William Thomas Patch, and Hilda Ann, his wife. So why would I want to be anywhere else?

I am very fortunate to have such good friends who take me out. I know the area so well that I show them little cuts through, and back lanes that most people do not know. I usually give a running commentary. History, geology and archaeology have been my fascination all my life, and I can give a guided tour to whoever happens to be taking me round. There are Roman remains everywhere, there are rock formations that are two million years old, and further away in the Mendip Hills there is an extinct volcano, Emborough Pool, and the other extinct volcano is Bath itself, hence the famous springs. Going back to my home village of Combe Down is lovely. Nick Fear has taken me back on a couple of occasions to the house I was born in, and I can look up to my childhood bedroom and to the little ornate Victorian grill my father placed on the concrete sill outside to stop his toddler son from falling out. Last time I was in Combe Down I saw that the war memorial is in the middle of a construction site. They are not building; rather, they are filling the empty quarries below with concrete. The council is pouring concrete – and tens of thousands of pounds – into the old workings to shore them up, and at the same time thirty-ton lorries pass over these quarries and shake the roof to pieces. Best of luck, is all I can say. According to one man I met, it would take a ten-ton lorry every ten minutes for eleven years to fill it up. There are sixty-two acres of quarries underneath Combe Down, and that's only one part of the entire system which stretches for thousands of yards in every direction.

I am fortunate to have kept my eyesight so I can enjoy all these things. Otherwise, you'll have to ask the doctor how I am physically. All I can say is that I feel all right. I've currently got an infection on my arm which I went to see the doctor about. Whatever I had, it was itching like mad, and in scratching my arm I've managed to infect the skin, so he tells me, but a bit of cream in the morning is clearing that up. Otherwise, I'm in pretty good shape.

When I was wounded, well, it must have been as I fell down, this ankle here, I don't know whether I sprained it or fractured it; either way it has never been right since. It has always been swollen, and if I used to walk on it too long, it was a bit painful. I also have a small scar where the shrapnel was taken out. When I told a doctor recently and showed him where it was, he told me that a quarter of an inch deeper and I would have bled to death. Even now I occasionally get pain from it. Sometimes if I stretch, I can feel there is something there, an ache, that's all, nothing regular about it. It comes and goes when it wants to.

And that's about it. The memories remain, of course. In the home right opposite my room upstairs there's a linen cupboard and the girls who are on night duty often go to store away folded sheets and, until recently, when I was lying in bed at night and the nurse switched the light on outside my room, if I was half asleep and half awake, I was back on that battlefield; there was the flash. Now the staff have blacked out that top window, so I don't have that problem any more.

I don't take any tablets, except one for iron; they say I'm short of iron. I see other residents here swallowing handfuls of tablets, and they are thirty years younger than I am. I have hearing aids in both ears, and I have reading glasses, but I don't use them now, not since my cataracts were done. I went into hospital for that small operation and I was quite tense about it as it was the first time I'd had an operation since 1917; otherwise I have never been in hospital, not as a patient, anyway. I have lived in the countryside all my life; fresh air, perhaps that's the secret. I've hardly ever seen a doctor either, no broken bones as a child.

I don't drink alcohol any more; I saw what it did to my boys. I smoked a pipe until I was sixty, Royal Seal tobacco, but I gave it up after I was taken ill at work and had to go home. My wife called a doctor; it wasn't my own doctor, he was a Czech. Anyway, he gave my wife a tablet, and said, 'Give him this and on no account wake him. Let him wake naturally.' She gave me that tablet Thursday night, and I woke Saturday morning as right as rain. What I had, I don't know.

What is the secret of a long life? No idea. I wish I could tell you. I'm happy and that is all that concerns me today. I don't have any ambitions now. I achieved what I wanted when I became a Member of the Royal Sanitary Institute, when I wanted to be either a building inspector or a sanitary engineer. I am glad to see my family and friends, and I'm glad that I have had the chance to be reunited with relatives with whom I had lost contact. Otherwise, it's a day at a time.

They will have written their pieces in the papers for when I finally go; the last trench fighter has to be newsworthy. I've seen obituaries of other veterans and there is now only Henry Allingham and myself in this country who served on the Western Front, and one British man in Australia, so you tell me. Can you imagine how it feels to be one of the last ones? Always hearing that another has just died, then another and another, waiting to hear who's gone and always wondering if you're next. Well, if they've written the obituary, all I can say is that I hope to live long enough that they will have to update it, and more than once! Then I can fade away. Isn't that what old soldiers are meant to do?

EPILOGUE

HARRY: HIS FAMILY AND FRIENDS

The author talked to Harry's friends, family and, in one case, a work colleague. Each had a different perspective on Harry's life and personality; together they represent over three hundred years of personal and affectionate contact. Their insights help to complete the picture of Harry and the influence he has had on a wide range of people throughout his long life.

May Cooper, daughter of George Patch, and Harry's niece, born 1918

I got a letter recently from Uncle Henry. I've not seen him since he was about 103, as my health is not good and it's difficult for me to get out. I'll be eighty-nine next birthday myself. He signed the letter 'Uncle Henry' which pleased me, because I notice everyone refers to him as Harry now on television, or Hal. Well, he was always Uncle Henry as far as I was concerned.

The Patch family was what I would call a proper nature family because they all loved and understood the natural environment. This stemmed directly from Granddad. From my earliest childhood, I can remember a big glass case in the sitting room of my grandparents' house and inside was every kind of stuffed bird you could think of, perhaps forty or fifty that he had collected over the years: jays, robins, blackbirds and goldfinches, and another case had a squirrel inside. As a child I used to look intently at all these creatures and learn about the wildlife.

Granddad was a wonderful gardener. He grew fruit, even grapes, and vegetables, and the two greenhouses were always full of flowers, geraniums and orchids. As well as the bees he kept and the animals he reared, I know that Granddad was keen on rabbiting. It was only after he died, when his sons were sorting out his affairs, that they found his gun. No one was sure whether it had ever been licensed, so they threw it down Granny's well.

This love of the countryside was transmitted to all three boys. Father and I walked for miles around Combe Down and Midford, and I don't suppose there's a walk around here that we didn't cover. He would talk to me about the flowers and the wildlife, show me the different leaves, and the mushrooms you could eat safely and those that were deadly. We'd walk down the valley to Tucking Mill and the canal. It wasn't as overgrown as it is today, and we'd pick sloes and make sloe gin.

Granny was a lovely person, too. After Granddad died, I used to pop round two or three times a day and would often find her sitting contentedly in her arbour near the back door, a shaded place surrounded by sweet-smelling jasmine. I always went in very gingerly so as not to frighten her, as she was stone deaf. She lived on her own until she died aged ninety-four, and managed to look after herself very well. Uncle Bill could get to Granny's house by a little path that ran directly to her back door, and he would often walk over and help put her to bed. Only when she was nearing the end of her life was her bed brought downstairs into the sitting room, and then everything else was moved out to make space, including that glass case with the birds in. I think it was eventually given to the Scouts.

We all used to visit Granny to make sure she was all right. She lived on a pension of just five shillings a week, so if she needed a new pinafore I would go to Bath and buy one, knocking a bit off the price as she would have been horrified had she known what they cost.

I'm making it sound like village life was idyllic, which it wasn't. It was wonderful in many senses, but just ordinary, too, nothing special. The world has changed so much even since the 1950s when all the family looked after one another, and it was all part and parcel of village life. When I was a child, there were thirty shops in Combe Down, including a butcher, baker, tailor, a dairy, but they've slowly disappeared and now there are just two, the Co-op and a newsagent. There were once five pubs; there are just a couple now and the Post Office closed two years ago. The only shop that has opened up since then is an estate agent's; it's a sign of the times.

The quarries and the work they gave were once the lifeblood of the village, but even when I was a child they had practically all gone as a viable industry. Now, those same quarries are threatening the village and the council is spending millions to shore them up. There's a quarry underneath my sitting room, and I get letters all the time from engineers wanting to inspect my house for subsidence. It's always been a threat. Granddad had a problem with some building work years before I was even born. He went to check under the house and found a large amount of cut stone down there, abandoned, so he used it in the building of nos 4 and 5 Gladstone Place; he clearly wasn't overly concerned about the quarries back then and he was a master mason.

His sons followed him into the building business, all with different skills. My father was a wonderful joiner. Like Uncle Henry, he served an apprenticeship at J. Long and Sons and he made some beautiful furniture. I have a wonderful fireguard here with me now, and he also made me a doll's house with all the individual pieces, chairs and tables, in minute detail. I often thought that perhaps the three boys could have gone into partnership together, but they never did.

Margaret Ffoulkes, George Atkins' daughter and Harry's god-daughter

Harry, or Henry, as I know him, has always called me 'my little girl' from as far back as I can remember, and he refers to me in the same way today, and I'll be eighty-five later this year. Last year, on Henry's 108th birthday, he had a party at a restaurant and he gave his 'little girl' a bowl of flowers, roses and carnations. I cried for several minutes and he cried too, I don't know why, but it meant such a lot. I placed the flowers in the memorial window in our local church in North Wales, and I was delighted to see that they lasted for several weeks.

Uncle Henry was lifelong friends with my father, George Atkins, right from school days, and was best man at my parents' wedding in 1921, and so a natural choice as my godfather. He held me, so he has told me, when I was just half an hour old, and we have remained close ever since. He is a very, very loyal and honest friend and a counsellor to me even now, and very witty as well. To me he was always Uncle Henry, and his wife, Aunt Ada, indeed our families were so close that it wasn't until I was about twelve that I discovered they weren't blood-related at all.

I was a very naughty child, pulling the heads off four rows of leeks in a neighbour's garden, or letting mother's canary fly free from the cage; I had a thing about cages and so did the canary, because it never came back. I would get a good wallop, of course, and Mother would tell me, 'Your sister wouldn't do it.' My sister was terribly spoilt, and I frequently fought with her and when things got too much I would say that I was going to run away, but I would go no further than down the lane to Uncle Henry's house. Aunt Ada was always sympathetic. 'Oh, she's a little cat,' she would always say of my sister, in her strong Birmingham accent. Of course, my parents always knew where I was going and in due course Dad would come and get me.

Each year we went to Uncle Henry's for Boxing Day, and in the summer we would all holiday together at Boleaze's Cove, near Weymouth. At the end of his garden, Henry had built himself a little caravan which he hitched on to the back of his Austin Seven, with Terry, the white-and-brown spotted wire-haired terrier, in the back. We thought Henry was very posh, camping in a caravan. My father followed in a Morgan. My sister and I were sent by trailer as our seats in the car were used to carry the large ex-army bell tent and its gear that my family slept in. It was a blissful childhood, walking and cycling for miles, every year, all of us together. In fact, when war broke out in September 1939, that was the first year that the Patch family was not with us. During the war, my father was an air-raid warden manning the telephone in the church hall, while Uncle Henry was in the fire service with its head-quarters at the vicarage stables.

My father spoke very little about the First War unless asked. He joined the Somerset Yeomanry but transferred to the Royal Army Medical Corps because he wanted to be a non-combatant. I don't think Henry wanted to fight either, but he went in any case. Henry was a quiet man, in fact I never saw him get annoyed – I don't know if he could get angry, because he would always want to reason – but I would see him often having very long and meaningful conversations with my father. What about, I don't know, but I never heard Henry speak about the war either, and I somehow doubt they ever spoke about it. We were to forget about the war, and although I remember seeing Dad wearing his medals on Armistice Day, the day of remembrance itself was something for the men; children were not involved that I can recall.

Derek Andrews, apprentice plumber under Harry Patch

School broke up at the end of July, and two weeks later, on 14 August 1943, my fourteenth birthday, I started work for E.R. Carter's, then the biggest plumbing and heating firm around. When I started, the boss had only three or four men actually at work, because all the rest had been called up in the forces. There wasn't too much heating to do, more plumbing jobs, because there weren't new buildings or installations going up because of the war. While the scope of jobs was reduced, there was, nevertheless, so much demand that you were forever running from one job to another; because there weren't enough plumbers around for you to take your time, you had to rush into everything.

I was what was known as a boy mate. The boss gave evening classes to the young lads to show them the As and Bs of the business, but he never signed on apprentices, not officially, because that way he could get rid of you if you were no good. That's how he looked at it. As a consequence, my wages were very little indeed, not much more than one shilling and two pence a day, so I was on an apprentice's wages without ever being called an apprentice.

There were always half a dozen of us boy mates to go with one of the experienced heating engineers or plumbers. As the war ended, more plumbers became available to be taken on and I was sent with Harry Patch who had recently joined the firm. My job was to watch what Harry was doing, and eventually I would go and practise it myself. It wasn't his job actually to show you as such, because you could see what he was doing. Nevertheless, you had to have confidence to do plumbing, especially when you are dealing with water in private houses! So you've got to be really confident in what you are doing before you start.

Harry never had any transport, not that I can remember. He always came in on the bus from Compton Dundon, where he lived, and whenever possible he preferred to walk everywhere, and was a quiet man. We had a pick-up driver. He drove the van and would take all the materials to the next job, and would take you too if he had room. Otherwise, I can remember carrying Harry's tool bag all round Yeovil; you couldn't get any lower than that, walking round Yeovil with a tool bag.

A plumber's tool bag was pretty weighty back then. There were wrenches for the steel pipes: you could get them in different sizes, 8-inch, 10-inch, 12-inch, 14-inch, right up to 24-inch, and you carried three or four of these as well as pliers, hammers and wood chisels, and a blowlamp for the lead joints, because it was all lead or steel then, no copper piping; even the waste pipes underneath sinks were lead, not plastic like today. Yeovil is quite a big town and our business place was right down one end, in Henford. If you had to climb an incline like Mudford Road, you had half a mile uphill carrying this bag, and by the time you got halfway up, you were looking to Harry to take the bag out of your hands.

The boss's mate was the Somerset County Engineer, a chap he went to college with, so we had all the educational buildings in this area to maintain because his mate gave them to him. I would be assigned to the plumbers according to what jobs were available on the day. I could be with Harry for weeks, until such time as someone else needed two mates on another job. Harry would be given a job card, and we would tackle one job after the other, I suppose six or seven in a day. If Harry was working underneath a sink, he would want this tool and that, and I would hand him the tools, and similarly if he was up a ladder or a pair of steps; wherever the plumber went, you went. That was the life back then of a boy mate.

If you see Harry, remember me to him and tell him my arm still bloody aches from carrying his tool bag.

David Isaacs, son of Betty Isaacs, Harry's neighbour
Harry was great friends with both Mum and Dad, and, when Dad died, Harry more or less took over the care of

Mum. He'd known them both for many years, through the church and clubs, and I know that the day Dad died, Harry brought Mum up to see him.

They were all neighbours in a sheltered housing scheme in Wells. Harry was ninety-three at the time of Dad's death, and he took it upon himself to mow not only his own lawn, front and back, but Mum's too. In fact, as Mum became less and less able, he did everything for her, washing, ironing, shopping. He looked after Mum for many years and he was devastated when she died in 2001. His second wife had died many years before. She had been bed-ridden with cancer for a long time and Harry looked after her with total devotion. I think that is Harry through and through. He needs someone to look after, someone he can concentrate on, and this is when the gentleman in him comes out best. I was so pleased when Doris arrived at the home later that year, after Mum died. I think that saved him.

There is a natural fighter in Harry. His experiences in the war made him want to fight for justice, and I think they changed his attitude to life. But his instinct to fight is not something entirely derived from the war; I think it comes from his nature when, as a child, he learnt to stand on his own two feet.

When I first knew Harry, in the early 1980s, he was the champion of local causes. He hates injustice and because of that he never hesitated to write letters to the council or the local newspaper, usually firing on all cylinders when he did so. On the ring road, the council proposed to put in traffic lights which Harry felt would only hamper and not relieve congestion, causing more problems for local people. Harry and Mum did their shopping down the high street and frequently struggled to get across the road. So he fought the proposal. In the end, he lost. Nevertheless, a pedestrian crossing was put in. There was another time when permission was sought by local people to erect a communal hut on some open ground. The council refused the proposal and Harry took up the cause but lost that, too. You'll have to ask him which campaigns he won! He was a one-man band, and that helped him remain active.

One day, Harry and Mum went on an outing. As they came through the front door, Mum tripped and fell, damaging her hip very badly. Harry redoubled his efforts to look after her, but he was probably ninety-eight by this time and I was frequently called to go up and help. Then one day he said, 'David, I want you to make arrangements for us to go into the residential home, we've decided that it's time.' As it happened, a double room was available and Harry and Betty moved in. Both homes had to be cleared quickly. I called in a house-clearing company and they came round and took all the furniture from both houses. It was heartbreaking; a lifetime's possessions gone. The men were breaking the furniture up as it was being taken from the house. They offered £100 for the lot, but Harry wanted to get rid of everything; as he said, he couldn't use it any more; but I don't know what he thought of the money, I really don't.

June Beeching, niece of Harry's first wife, Ada, born June 1933

My mother, Winifred, was the youngest of six children, one of whom was Ada, my aunt, who married Harry in 1919. When I was a child we often went to visit my aunt, but over time, as Ada died and then my mother died, we somehow

217

lost touch with Uncle Hal, as we called him. I don't quite know how it happened. I suppose people move house; I know we moved to Devon, and after a while you just assume that all that generation has gone.

When the BBC1 programme *The Last Tommy* came on, I'd actually seen the name Harry Patch on the screen, but as he had always been Uncle Hal to us the penny did not drop that it could actually be him. I was in the living room with my back to the television, as I had turned to get something out of the bureau. Suddenly, I heard his distinctive voice and it made me feel quite peculiar; it was quite a shock, and I was very still for a moment. I remember thinking, 'Oh my goodness, it's Uncle Hal, but then it can't be.' Hal had quite a few relations in Somerset and I wondered if it could be one of them. So I picked up the phone and rang my daughter, and Daniel, my grandson, answered. I said, 'Get your mother to put the TV on to BBC1 straightaway and I'll ring a bit later.' I didn't say anything else because I didn't want her view to be coloured by anything I said. I went back and watched again, and the more I watched, the more I thought, it is him, it is, but at the same time I thought it can't be, because of his age. We thought he had died a long time ago. My daughter rang back. 'Do you think Uncle Hal is still alive?' I asked. She said, 'Surely not', and my husband doubted it was Hal, too, but I was convinced it was him. It wasn't what he looked like, it was his voice that convinced me; that hadn't changed at all since we'd last met in the late 1970s. In the *Western Morning News* there was an article about Hal. Other newspapers ran stories and we took a look at everything. One newspaper said Hal had lost touch with all his relatives and that his two boys had died. I had no idea of any of this; it was very sad. Another went on to mention his friend Nick Fear. I went to the local library and explained the situation and they gave me two telephone numbers, neither of which was correct, and after that the trail went cold for a while. Then, when it was Uncle Hal's birthday, he appeared again and I went back to the library, explained the situation once more and asked if there was a local British Legion which could help. They gave me the number of the Bridgwater branch, and one of the members, as it turned out, visited Harry. I explained I wanted to send a birthday card and he promised to see that he got it. I wrote and put one or two things in about the past, just to prove it was me. I mentioned the thatched cottage near Somerton where we'd all been as a family, and where I used to cook up baby potatoes in a large copper for Uncle Hal's pigs. I thought, 'It will tell him that I am who I say I am.' Shortly afterwards, I got a letter which said how pleased he was to hear from me.

A visit was arranged, and we went to his residential home. He was sitting on a sofa and I just walked straight up to him and said, 'Hello, Uncle Hal, you look very well . . .' And we went from there. It was marvellous to see him looking so fit and well. Nick brought Hal down to see us, and we've been each month since then and hope to go again before Christmas. He seems to have perked up even more since we got in touch; I don't know, perhaps it's my imagination, but it feels like that.

Jeremy Banning, close friend

Harry was always adamant that he wouldn't meet a German veteran, so it was a surprise when he changed his mind. He doesn't make an instant decision, he needs space to think.

So he mulled over the idea and by the time he agreed to meet Charles Kuentz, he wasn't nervous at the prospect, he was looking forward to it. By 2004, he'd been back to Belgium twice, and he knew that the whole trip would be tailor-made to be as easy as possible for him.

The meeting was filmed for a BBC1 documentary, *The Last Tommy*, and the production company provided three of us with a people carrier as it was easy for Harry to get in and out. We kept an eye on him through the rear-view mirror, and when he fell asleep we were glad that he was at ease with his surroundings and with us.

When he's out of context, Harry doesn't necessarily stand out and isn't recognized, but when he's at the Menin Gate memorial in Ypres, he's mobbed, people standing six deep wanting to shake his hand and say how proud they are to meet him; one or two want to tell him about their own relatives who fought. It can get overwhelming, although Harry never seems to find it too much. On several occasions, I've been handed money by people, total strangers, who say, 'Make sure Harry has a drink on me.' But he doesn't drink, so he gives it to the British Legion. I always joke with him, that he's the most photographed man in Belgium, and he just smiles and says, 'yeah', as only he can.

The first time I looked after Harry was in 2002 when he went back to Pilckem Ridge. That day he was too distressed to leave the bus and lay a wreath. When I helped him to bed, he said, 'I was a bit wobbly today.' So we sat on the edge of the bed and talked about it for an hour, one to one, away from the hotel bar and the general hullabaloo downstairs. It's the time veterans are most likely to give you their thoughts, and that talk with Harry is a very precious memory.

In September 2004, we reached Belgium and stayed overnight in a small farmhouse in Elverdinghe. Of course Harry, being a countryman, was in his element; given a pregnant cat or a duck with one leg, he's just wonderful. I have a mental image of Harry surrounded by cats, and because his fingers are not as flexible as they once were, the cats pushed against his hand instead of being patted. One or two would get quite playful and Harry would hold up his index finger as if to say, 'Now, that's enough.'

If Harry has a big day ahead of him, such as meeting Charles Kuentz, he'll choose to go to bed at 7 p.m. He's very much in tune with his body and with himself. He knows what pills he needs to take and that he likes to eat little but often. He is also used to a routine, so it's good to keep to that as far as possible.

The following morning, Harry had a big breakfast and was raring to go. The film crew came to see what his thoughts were at meeting a German veteran, but Harry just said, 'I'm all right, looking forward to it.' I think they were hoping he would say much more, but that isn't his way. After the event, he'll give a measured response. I think the meeting with Charles Kuentz helped Harry enormously. It wasn't a momentous occasion, just two very old men meeting, shaking hands and smiling broadly. Charles was very deaf and everything had to be written down and then translated. Perhaps the symbolism of the meeting was more important than what they actually said. At one point Harry was asked if he would still have met Charles Kuentz if Charles had been the one who fired the shell that killed his friends, and without hesitation he said 'Yes.'

Later that day, we drove to Tyne Cot, the largest British cemetery on the Western Front. Harry was much more depressed there, sitting with his hands together under his chin, as if in silent prayer. As he looked around, he could see nearly 12,000 graves, all of them of men who will always remain his peers. Behind, there are panels with the names of another 35,000 men, who simply disappeared in battle. Harry sat there, hunched over, looking almost haunted, deep in thought. It was clear to see in his eyes that he was back in time. It's hard. You don't want to break into his thoughts but you have responsibilities as a carer and you can't leave him there for too long in the cold. It took quite a while for him to perk up.

There are three places at Ypres that Harry is always going to struggle with: Tyne Cot, the Menin Gate and Pilckem Ridge. We always tell Harry, 'We're going to Pilckem Ridge now, OK?' It's only fair to give him warning. To me, it feels as if it is something he has to do. I don't think he gains comfort or pleasure by being there, by seeing that it has been rebuilt or that kids are playing nearby; rather it is simply that he feels he must go. In 2004 there was a grey, leaden sky, and just as he laid the wreath and sat there in contemplation, a shaft of sunlight came out from behind the clouds, and touched Harry's head and the wreath.

Pauline Leyton, manager at Harry's residential home
Harry the soldier, the war veteran, was someone everybody wanted to talk to, but only about the war. They wanted to hear what his experiences had been, and I thought there was nobody who was really just interested in Harry as the whole person. There's an awful lot of Harry as the husband and the father, and as a resident in an elderly persons' home, so I organized with Age Concern that someone would come

down, what they call a befriender, and talk to Harry, to support him.

I often sit down with Harry and we talk and put the world to rights. Equally, if he has a problem, he always comes to the top, to the manager. A few years ago, he said that he was having bad dreams, and that it was all coming back to the fore, memories which he had suppressed or put to the back of his mind. I think it was after his 100th birthday, when people began to come and talk to him, and there was all the interest in the press and the media.

One of the most moving things for me was when he paid his first visit to the Wills Memorial Building in Bristol, the building he had helped construct in the 1920s, and for the first time I really had a realization of what he'd gone through, because he was talking to the television crew, and I saw that so much of his war was inside him, and had never come to the top. It upset me to hear it.

I knew Harry as the man who had come in with his friend Betty back in October 1996. He had made a pact with her husband, before he died, that he would look after Betty. They came in for a trial, for day care, and that didn't quite work, as they were coming in and going home, and it was a lot for them. So we invited them to come in and live here for a while, and that was when I first met him, but of course I had no idea of what he had been through.

I took him twice to launch the Somerset Poppy Appeal at Weston-super-Mare. They always have a different way of launching the appeal and on one visit they had a great big cannon that shot, or rather exploded, the poppies out of the muzzle. Harry had to press the button and of course everybody jumped in shock and Harry didn't stir a muscle. He just said, 'You haven't heard the guns like I have.'

One of the best feelings in life is when you actually achieve something, and in Harry's case it was receiving his honorary degree from Bristol University; at that moment he was right at the top of the pinnacle. When it was offered to him, seeing him there, I'll never forget that as long as I live, his eyes sparkling, looking down on the assembled congregation. The recognition meant so much to him.

Another example was meeting the German soldier, Charles Kuentz. We applied for a passport for Harry, and when it arrived he not only got the passport but an enclosed note from someone at the office saying, 'Dear Harry, I hope you have a wonderful time.' It was funny, no one queried the application to check we'd got his birth date right. It was lovely. I think the trip abroad helped him come to terms with his past.

Nick Fear, close friend

Harry is such a capable and caring man that he likes to answer as many of his letters as he can. In the week after *The Last Tommy* was shown in 2005, he had something like 180 letters from the public. A lot of them were fan mail of the sort that says 'We loved you on the programme, thank you for what you did for us in World War I', but quite a few were asking for answers that Harry couldn't possibly know. Some people were asking, 'My grandfather was in the Great War, did you know him?' Some were in Harry's regiment, the DCLI, but in another battalion; sometimes they were in a completely different regiment, fighting in a different battle on a different continent! But fair enough; some people didn't realize that Harry didn't fight on Gallipoli, or that he didn't know East Africa.

There is a side to Harry that likes the attention, but it can get too much. Harry was concerned to answer his letters and he just needed a bit of help. I now visit him every couple of weeks and come away with mail that needs answering. He had his double cataract operation on the NHS two years ago, and his eyesight is remarkable. I know that we moan about the NHS, but I am rather proud of that investment in a gentleman of advanced years because it has improved his quality of life tenfold.

Nevertheless, he gets asked the strangest things, such as, 'What cigarettes did you smoke in the trenches?' Recently a gentleman sent a cassette tape and wondered if we could ask Harry about World War I. A few years ago he was happy to talk about it, but now he's fed up, because there was a lot more to his life than just the Great War. The man asked if we could interview Harry on his behalf because he thought it might be therapeutic. It was very kind, but that was the last thing he wanted. We sent the tape back and said we were very sorry but we couldn't help him. Harry has had a request recently from abroad asking for his autograph, or, more accurately, asking for fifteen copies of his autograph, on photographs or book-plates; the writer even included a special pen that signs pictures, but Harry has a problem with arthritis in his writing hand and it pains him to write, so he will nowadays dictate the letter to me and then I'll send it off. Requests for autographs have come so often in the last two years that he's saying no, because he just can't do any more. Inevitably, we have had one or two strange letters, not in a harmful way, but ones where you couldn't quite understand what the writer is talking about. The upside to all the letters is that Harry cuts off the stamps for the Royal National Lifeboat Institution, and of course foreign stamps are the most useful.

ACKNOWLEDGEMENTS

I would like to thank everyone at Bloomsbury, particularly Bill Swainson, the senior commissioning editor, for his belief in the project and his unstinting encouragement, and Emily Sweet for her expert editorial advice and support. I am also grateful to Nick Humphrey, Colin Midson, David Mann, Jessica Yarrow, Lisa Fiske and Polly Napper, all of whom have worked hard to produce and market this book.

I would also like to thank Jason Williams for the rear cover photograph, as well as my good friends Jeremy Banning, Peter Barton and Taff Gillingham for their help and expert knowledge on the Great War.

I would particularly like to thank my agent, Jane Turnbull, for all her enthusiasm and constant support throughout this project.

Thank you, too, to the large circle of friends of Harry Patch, many lifelong, including his niece May Patch, the daughter of Harry's eldest brother George; his god-daughter, Margaret Ffoulkes, who has 'known' Harry since she was half-an-hour old; David Isaacs, the son of Harry's beloved neighbour Betty Isaacs; Nick Fear and Lindsay Vasey, his close friends; Jim and Lesley Ross, his frequent visitors; and June and Richard Beeching, who, owing to Harry's numerous television appearances, have been reunited with a relative they both assumed had died a long time ago.

I am grateful to Pauline Leyton, the senior manager of Harry's residential home in Somerset. She has been unfailingly considerate and, with her excellent staff, has been enormously helpful in facilitating my visits and supplying me with numerous cups of coffee and tea.

A big thank you is due to the late Doris Whitaker, Harry's feisty confidant and soulmate, who has been kind enough to let me interview Harry on innumerable occasions. She would have had no need to read this book, as she must have heard every story five times over.

As always, I must thank my wife, Anna, for all her unstinting enthusiasm and her understanding as I disappeared to my study to write. A special thank you to my indomitable mother, Joan van Emden, whose superb knowledge of the English language has helped get rid of errors, daft and otherwise, which crept in.

Lastly, I am grateful to Harry himself. He has been a willing participant in this project from the first day, but could not have expected the regular and extended grilling he underwent as we revisited his 108-year life in detail. 'It's a long time ago,' he would sometimes say, when tiredness stopped him from remembering an event that had taken place perhaps one hundred years earlier. This did not stop him thinking about it, and on my next visit he would often have the answer. Thank you, Harry. It has been a great pleasure to help write your story, or rather, your story so far.

PICTURE CREDITS

I would like to thank the *Bath Chronicle* for their kind permission to use three images taken during the Bath Blitz of 1942, as well as the Imperial War Museum for permission to use the following images: Q2751, C.O.2253, Q5865, Q17654, Q2708, Q2706 and Q8460. Thank you to the Hauptstaatsarchiv, Stuttgart, for permission to use the German aerial image of the Steenbeek taken on 22 July 1917, and to Bristol University for permission to reproduce the image of the topping-out parade at the Wills Memorial Building in 1925. I am grateful to The National Archives for permission to reproduce the aerial image of the battle-field close to Langemarck, August 1917; the image from the 1901 Census return; and a page from the Medal Roll for the Duke of Cornwall's Light Infantry. I should also like to thank Jason Williams for his pictures of Harry Patch and Doris Whitaker, and Harry holding his Légion d'Honneur. All other images are courtesy of friends and close relatives of the Patch family or from the author's personal collection.

INDEX

A NOTE ON THE AUTHOR

Harry Patch served as a private in the Duke of
Cornwall's Light Infantry at the Battle of
Passchendaele in 1917. He was married in 1919
and had two sons. Between the wars he worked
as a plumber and on building sites in the Bristol
area, and when the Second World War broke out
he served as a firefighter throughout the Bath Blitz
and later alongside American troops in the run-up
to D-Day. In 2002 he attended the seventy-fifth
anniversary of the inauguration of the Menin Gate
at Ypres, and in 2005 he took part in the BBC TV
documentary *The Last Tommy* and was awarded
an honorary degree by the University of Bristol.
He lives in Somerset.

Richard van Emden has interviewed over 270 veterans
of the Great War and has written widely on the
1914–18 conflict. His previous books include *Britain's
Last Tommies*, *Boy Soldiers of the Great War*, *All Quiet
on the Home Front*, *Prisoners of the Kaiser* and the
top five best-selling *The Trench*. He has visited the
Somme and Ypres every year since 1985 and has
an expert knowledge of the First World War
battlefields. He lives in London.

B L O O M S B U R Y

The Soldier's War

The Soldier's War by Richard van Emden will be published by
Bloomsbury in November 2008

*A personal history of The Great War told using never-seen-before
interviews, letters and photographs.*

November 2008 sees the 90th anniversary of the end of the Great War
that still haunts and fascinates in equal measure. Richard van Emden's
new book tells that story as never before through the voices of more
than 270 veterans and reveals the true stories of a lost generation.

The Soldier's War traces the war chronologically, taking stories from
each year of the fighting and following the British Tommy through
devastating battles and trench warfare to the armistice in 1918. The
book also reflects on other lesser-known and more personal aspects of
the war, such as the work of stretcher-bearers, army chaplains, and
burial parties. Central to *The Soldier's War* are the original and as-yet-
unseen photographs that punctuate the narrative. Many soldiers
carried lightweight VPK cameras (Vest Pocket Kodaks) and used them
(illegally) to photograph the war as it unfolded. Between seventy-five
and a hundred remarkable images will for the first time show trench-
warfare as it really happened.

ISBN: 978 07475 9780 3 / Hardback / £20.00

Order your copy:

Order by phone: 01256 302 699

By email: direct@macmillan.co.uk

Delivery is usually 3–5 working days.
Postage and packaging will be charged.

Online: www.bloomsbury.com/bookshop

Free postage and packaging for orders over £15.

Prices and availability subject to change without notice.

Visit Bloomsbury.com for more about Richard van Emden

Three Cheers for Wales

Wendy White

Illustrated by
Helen Flook

Pont

For

Mam and Dad,

Susan and Stephen

First published in 2015 by Pont Books, an imprint of
Gomer Press, Llandysul, Ceredigion, SA44 4JL
www.gomer.co.uk

ISBN 978 1 84851 917 6

A CIP record for this title is available from the British Library.

This book is published with the financial support of the Welsh Books Council.

Printed and bound in Wales at Gomer Press, Llandysul, Ceredigion

A Trip Back in Time

Emyr Rhys waved out of the bus window at Da-cu.

'Have fun on your trip,' Da-cu called from the school gate. 'Enjoy being a Victorian schoolboy!'

'I will,' Emyr Rhys called back.

Betsi Wyn sat down next to Emyr Rhys. She waved to Carys and Anwen sitting in the seat behind them. They were all very excited. They loved going on school trips.

'I've got some chewy sweets in my bag,' Betsi Wyn told Emyr Rhys, as she waved goodbye to Mam-gu. 'We can share them on the way.'

'And I've got some crisps,' Emyr Rhys said. 'We can share those too.'

Mr Evans, the head teacher, climbed onto the bus and stopped at the top of the steps. He looked very worried. Everyone had been chatting excitedly, but they were soon quiet when they saw his serious face.

'I'm sorry to say that we can't go on the trip after all,' Mr Evans said. 'Mrs Philpot and Mr Thomas have both gone down with 'flu. They were supposed to be our helpers today.' He shook his head. 'We can't have a trip without helpers,' he said. 'I'm afraid we'll have to cancel it.' And he got off the bus.

Everyone was disappointed. Betsi Wyn and Emyr Rhys picked up their backpacks sadly.

'I was really looking forward to going to a Victorian school,' Emyr Rhys said.

'So was I,' said Betsi Wyn. 'I've been looking forward to it for ages.'

There was a knock on the window.

'What's happening?' Da-cu asked through the glass.

'Mr Evans says we can't go after all,' Emyr Rhys told him. 'We haven't got enough helpers.'

Da-cu thought for a minute. 'I can do something about that,' he said, and he rushed off.

When Mr Evans got back on the bus he was smiling. 'Sit down again everyone, please,' he said. 'I've got good news. We have two new helpers.'

With that, Da-cu climbed onto the bus and everyone cheered.

Emyr Rhys waved to him.

Then Mam-gu got onto the bus too, and everyone cheered again.

Betsi Wyn waved to her.

Da-cu and Mam-gu sat down near the front of the bus with Mr Evans and Miss Khan, and the driver started the engine.

'*Bant â ni!*' Mr Evans called. 'Off we go!'

Betsi Wyn and Emyr Rhys chewed their chewy sweets and crunched and munched their crisps all the way to the Victorian school. At last the bus stopped outside a big, old building.

'First of all,' Miss Khan said, 'we need to put on our Victorian clothes.' And she led the children off the bus to a room that was full of white shirts and long skirts.

It was fun finding the right outfits. Emyr Rhys put on a brown waistcoat over a shirt that buttoned right up to his chin.

'You look a bit squashed in that shirt,' Betsi Wyn told him.

'It's alright,' Emyr Rhys said, pulling at the collar. 'But I'm glad I don't have to wear it every day.'

Betsi Wyn pulled on a brown dress over her T-shirt and trousers. The dress was very long.

It dragged on the floor. It was a bit scratchy too.

'And I'm glad I don't have to wear this every day,' she said.

Gwion came running up. He had a flat cap on his head.

'Here you are,' he said to Emyr Rhys, and he held out a cap. 'And there are white caps for the girls,' Gwion told Betsi Wyn.

'Thanks, Gwion,' she said.

'*Croeso*,' said Gwion.

'You mean "you're welcome",' said Betsi Wyn. 'Remember what Miss Khan told us? We're not allowed to speak Welsh at the Victorian school.'

'Not allowed to speak Welsh?' Gwion said. 'That's terrible!'

'Yes,' said Betsi Wyn. 'But while we're here we have to speak in English all the time or we'll have to wear the Welsh Not.'

'The Welsh Not?' said Gwion. 'What's that?'

'Oh, Gwion!' Emyr Rhys said. 'Didn't you listen to what Miss Khan said yesterday?'

With that Miss Khan came into the room. She was wearing a long black dress with a tight white collar.

'When everyone's ready,' Miss Khan said, 'line up at the door.'

They followed Miss Khan across the yard to the school house.

Mr Evans, the head teacher, was waiting for them in the school doorway. He was wearing a long black coat and a strange flat hat. It was like a black square sitting on his head.

'Now,' he said, in a strict voice, 'we will go into the classroom silently.' He looked at the children with a serious face. 'Not one word.'

'What's wrong with Mr Evans?' Gwion asked Emyr Rhys. 'He looks so cross.'

Emyr Rhys had been listening to Miss Khan in class the day before. He knew that Victorian teachers were very strict. And he knew that

Mr Evans was pretending to be a Victorian teacher. So Emyr Rhys didn't answer Gwion.

'Not one word!' said Mr Evans again, very loudly. And even Gwion was silent.

The Victorian classroom seemed very odd. It had rows of wooden desks with wooden seats joined on to them. There was a big blackboard on a stand next to the teacher's desk.

Betsi Wyn and Emyr Rhys were pleased to see Mam-gu and Da-cu in the classroom. Mam-gu wore a long skirt and a shawl, and Da-cu had a waistcoat and a flat cap like Emyr Rhys. They were putting a small square of slate onto each desk. Mam-gu smiled at Betsi Wyn, and Da-cu gave Emyr Rhys a wink.

When all the children had found a desk and they were sitting down quietly, Mr Evans picked up a long stick.

'What's that?' Gwion whispered.

'It's a cane,' Emyr Rhys whispered back.

Mr Evans tapped the blackboard with the

11

cane. 'Times tables first,' he said. He pointed to the two-times-table written on the blackboard, 'Repeat after me . . .'

They recited lots of times tables, then Mr Evans gave the class sums.

'Write your answers on your slate,' Mr Evans said, and Mam-gu and Da-cu began handing out pieces of chalk for the children to write with.

'Thank you,' Betsi Wyn said, as Da-cu handed her some chalk.

'*Croeso*,' said Da-cu.

Mr Evans banged his desk with the cane and everyone jumped.

'Did I just hear a Welsh word?' he asked. He looked cross.

Da-cu slowly put up his hand. 'It was me, Sir,' he said.

Mr Evans took something off a hook on the wall. It was a loop of string with a rectangle of wood on it. On the wood were written the letters W and N.

'Oh,' gasped Betsi Wyn, 'the Welsh Not!'

Mr Evans put the strange necklace around Da-cu's neck.

'No Welsh in my classroom,' said Mr Evans. He sounded very cross, but Emyr Rhys saw Mr Evans wink at Da-cu. He saw Da-cu wink back too.

'Now then, more sums,' Mr Evans said, and he gave them some very hard numbers to add up.

They all tried their best to work out the sums. They wrote their answers on the squares of slate.

Mr Evans walked around the classroom and checked what they'd written. He stopped at Gwion's desk.

'Good work, Gwion,' he said.

'*Diolch*,' said Gwion, and he smiled up at Mr Evans.

'No Welsh in my classroom,' said Mr Evans. And he took the Welsh Not from Da-cu's neck and put it around Gwion's.

'It's not fair,' Gwion muttered to Emyr Rhys, as Mr Evans went back to his blackboard. He didn't like having the piece of wood hanging around his neck. 'I was only saying "thank you". I don't like Mr Evans any more.'

'He's acting,' Emyr Rhys said.

'Handwriting next,' said Mr Evans in a loud voice. 'Wipe your slates.'

And Mam-gu began giving out pieces of cloth to everyone, so they could clean their slates.

As she got near Betsi Wyn's desk, Mam-gu dropped a cloth on the floor. Betsi Wyn picked it up.

'Thank you, *cariad*,' Mam-gu said.

'Oh, Mam-gu,' Betsi Wyn whispered. 'You used a Welsh word.'

Gwion took off the Welsh Not. He handed it to Mam-gu.

'*Diolch*, Gwion,' said Mam-gu, and everyone gasped. 'Well, if I've got to wear this thing,'

Mam-gu said, 'I might as well make it worth my while. *Diolch. Diolch. Diolch.*'

And she took the Not from Gwion and put it around her own neck.

Betsi Wyn saw Mr Evans give Mam-gu a little smile.

They did a lot of curly handwriting on their slates. It was hard to make the letters look like the ones Mr Evans had written on the blackboard. Now that everyone knew Mr Evans was just pretending to be very stern, they began to enjoy their day at Victorian school. He banged his cane against the blackboard lots and lots, and the Welsh Not was passed around every time someone spoke Welsh. By the end of the afternoon, it was back around Da-cu's neck. Miss Khan popped her head into the classroom.

'The bus is here,' she said.

Mr Evans took off his black coat and his funny square hat. He put them on the desk.

'We're at the end of our Victorian school day,' he said. 'And I'm glad to say that now I'm your friendly head teacher again.'

Everyone cheered. They all thought Mr Evans was the best head teacher in Wales.

He called Da-cu to the front of the class and took the Not from around Da-cu's neck.

'You are the last person to be wearing the Welsh Not at the end of today's lessons,' Mr Evans said. 'You should be punished. That's what happened in Victorian times.'

Emyr Rhys looked a bit worried. Was Mr Evans going to punish Da-cu?

The head teacher looked around at everyone. Then he smiled. 'Thankfully, we aren't living back in Victorian times,' he said, 'so there will be no punishment. Now, what do we think of the Welsh Not?'

'Horrible!' everyone shouted.

'It's not fair,' said Gwion.

'You're right, Gwion,' Mr Evans said. 'It wasn't fair. And that's why we're leaving it here, in Victorian times.' And he hung it back on its nail.

Everyone cheered.

'Thank you for being a very good class,' Mr Evans said. '*Diolch. Diolch yn fawr.*'

'*Croeso*,' everyone shouted. And then they laughed and cheered again.

'And *diolch yn fawr* to Mam-gu and Da-cu, too,' Mr Evans said, before they all went off to get changed. 'We wouldn't have had this trip without you. *Un, dau, tri*! Hip, hip hooray!'

Betsi Wyn
and the Monster

'Well, that's all the flowers planted,' Mam-gu said, as she stood up and dusted off her knees. She smiled at the sunshine. 'What a lovely day.'

'Quick, Mam-gu, quick!' called Betsi Wyn. 'The frogs are jumping out of the pond!'

Mam-gu rushed across the lawn to where Betsi Wyn was trying to catch the tiny frogs and put them back into the water. They kept slipping through her fingers.

'Oh no!' said Betsi Wyn. 'They're all escaping!'

'Don't worry,' said Mam-gu. 'They'll have a little hop around the garden, but they'll go back to the pond later. Shall we have a cup of tea and a think about what you can wear to the fancy dress party on Saturday?'

Mam-gu sipped her tea and Betsi Wyn licked a lollipop as they sat on the garden chairs.

'What would you like to wear to Anwen's party?' Mam-gu asked.

'I'm not sure yet,' said Betsi Wyn.

A butterfly fluttered by. It flitted around the flowers that Mam-gu had just planted.

'Oh what a lovely *pili-pala*,' Mam-gu said. 'Shall we make a butterfly costume for you to wear to Anwen's party? That would be pretty, wouldn't it?'

The butterfly was beautiful, but Betsi Wyn shook her head. 'No, thank you,' she said. 'I don't want to be a butterfly.'

Mam-gu looked around the garden at all the flowers.

'How about a sunflower outfit?' she asked. 'That would be good.'

Betsi Wyn loved the sunflowers in Mam-gu's garden, but she shook her head again.

'I don't want to be a sunflower either, thank you,' she said.

'Well then,' said Mam-gu, 'would you like to be a pirate, like you were for Gwion's party? Or a princess?'

'No, thank you. I don't want to be a pirate or a princess,' said Betsi Wyn, as she watched the frogs hopping in and out of the pond. If she listened very hard, she could hear them making tiny sounds.

'What are the frogs saying?' asked Betsi Wyn.

Mam-gu listened hard too.

'I think they're saying, "rrribit, rrribit",' she said.

'Oh,' said Betsi Wyn. She went closer to the pond to hear them better. 'Rrribit, rrribit,' she croaked.

'I know what I want to dress up as for Anwen's party,' she said.

'Oh yes?' said Mam-gu. 'What's that, *cariad*?'

'A frog,' said Betsi Wyn.

'What?' said Mam-gu. She was surprised at Betsi Wyn's choice.

'Yes,' said Betsi Wyn. 'A frog. Rrribit, rrribit.'

'Well,' said Mam-gu, 'we'd better start thinking how we can make your costume then.'

And that's what they did.

On Saturday, Betsi Wyn pulled on her green trousers and her green sweatshirt. Mam-gu dabbed green face paint onto her cheeks and the back of her hands. Betsi Wyn looked at herself in the mirror. She hopped up and down a bit.

'Rrribit, rrribit,' she said. 'I think I need a green hat too.'

So Mam-gu found an old, woolly, green

hat and stitched a pompom on each side to make two bulgy eyes.

'*Diolch*, Mam-gu,' said Betsi Wyn. 'Now I feel just like a frog.'

On the way to Anwen's house, Betsi Wyn and Mam-gu met Emyr Rhys and his grandfather.

'I like your fireman's costume, Emyr Rhys,' Betsi Wyn said.

He grinned. 'Thank you,' he said. 'It's like my Uncle Gareth's. He's a real fireman.' Emyr Rhys looked at Betsi Wyn. 'I like your alien costume,' he said.

'I'm not an alien,' she said. 'I'm a frog.' And she hopped up and down. 'Rrribit, rrribit.'

'Oh yes,' said Emyr Rhys, 'I can see that now.'

A little further along the road they met Carys and her mum. Carys was wearing a clown outfit.

'I like your clown costume,' Emyr Rhys said.

'I like your fireman's costume,' Carys said. 'And I like your alien costume, Betsi Wyn.'

'She's not an alien,' Emyr Rhys said.

'No,' said Betsi Wyn. 'I'm a frog.' And she hopped up and down. 'Rrribit, rrribit,' she said.

'Oh yes,' said Carys. 'You look great.'

They arrived at Anwen's house. Anwen's dad opened the door.

'*Helo 'na*,' he said. 'What have we got here? A fireman, a clown and an alien.'

Betsi Wyn shook her head. 'I'm not an alien, I'm a frog,' she said, and she hopped up and down. 'Rrribit, rrribit.'

'Sorry, Betsi Wyn,' Anwen's dad said. 'Come in Miss Frog, Miss Clown and Mr Fireman.'

They all waved goodbye to Mam-gu, Da-cu and Carys's mum, and went inside.

'Anwen's in the garden,' her dad said, and he led them all outside.

Anwen was excited when she saw her friends. She twirled her princess skirt.

'*Penblwydd hapus*!' Betsi Wyn, Emyr Rhys and Carys called. 'Happy birthday!'

'*Diolch*,' Anwen said. 'I like your fancy dress outfits.' She looked at Emyr Rhys. 'You're a fireman,' she said. She looked at Carys. 'You're a clown.' Then she looked at Betsi Wyn. 'And you're an alien.'

Betsi Wyn rolled her eyes. 'I am NOT an alien,' she sighed. 'I'm a frog.' And she hopped up and down. 'Rrribit, rrribit,' she said.

'Hey, that's good,' said Anwen. 'Hop over here.'

Anwen's dad went back inside to help get the party food ready, and Betsi Wyn, Emyr Rhys, Carys and Anwen ran off to play on the climbing frame.

When they had all climbed to the very top, they suddenly heard a terrible roaring sound. 'Rrroaaarrr! Rrroaaarrr!'

'Wha . . . wha . . . what was that?' Carys asked.

'It must be a monster,' Emyr Rhys said.

'Quick!' said Anwen. 'Let's hide in the play shed.'

They climbed down from the climbing frame as quickly and carefully as they could. Then they all ran into the play shed and closed the door tightly. It was a bit of a squeeze with Betsi Wyn, Emyr Rhys, Carys and Anwen all squashed inside. They listened hard.

'I can't hear anything,' Betsi Wyn said. 'Shall I peep out of the door?'

She opened the door a tiny bit and put her green face outside. 'I can't see the monster,' she said. 'It must have gone.'

Suddenly, there was another huge roar. It came from down the path.

'Rrroaaarrr!'

'The monster!' said Emyr Rhys. 'It's still out there.'

Betsi Wyn pulled her green face back into the shed as quickly as she could, and closed the door tightly.

They all stood very quietly in the play shed and listened hard. They couldn't hear a thing.

Suddenly, there was a knock on the door. They all jumped.

'Who's there?' Betsi Wyn asked, bravely.

'It's me,' a loud voice said from the other side of the door. 'Gwion.'

'Shsh, Gwion,' Betsi Wyn said, opening the door. 'Come in quick. There's a fierce monster out there.' Gwion squeezed into the play shed. He was wearing a red costume.

'*Penblwydd hapus!*' he whispered to Anwen. 'Happy birthday!'

'*Diolch,*' Anwen whispered back.

Betsi Wyn, Emyr Rhys, Carys, Anwen and Gwion were very, very squashed in the play shed. They all stood quietly and listened hard. They couldn't hear the monster outside.

'I like your fireman's costume,' Gwion whispered to Emyr Rhys. 'And I like your clown costume,' he whispered to Carys. 'And I like your princess costume,' he whispered to Anwen. He looked at Betsi Wyn. 'And I like your alie . . .'

'She's NOT an alien,' Emyr Rhys, Carys and Anwen said, very, very quietly.

Betsi Wyn rolled her eyes. She sighed. 'I'm a frog,' she said, and she tried to hop up and down but there was no room. So she just said a quiet 'Rrribit, rrribit.'

What Gwion did next terrified everyone. He rrroaaarrred! It was so very, very loud that everything in the play shed rattled.

'You're the monster, Gwion!' Betsi Wyn shouted. She opened the door and everyone squeezed passed Gwion and ran off into the garden.

Gwion climbed out of the shed. 'I'm not the monster,' he said, running after them.

'You are!' Betsi Wyn said. 'You made that terrible roaring noise!'

'I'm just doing my sound effect, like your

"rrribit, rrribit",' he said. 'I'm not a monster, I'm the *Drai* . . .'

But no one was listening to him. He tried to catch up with the others, but his red costume was too heavy. 'Please stop and I'll show you,' he gasped.

But no one took any notice. They ran away from Gwion and hid behind a big tree.

They stayed there for a long time. The garden had become very quiet. Some ants were climbing up and down the tree's trunk. Betsi Wyn thought the ants were very clever – they could walk up a tree and not fall off. Watching the ants made her forget why they were hiding.

Then Anwen said, 'I wonder where the monster's gone?'

'I'll take a look,' said Betsi Wyn, and she peeped out from behind the tree trunk.

Gwion was sitting in the middle of the lawn. He seemed very sad, sitting there by himself.

Betsi Wyn felt sorry that they had all run away from him.

'There isn't a monster,' she told the others. 'It's only Gwion.'

She stepped out from behind the tree. 'Gwion,' she said, 'do you promise not to roar again?'

Gwion nodded sadly. 'OK,' he said.

'It's safe to come out,' Betsi Wyn said. 'Gwion isn't going to be a monster any more.'

Just then Anwen's dad came into the garden.

'Pizza's ready!' he called. 'Come along, Mr Fireman, Miss Frog, Miss Clown, Miss Princess and Mr *Draig Goch*.'

'*Draig Goch*?' said Betsi Wyn. 'Gwion is the red dragon!'

'Yes,' said Gwion. 'I was trying to tell you, but you all kept running away.' And he pulled up his hood.

He made a magnificent dragon, with a fierce red face and a forked red tongue.

'*Y Ddraig Goch*!' said everyone. And they all patted Gwion on the back.

'Aren't you going to roar?' said Betsi Wyn.

Gwion looked from Betsi Wyn to Carys to Emyr Rhys and to Anwen. 'Will you all run away again if I do?' he asked.

'Oh no,' said Emyr Rhys, 'not now we know you're the Welsh dragon.'

'OK,' said Gwion, and he roared his loudest roar yet. 'RRROAAARRR!'

And no one ran away.

'Well,' said Mam-gu, as she and Betsi Wyn were walking home after the party, 'did you enjoy being a frog?'

'Oh yes,' said Betsi Wyn. 'It was great fun.' She skipped along next to Mam-gu. 'Carys is having a party next week. That's a fancy dress party too.'

'Another fancy dress party?' said Mam-gu. 'Well let's see, you could be a pirate. Or a princess. Or a frog again.'

Betsi Wyn shook her head. 'I don't want to be a pirate, or a princess, or a frog,' she said. 'I'm going to be something else.' She smiled up at Mam-gu. 'I'm going to wear my brown trousers and my brown sweatshirt,' she said, 'and I'm going to be . . . an ant!'

Emyr Rhys
on the Big Screen

'It's the big match today, Da-cu,' Emyr Rhys said. 'I bet Betsi Wyn and Gwion will have a great time watching it in Cardiff.' He shook his head sadly. 'It's a shame there weren't any seats left on the minibus for us.'

'We'll have a good time watching the match at home,' said Da-cu. 'We've got our red shirts on, we've got our scarves ready to wave and we're going to have something special for lunch.'

'Something special?' asked Emyr Rhys.

'Welsh rarebit,' said Da-cu. 'I thought we could get it ready while Nain and Lowri Haf are out. It'll be a nice surprise for them when they get back, just in time for the rugby.'

He found his recipe book. 'Now then,' Da-cu said, turning to the right page, 'first we need some butter.'

He took a big bowl from the high shelf and put a blob of butter into it. He gave Emyr Rhys a wooden spoon.

'You squash the butter with this,' he said. 'And I'll grate the *caws*.'

Da-cu found a block of cheese in the fridge and the grater in the cupboard.

It was hard for Da-cu to grate the cheese. Little chunks kept flying off and getting lost on the kitchen floor. So he chopped up the rest of the cheese and put it in the bowl with the squashed butter.

'What's next?' he asked.

Emyr Rhys checked the recipe. 'Two spoonfuls of milk,' he said, 'and a little bit of mustard.' He added them to the bowl.

'Now for *halen a phupur*,' said Da-cu, adding a pinch of salt and pepper.

Emyr Rhys gave the mixture a big stir. Squidgy, cheesy chunks slipped from the bowl and splattered onto the worktop.

'What do we do with this mixture, Da-cu?' Emyr Rhys asked.

'We spread it on toast,' Da-cu said, 'and then we pop it under the grill until the cheese melts and turns golden brown. I'll just slice some bread ready to make the toast.'

But when he looked in the bread bin, it was empty. 'Oh, *dim bara!*' he said. 'No bread! We can't have Welsh rarebit without bread.' He scratched his head. 'I've seen Nain make bread a hundred times,' he said. 'I'm sure we could make some, too.'

Da-cu opened the cupboard. 'We've got all the ingredients we need.' He passed Emyr Rhys the flour and a packet of yeast. 'We just have to tip everything onto the worktop, like Nain does.'

Da-cu's Rarebit Recipe

Ingredients
25g soft butter
150g grated cheese
A pinch of mustard powder
2 tablespoons of milk
A pinch of salt and pepper
4 thick slices of bread

Method
1. In a bowl, beat the butter with a wooden spoon until it is very soft.
2. Add the grated cheese to the bowl and mix with the butter.
3. Add the milk and mustard powder. Mix into the cheese and butter.
4. Add a pinch of salt and pepper and mix well.
5. Ask a grown-up helper to toast the bread under the grill on one side only.
6. Spread the cheese mixture onto the untoasted side of the bread.
7. Ask your helper to toast the cheese mixture under the grill until it is light brown and bubbling.
8. Allow to cool slightly and enjoy.

And Da-cu emptied all the ingredients into a big heap. 'Now we need to add some water,' he said. And he poured a cupful on top of the flour and yeast.

Lots of water ran off the worktop and made floury puddles on the floor.

'Are you sure this is how Nain makes bread?' Emyr Rhys asked, as he watched Da-cu mix the flour, yeast and water with his hands. 'I don't think it looks right.'

'Mmm,' Da-cu said, looking down at the sticky mess on the worktop. 'You're right. This doesn't look much like Nain's bread dough. I might have done something wrong.'

Emyr Rhys looked into the cupboard. 'We've got more flour,' he said. 'Shall we start again?'

'Good idea,' Da-cu said. 'Now if I could only get this sticky stuff off my fingers . . .' And he shook his hands. Big lumps of gluey dough flew around the kitchen.

Suddenly there was a loud knock at the door. Da-cu went to answer it. Gwion's dad was standing on the door step.

'Would you and Emyr Rhys like to come with us to the match?' he asked. 'We've got two spare tickets and two free seats on the minibus.'

'Oh yes, we'd love to come,' Da-cu said. '*Diolch*! Thank you, thank you!' Then he shouted, 'Emyr Rhys, grab our scarves. We're going to the match after all!'

It was great fun on the minibus with Betsi Wyn and Mam-gu, Carys and her mum, and Anwen and her aunty. Gwion and his dad knew lots of songs. Their favourite was '*Sosban Fach*' and everyone joined in loudly. The time flew by until they arrived in Cardiff.

'Here we are,' Gwion's dad said, '*Stadiwm*

y Mileniwm. We'll have to get to our seats quickly. There's not long before kick-off.'

As they rushed passed all the stalls selling hats and scarves and hotdogs, Emyr Rhys remembered something.

'Da-cu,' he said, 'we haven't told Nain where we are.' And then he remembered something else. 'And we didn't tidy up the kitchen before we left!'

'You're right,' Da-cu gasped. 'She'll be wondering where we've gone. Don't worry,' he said, checking his pockets, 'I'll send her a text.' But no matter how hard he searched, he couldn't find his phone.

'I think I left it on the kitchen table,' he said.

'What shall we do?' Emyr Rhys asked. 'The match is going to start soon.'

Da-cu scratched his head. 'You go to your seat with Gwion and his dad,' he said. 'I just need to get something.' He smiled at Emyr Rhys. 'I'll be with you in a minute.'

It was noisy in the stadium. Everyone was very excited about the match.

'Look!' said Gwion. 'There's the Welsh team.'

From their seats high up in the stadium, they could see the team in their red jerseys running onto the pitch. Emyr Rhys and Gwion clapped and cheered. Then a brass band began to play and suddenly the crowd became very quiet.

Da-cu slipped into his seat just in time to start singing '*Hen Wlad Fy Nhadau*'.

He put down a big bag near his feet. Emyr Rhys could see some yellow material peeping out of the top of it.

'What have you got in the bag?' Emyr Rhys whispered.

'You'll see,' said Da-cu quietly, as they all stood up to sing the Welsh national anthem, loudly and proudly.

The match was very exciting. Wales scored the first try and Emyr Rhys and Da-cu cheered and cheered and waved their scarves in the air. It was fun to watch people cheering on the big screen. Some had red dragons painted on their cheeks and some were wearing Welsh hats. Some people were dressed as leeks. They looked very funny.

When Wales scored a second try, Emyr Rhys, Betsi Wyn, Carys and Anwen jumped up and down with joy. Gwion started to sing '*Sosban fach . . .*' and everyone in the stadium joined in.

At half time, Da-cu began rummaging in the bag. He took out some pieces of white card and a big, black marker pen.

'I borrowed these from the stall outside,' Da-cu told Emyr Rhys.

He started writing.

'What are you doing, Da-cu?' Emyr Rhys asked, through a mouthful of hotdog and tomato ketchup.

'You'll see,' said Da-cu, and he carried on writing.

The second half was just as exciting as the first. There was lots of singing and cheering, and Wales scored twice more. Every time they scored a try, the big screen showed people in the crowd celebrating.

'I wish we could be on the big screen,' Emyr Rhys said. 'It would be great.' Then he suddenly remembered something. 'We still haven't told Nain where we are!'

'I've got an idea how we can get a message to her,' Da-cu said, as he took something from the bag.

He handed Emyr Rhys a big, yellow thing. It was made of soft material.

'What this?' Emyr Rhys asked.

'It's a daffodil hat,' Da-cu said. 'And I've got nine more of them. We're going to be the biggest bunch of daffodils here today.' And he gave one each to everyone – to Gwion and his

44

dad, Betsi Wyn and Mam-gu, Carys and her mum, and to Anwen and her aunty.

They all put them on.

'Now,' said Da-cu, putting on his own yellow hat, 'if you wouldn't mind holding up these.' And he handed out the pieces of card. Each piece had a different big black word on it.

'Right,' said Da-cu, 'when Wales score next, hold up your card for the camera, *os gwelwch yn dda.*'

They waited and waited. And waited and waited. And they shouted, 'Come on, *Cymru*!'

There were scrums and lineouts, and Wales needed two points to win. Just as the referee was about to blow the final whistle, Wales charged for the try line. They scored!

'We've won. We've won,' Emyr Rhys and Gwion shouted. 'Three cheers for Wales!'

All the Welsh supporters stood up and cheered. Emyr Rhys, Da-cu and everyone from the minibus stood up too. They were all wearing the flower hats Da-cu had given them. They looked like a big bunch of daffodils. They waved their pieces of card in the air. Suddenly, the cameraman spotted them.

And there they were on the big screen – a bunch of smiling, cheering daffodils, holding up a message. The message said: 'Sorry about the mess, Nain. We'll tidy it up later!'

'Da-cu,' Emyr Rhys said, as they left the stadium, 'do you think Nain saw our message?'

'Of course,' Da-cu said 'She never misses one second of Wales playing rugby. She'll have been watching in the *lolfa* with Lowri Haf.'

'You know,' Gwion's dad said, as they all walked through the crowd back to the minibus, 'there was a much easier way to get a message home.' He took something from his pocket. 'You could have borrowed my mobile phone.'

'Oh,' said Da-cu. 'I didn't think of that!'

'Never mind,' said Emyr Rhys. 'It was fun being a bunch of daffodils.'

'And it was great being on the big screen,' said Gwion. He hooked his arm around Emyr Rhys's shoulder.

'*Sosban fach yn berwi ar y tân . . .*' he began loudly.

And everyone else joined in too.

GWION'S SONG

Sosban Fach

Sosban fach yn berwi ar y tân,
Sosban fawr yn berwi ar y llawr,
A'r gath wedi sgramo Joni bach.

Little Saucepan

Little saucepan, boiling on the fire,
Big saucepan, boiling on the floor,
And the cat has scratched little Johnny.

Traditional

Quick, Quick, Betsi Wyn!

'Quick, quick, Betsi Wyn,' Mam-gu called. 'Fetch our buckets and spades. We're going to the seaside!'

Betsi Wyn looked out of the window at the raindrops splashing the pavement. 'To the seaside?' she asked. 'In the rain?'

'That nice weatherman on the telly says it's sunny in Tenby,' Mam-gu said. 'If we're quick we can catch the next train there.'

'Hooray!' said Betsi Wyn, running off to find the buckets and spades. It had rained every day so far this summer holiday. And Betsi Wyn had had enough of rain.

Mam-gu made a stack of sandwiches and put them into a cool bag. She packed a tin of Welsh cakes too. Then they found their swimsuits and put them on under their clothes. They plonked on their sun hats and hurried out of the house.

'Quick, quick, Betsi Wyn!' Mam-gu said, as they neared the station. 'The train's at the platform.'

They found two empty seats.

'Sit by the *ffenest*,' Mam-gu told Betsi Wyn. 'That way you can look out and spot the sea.'

Betsi Wyn took off her backpack and sat next to the window.

'I can't see the sea, Mam-gu,' she said.

'Give it a chance, *bach*,' Mam-gu smiled. 'We haven't left the station yet.'

Soon the train was rushing through the countryside. Betsi Wyn watched trees and fields gliding past the window. It was still raining, but only a little bit.

A lady in a blue uniform came down the aisle of the train.

'Tickets, please,' she called.

'That's the ticket inspector,' Mam-gu told Betsi Wyn. Mam-gu held up their tickets and the lady stopped to check them.

'*Iawn*,' she said. 'That's fine.' She handed back the tickets to Mam-gu. 'Off to Tenby for the day, then?'

'Yes,' said Mam-gu. 'That nice weatherman on the telly said it's sunny there. And we're fed up with the rain, aren't we, Betsi Wyn?'

Betsi Wyn nodded.

'You'll have a lovely day at the seaside,' the ticket inspector said. 'And if you look out of that window, any minute now you'll be able to see the sea.'

Betsi Wyn looked out of the window. 'I can't see it,' she said.

'Keep watching,' said the ticket inspector, as she went off down the aisle.

'I still can't see it,' Betsi Wyn sighed.

Then she jumped to her feet. 'I can see it. I can see it! Look, Mam-gu.' And she pointed to a silvery shimmer in the distance.

'*Da iawn.* Well done,' Mam-gu smiled. 'Now, you keep watching the sea, and I'll have a little nap.' And she put her head back on the headrest and closed her eyes.

The weatherman was right – it was beautifully sunny in Tenby.

'Hooray!' cheered Betsi Wyn, as they got off the train.

'It's lovely and warm,' smiled Mam-gu. 'We'd better put on our suntan lotion.'

They headed for the beach.

'We should have a swim first,' Mam-gu said, putting down the cool bag. 'And then we can eat our picnic.'

The sand was warm under Betsi Wyn's toes as she and Mam-gu skipped down to the sea. They ran straight into the water without stopping.

'Ooh!' laughed Betsi Wyn, hopping about. 'It's cold!'

'Aah!' laughed Mam-gu, hopping about, too. '*Mae'n oer!*'

But once their toes and feet and legs got used to the cold, they quite liked being in the sea. They splashed around and kicked the waves.

'I'm going to sit down in the water,' Betsi Wyn said.

'So will I,' said Mam-gu.

They held hands and sat down with a big splash.

'Ooh!' Betsi Wyn laughed, and she stood up again quickly.

'Aah!' laughed Mam-gu, and she stood up quickly too.

But now that they were wet all over the water didn't seem so cold. Soon they were lying down in the sea and swimming through the little waves. Being in the sea was making them feel very hungry.

'Time for our picnic,' Mam-gu said, and she and Betsi Wyn ran up the beach to the cool bag.

'*Blasus*,' Betsi Wyn said. 'Delicious. Those were the best sandwiches ever.'

Mam-gu smiled. 'Food always tastes better on the beach, especially after a swim.'

Mam-gu began packing away the empty picnic things.

'I know,' she said, 'why don't we build some sandcastles next?'

They built a whole row of sandcastles. Betsi Wyn knocked the tops off some of them.

'Look, Mam-gu,' she said. 'They're just like the tumble-down castles I saw from the train when you were asleep.'

'Well, well,' said Mam-gu. 'You'll have to show me those castles on the way home.'

Betsi Wyn frowned. 'We're not going home yet, though, are we?' she asked. She was having a lovely time at the seaside. She didn't want it to end so soon.

Mam-gu smiled. 'Oh, no, *bach*,' she said. 'We've got something special to do first.'

'Something special?' asked Betsi Wyn. 'What is it? What is it?'

'You'll soon find out,' Mam-gu said. 'Pack away the bucket and spades. We haven't got much time, so quick, quick.'

They pulled their clothes over their swimsuits, put on their hats and picked up their bags. Then they headed down to a wooden walkway.

'Where are we going?' Betsi Wyn asked.

'To the *cwch*,' Mam-gu said.

'The *cwch*?'

'The boat,' said Mam-gu, and she pointed to a small blue and white boat that was bobbing on the water at the end of the walkway. The engine started and the boat began to rock.

'Quick, quick, Betsi Wyn,' Mam-gu said. 'Or it'll go without us.'

They rushed down the walkway and stepped into the boat. A friendly man held out his hand and helped them climb aboard.

'Where will the boat take us?' Betsi Wyn asked.

'Over there to Ynys Bŷr,' said Mam-gu. And she pointed to a blob of green across the sea. 'Caldey Island is another name for it,' she said, as the boat gently carried them away from the wooden walkway and out into the sea.

It didn't take long for them to arrive at the little jetty on the island. The friendly man held out his hand again, to help them off the boat.

Betsi Wyn and Mam-gu walked up the sandy

pathway to some trees and then out into bright sunlight. There was a huge building in front of them, with white walls and a red roof. Betsi Wyn gasped.

'Oh!' she said, 'what's that?'

'It's Caldey Abbey,' Mam-gu said. 'It's where the monks live.'

And with that, a man crossed their path. He was wearing a brown tunic over a long, white robe. He smiled and nodded at them.

'*Prynhawn da,*' he said. 'Good afternoon.'

'*Prynhawn da,*' said Betsi Wyn and Mam-gu together. They nodded and smiled too.

The man went through a gate into the abbey's garden.

'Was that a monk?' Betsi Wyn asked Mam-gu. 'Does he live there?'

'Yes,' said Mam-gu. 'What a wonderful place to live.'

They had a lovely time on the island. There was a café and a gift shop. There were ponds to peer into, and an old chapel and a lighthouse, too. And everywhere they looked were birds and beautiful flowers.

'This is the life,' said Mam-gu, as they reached the very top of the island. They sat down on a patch of soft grass to finish off their Welsh cakes. Mam-gu sighed. 'Nothing but blue sea around us,' she said, 'and blue sky above.'

'And a little blue boat in the distance,' said Betsi Wyn, pointing out to sea.

'A blue boat?' Mam-gu said. She jumped to her feet. 'That's our boat back to Tenby. Quick, quick, Betsi Wyn!'

Betsi Wyn grabbed Mam-gu's hand and they ran as fast as they could down the hill. They had to hold tight to their hats. Betsi Wyn's backpack bounced on her back and the cool bag knocked against Mam-gu's knees. At last they arrived at the little jetty.

But the boat was long gone.

'Oh no,' Mam-gu sighed. 'That was the

last boat back to Tenby today. And we've missed it.'

'What shall we do?' Betsi Wyn asked.

'The first thing we'll do is have a rest,' Mam-gu said, and she sat down on the jetty wall. 'And then we'll have a think.'

'Hello again,' said a cheerful voice. It was the monk they had seen earlier. He smiled. 'If you don't mind me saying, you two look out of puff.'

'We are,' said Betsi Wyn. 'We were running for the boat, but we missed it.'

'Oh deary me,' said the monk. He smiled. 'I'm Brother Tomos, and it's just as well that I'm off to Tenby myself, in the abbey's little boat. Would you like a lift?'

'Oh, yes please,' said Mam-gu. '*Diolch, diolch.* Thank you so much.'

They climbed into Brother Tomos's boat. It was smaller than the blue and white boat, but with its little engine it went just as fast.

'What a day out this has been,' said Mam-gu, as they sat down.

'It was great,' Betsi Wyn said. 'Can we do it all again tomorrow?'

Mam-gu smiled. 'I think I need a good rest after today,' she said, and Brother Tomos chuckled.

Soon they were climbing out onto the beach at Tenby.

'Now, don't tell everyone about this,' smiled Brother Tomos, 'or they'll all be wanting lifts.'

'We won't,' said Betsi Wyn. 'Thank you, Brother Tomos. *Diolch yn fawr.*'

'Yes, thank you very much,' said Mam-gu. 'But I'm afraid we'll have to dash. I think our train is about to leave the station.'

She climbed out of the boat as fast as she could. 'Come on, we'll have to run.' She grabbed Betsi Wyn's hand, as Brother Tomos waved and chuckled again.

They left the sea and the boat behind, and they headed for the station. All the way there Mam-gu cried, 'Quick, quick, Betsi Wyn! Quick, quick!'

And just as the whistle blew, they climbed aboard the train. They flopped down into two empty seats.

'Remember to show me those castles,' Mam-gu said, 'like the ones you made on the beach.'

But when the train rumbled past the tumble-down castles, Betsi Wyn and Mam-gu were both fast asleep.

Good Thinking,
Emyr Rhys

'Now,' Nain said, as she checked her lipstick in the hall mirror, 'you won't forget those flowers need planting, will you?'

She picked up her handbag. 'And you'll remember to peg out the sheets?'

She popped her umbrella inside her bag. 'And you will get them in again if it starts raining?'

She looked sternly at Da-cu. 'And you're going to take good care of Lowri Haf all day, aren't you?'

Da-cu smiled. 'Don't worry,' he said. 'We'll do just what you've asked us to.' He winked at

Emyr Rhys. 'And we might even have time for a game of football.'

Nain looked at Da-cu and lifted her eyebrows. 'You won't go crashing through Mrs Morgan's hedge again, will you?' she asked. 'Like you did last time?'

Da-cu laughed. 'Oh no,' he said. 'That was just a little mistake.'

'You were only diving to save a goal, weren't you, Da-cu?' Emyr Rhys said. 'You didn't mean to land on Mrs Morgan's bird bath.'

'Well,' Nain said, buttoning up her coat, 'just be careful. I don't want to come home and find you've got an injured elbow again.'

'Don't worry,' Da-cu said. 'We'll be fine, won't we Emyr Rhys?'

'Yes,' said Emyr Rhys. 'We promise – no injured elbows.'

They heard a car toot-tooting its horn.

'They're here!' Da-cu said.

He opened the front door, and he and Emyr Rhys stood on the step as Nain rushed out, waving all the way down the front path.

'Enjoy your day shopping,' Emyr Rhys called after her.

'*Diolch*,' Nain called back. 'I will.'

'Try not to buy everything you see,' added Da-cu.

Nain climbed into the back of a car. It was filled to the brim with excited, smiling ladies. The ladies waved to Da-cu and Emyr Rhys, who waved back as the car disappeared down the road.

'Right,' said Da-cu, 'we'd better peg out the sheets before Lowri Haf wakes up.' And he shut the front door.

As they were pulling the sheets from the washing machine, they heard a loud cry.

'It's Lowri Haf,' Da-cu said. 'I'll go and fetch her.'

'Put her in the pushchair,' Emyr Rhys said. 'Then she can watch us doing our jobs.'

'Good thinking, Emyr Rhys,' said Da-cu.

Lowri Haf enjoyed watching Da-cu and Emyr Rhys in the garden. She thought it was very funny when they got tangled up in the sheets as they tried to peg them on the line.

And she thought it was even funnier when Da-cu sprayed Emyr Rhys with water from the hose-pipe, as he tried to water the flowers they'd planted in Nain's flower bed.

And she thought it was absolutely hilarious when they had finished their jobs, and began charging around and around the garden, chasing a red football.

They got wrapped up in the sheets blowing on the line.

They ran into the flower beds and almost trampled over Nain's flowers.

And they got covered in mud.

Lowri Haf laughed and laughed and waved her feet in the air.

Suddenly Emyr Rhys kicked the ball very hard. It flew across the garden and up and up towards the top of Mrs Morgan's hedge. Da-cu put his hands out and tried to grab the ball. His fingers stretched and stretched but he couldn't quite reach it. He jumped to make himself taller and his fingers touched the football. But then he began tumbling backwards.

'Oh no,' Emyr Rhys shouted. 'You're going to fall through Mrs Morgan's hedge again!'

But Da-cu was ready. With one hand he grabbed a thick branch and with the other he caught the ball.

'Phew,' Emyr Rhys said, as he helped Da-cu pull twigs out of his jumper, 'that was a close one. I thought you were going to land on Mrs Morgan's bird bath again.'

Da-cu smiled. 'Oh no,' he said. 'I was lucky this time. I saved the goal and myself.'

With that, there was a loud clap of thunder.

'Quick!' Da-cu said, taking the brake off Lowri Haf's pushchair. 'Let's get inside before we get soaked.'

They ran into the kitchen, with Da-cu wheeling the pushchair, just as a big black rain cloud emptied over the garden.

'That was close,' Emyr Rhys said, as he watched the huge raindrops dancing along the path. 'What about the washing, Da-cu?'

'Oh no,' Da-cu said. 'I forgot about that. Quick!'

They rushed outside and dragged the wet sheets from the line. Then they dashed back into the kitchen. They dumped the sheets down in a heap.

'Oh no,' Emyr Rhys said, pointing at the floor. 'Look!'

Da-cu looked at the floor. There were muddy footprints all over the tiles, and muddy tyre marks, too, from Lowri Haf's pushchair. And there were muddy handprints on the sheets.

'Right,' Da-cu said, 'we'd better put this lot back in the washing machine and get the mops out.'

Lowri Haf watched from her pushchair as Da-cu and Emyr Rhys mopped and mopped. She didn't want to be in her pushchair any more. She wanted to mop the floor too. She began to cry. Emyr Rhys and Da-cu tried to cheer her up as they mopped and mopped, and mopped and mopped again. But she just kept on crying.

At last the kitchen floor and the sheets were clean. It had stopped raining, and Da-cu and

Emyr Rhys pegged out the washing once more. But Lowri Haf was still crying. Da-cu took her out of the pushchair. She was very cross and her face was as red as Emyr Rhys's football.

'Shush, shush, *cariad*,' Da-cu said, as he gave her a *cwtsh*.

But she was too cross to be cuddled.

'Whatever shall we do?' Da-cu asked Emyr Rhys.

'You could sing her that song,' Emyr Rhys said. 'You know – the one about riding a horse.'

'Good thinking,' Da-cu said. 'That always works a treat.' He sat down, balanced Lowri Haf on his knee and held her hands tightly. Then he began to sing:

'*Gee geffyl bach yn cario ni'n dau, dros y mynydd i hela cnau.*' And he bounced her up and down on his knee. She stopped crying at once and began to chuckle.

'*Dŵr yn yr afon a'r cerrig yn slic, cwmpon ni'n dau . . .*' Da-cu tipped her back gently and she laughed. Then he pulled her upright again as he sang, '*wel, dyna chi dric!*'

She kicked her feet when Da-cu stopped singing.

'She wants you to do it again,' Emyr Rhys said.

So Da-cu sang and sang the song, and bounced and tipped Lowri Haf on his knee until she began to yawn.

'Time for a nap,' Da-cu said, as he put her back into the pushchair.

All that crying had made her very sleepy, and her eyes closed straight away.

'Well done, Emyr Rhys,' Da-cu said. 'That song worked a treat.'

Emyr Rhys smiled. 'It was easy to think of it. I used to like you singing that song to me, Da-cu. It's a shame I'm too big for it now.'

'Too big?' asked Da-cu. 'What do you mean?'

'I can't sit on your knee anymore,' Emyr Rhys said. 'I'm too heavy.'

'Nonsense,' Da-cu said, sitting back down on the chair and tapping his knee. 'Come on. I'll be fine, you'll see.'

Emyr Rhys smiled and climbed onto Da-cu's knee. Da-cu made a bit of a face.

'Are you sure you're alright?' Emyr Rhys asked him.

Da-cu wriggled his leg. 'You're much heavier than Lowri Haf,' he said. 'But my knees are strong.'

He started to bounce Emyr Rhys and sing the song. Emyr Rhys tried to join in with the words, but he was laughing too much. Then they got to the part where Da-cu had to tip Emyr Rhys back.

'*Cwmpon ni'n dau . . .*' sang Da-cu, but before he could finish the song there was a loud CLICK.

'Ow! Ow!' Da-cu shouted.

Emyr Rhys jumped off Da-cu's knee at once.

'What is it? Are you OK?' he asked.

Da-cu got up off the chair and hopped about the kitchen. 'I don't think that was a good idea of mine,' he said. 'My knees aren't so strong after all.'

When Nain came home much later that afternoon, Emyr Rhys was waiting for her in the hall.

'Did you have a nice day?' Emyr Rhys asked, as he helped her in with all her shopping.

'Oh yes. Thank you, *cariad*,' she smiled. 'What about you and Lowri Haf and Da-cu?'

'We've had a lovely day too, *diolch*,' Emyr Rhys answered. 'We dried the sheets and planted the flowers. And we looked after Lowri Haf really well.' He opened the door to the kitchen a little bit. Lowri Haf was playing happily on the sparkling kitchen floor next to a pile of clean, dry sheets.

'So no injured elbows today then,' smiled Nain.

'No injured elbows,' Emyr Rhys said, and he opened the door a little bit more. Da-cu was sitting on the chair watching Lowri Haf play. His foot was resting on a stool, and he had a big, white pillowcase wrapped around his leg.

'Today Da-cu's got an injured knee.'

'Don't tell me,' Nain sighed, 'football again?'

'Not quite,' said Emyr Rhys. 'He wasn't trying to be a goalie this time – he was pretending to be a horse!'

After they got back from hospital, Nain put on the kettle and helped Da-cu into his favourite chair.

'At least there's no real damage done,' she said. 'A bit of a sprain, that's all.'

It was well past Lowri Haf's bed time, and she was very sleepy. Being sleepy made her cross. She began to cry.

'We know a song she likes, don't we, Emyr Rhys?' Da-cu said. 'It'll help her stop crying.'

Emyr Rhys shook his head. 'I think we should let Nain sort her out,' he said. 'You've only got one good knee, Da-cu. And you'd better keep that for football.'

Da-cu laughed. 'Good thinking, Emyr Rhys,' he said, and he laughed again. 'Good thinking.'

LOWRI HAF'S SONG

Gee Geffyl Bach

Gee geffyl bach yn cario ni'n dau,
Dros y mynydd i hela cnau,
Dŵr yn yr afon a'r cerrig yn slic,
Cwmpon ni'n dau, wel, dyna chi dric!

Gee Up Little Horse

Gee up little horse, carry both of us,
Over the mountain, hunting for nuts,
Water from the river makes the rocks slick,
We both fall – well, there's a trick!

Traditional

About the Author

As a child growing up in Llanelli, I loved spending time in the local library. On Saturday afternoons I'd browse the shelves, searching for books to borrow and lose myself in. When I was older, I was fortunate enough to work in that same library. It was amazing to be surrounded by so many books on so many different subjects. Later, when I was a primary school teacher, I enjoyed sharing my favourite stories with the children in my class. And they shared their favourites with me. We made up our own tales too.

I still live in west Wales, with my husband and children, and I still love books and making up stories. I hope you enjoy reading about Betsi Wyn and

Emyr Rhys. It was great fun writing about them again. I first wrote about them in a book called *Welsh Cakes and Custard* and was delighted when it won the Tir na n-Og Award 2014. If you'd like to read more stories about Emyr Rhys and Betsi Wyn, you might enjoy that book too.

Wendy White